The Journey Is the Goal

A Life Journey without Design

DISCARD

Jack Walker

D1522621

PAGE PUBLISHING, INC.
New York, NY

First originally published by Page Publishing, Inc. 2018

ISBN 978-1-64214-705-6 (Paperback)
ISBN 978-1-64214-706-3 (Digital)

Printed in the United States of America

Foreword

Memory is the connections. Meaning comes from what something is connected to. Something unconnected, unassociated with, unrelated to anything is literally meaningless. Conversely, something connected, associated, linked with many things is supercharged with meaning. And the farther back in time the connections go, the greater the meaning. By joining pieces of our lives together, we create ourselves. It's all in the order and the sequence. For this reason, memory may be more in the way things are stored, rather than what is stored.[1]

In trying to recall eight decades of my life, I find that my memory may be faulty and my ego may subliminally be recalling and coloring events to place me and those close to me in the best light. Being aware of these shortcomings and understanding that there are no absolute truths and that a life view is no more than the perception of the viewer, I have made a conscious effort to transmit to writing, to the best of my ability, my honest recollection of what happened, when, and where. I have also tried to place my role in these events in as humble a position as honesty demands and will allow.

"It is not always in the most distinguished achievements that men's virtues or vices may be discerned, but very often an action of small note, a short saying, or a jest, shall distinguish a person's real character more than the greatest sieges, or the most important battles."[2]

---

[1]   Excerpt is from *The Book of Words: Talking Spiritual Life, Living Spiritual Talk*, copyright 1993 by Lawrence Kushner (Woodstock, VT: Jewish Lights Publishing), www.jewishlights.com.

[2]   Plutarch's Lives, Alexander.

In the telling of my story, my viewpoints begin with those of a boy and migrate through adolescence, young adulthood, and middle age, to those of an elder. Personal viewpoints change as do the times, and the language describing people, places, and things. As a boy, I called my grandfather Grandpa; later on I stopped calling him that because, as a young adult, I thought it wasn't "manly," and I didn't vocalize any name when speaking to him but referred to him as EA, when speaking to other family members. A similar addressing progression took place from Uncle Walt to Walt, but for different reasons. In my adult years, Walt had become more like a big brother to me and less like an uncle. Also words like "Negro," "colored," "black," and "African American" have evolved with the times. For obvious reasons, much of the dialogue is approximated.

Book One

The Early Years 1931–1949

Memory clouds a clear understanding of childhood.
—Jean-Jacques Rousseau

My name is Jack. I first viewed the world in the historic town of Lexington, Virginia, on a cold November night in 1931; the same year the Empire State Building opened, and mobster Al Capone was convicted of income tax evasion. I was born the second of two children of Linwood and Lucy Belle Frazee Walker. Lexington, in the Shenandoah Valley, was established in the spring of 1778. The name chosen by the Virginia Legislature for the new seat of Rockbridge County was in honor of the great battle of the Revolutionary War, the battle of Lexington, Massachusetts, which had occurred three years earlier.

Local legend has it that Thomas Jefferson, who owned a tract of land in the county, played a part in naming the county as well as the town.

Almost from the beginning the city's main industry was education, what with the founding of Washington and Lee University in 1790 and the Virginia Military Institute in 1830. Robert E. Lee and Stonewall Jackson are buried there, and it is the birthplace of Sam Houston.

I am told that I was born with the caul over my face. A child "born with the caul" has a portion of the birth membrane remaining on the head. The caul is harmless and is immediately removed upon delivery by whoever is attending the birth. In medieval times the appearance of a caul on a newborn baby was seen as a sign of good luck. It was considered an omen that the child was destined for greatness. (Obviously the destiny considered became obscured in this case.) Born at home without an attending doctor, my guess is that my mother was aided by my father's mother. I was placed in my first baby crib, a tin washtub, and named Jack Stanley by my mother over my father's objection (he wanted to name me Mack, a family name in the Walker genealogy).

My sister Betty was born in Pueblo, Colorado, three years prior. I don't know much about my father since my parents were divorced when I was but two or three years old, and Mother, Betty, and I then moved back to Colorado to live with Mother's parents. I do know that Linwood was born in Lexington and that he and Mother lived in Pueblo, Colorado, shortly before my birth. He was an inmate of the Colorado State Prison, convicted on a charge of larceny. Mother was a nurse at the State Hospital at Pueblo. (The State Hospital was the repository for the state's insane, so judged as such by "County Lunacy Boards.") Mother, as an employee of the hospital, was privileged to give birth to my sister at the facility in 1928. (My half brother, Kenny, and I, as cruel as kids can be, often teased Betty by telling her she was born in the nuthouse.)

Mother was born in Oklahoma in 1906. She was the second of five children born to Elza Armstrong Frazee and Bertha Maud Dewald Frazee. She grew up on a farm in the Oklahoma territory and at age seventeen gave birth to my half brother, Kenneth "Kenny" Lankard. If she was married to Kenny's father, the marriage was short-lived. I'm sure that if she was married, it was a "shotgun' affair with Grandpa holding the shotgun. Lankard marrying her was known as "doing the right thing," or "doing right by her."

Mother left Kenny with her parents and attended nursing school in Woodward. Finishing nursing school, Mother met and married my father. I don't know when or how they met or when nor where they were married. In those days a young woman in her twenties who hadn't attached herself to a man was referred to as an old maid or a spinster. They were stigmatized as a pariah and were the awkward, odd person in any adult couples' activities. They were the subject of a lot of backhand gossip. Men would say, "She must be queer." Some men then and now say this about any woman who won't get in bed with them. Women would say (if she was attractive), "With those high heels and that short skirt clear up to her knees and that low-cut blouse, she looks like a street walker." And (if she was unattractive), they would say, "The poor soul, doesn't she know how she looks in those ugly shoes and those long skirts and that hairstyle?"

At the time of my birth, Herbert Hoover was president. The nation was in the depth of the worst economic depression in its history. The Wall Street stock market crash of October 24, 1929, known as "Black Thursday," was the most devastating stock market crash in the history of the United States, taking into consideration the full extent and duration of its fallout. Stock prices virtually collapsed and swept downward with gigantic losses by large and small investors alike. Many Wall Street princes were reduced to paupers. A rare few who anticipated the fall made millions by selling short on borrowed stocks and replacing them when they bottomed out. It was said that the deep and rapid market decline was responsible for several suicides. Myth has it that some stock brokers leaped to their death from skyscrapers. (I have found no hard evidence of this.)

The crash signaled the beginning of the Great Depression that affected all Western industrialized countries and did not end in the United States until 1947. It is difficult to imagine life during the Great Depression. While the Depression began at the end of the 1920s, the entire nation suffered most dramatically during the period 1929–1933. The unemployment rate rose to 25 percent. Food and jobs were hard to get and many people stood in lines to get government hand-outs. "Apple Annies" sold apples on the street trying to make ends meet. There were bread lines and soup kitchens set up by charities, missions, and churches." A lot of people lived on powdered milk, dried beans, and potatoes.³ Our family's economic well-being ebbed and flowed depending on Grandpa's employment status.

One Christmas I remember Mother and Grandma took me to a party given by the Salvation Army. (I think Grandpa, unemployed at the time, didn't go with us because he felt embarrassed asking for charity.) There was food and candy and gifts for all the children. I don't remember the gifts I received nor the food served, I only know the party made my Christmas a happy one. It was the only Christmas we had that year.

"If you find work, write," was an expression heard often during this time. Many young men (referred to as hoboes)⁴ hopped on freight trains to go find work wherever they could. I used to stand by the railroad tracks and wave at them. I often daydreamed of hopping on a freight train and sitting in the doorway of a boxcar, watching and waving at little boys as I go by. And of riding over trestles spanning canyons and rivers, and of pulling into big city stations, only to jump off and hop on another train to see lakes, rivers, and oceans, and wave at other little boys along the tracks. I would have taken a train by any means to any destination, near or far away. The journey was the goal. As a young man, I did travel by rail, but using the orthodox method to board: buying a passenger ticket. I did indeed ride the trestles and see the rivers and lakes and wave at little boys along the track. I imagined that each little boy waving at me had put a penny on the track to be flattened. Grandma used to give the hoboes food on the back porch steps when they would come by the house and offer to work for a meal. She never required them to work though. The population of hoboes increased tremendously during the Depression era. During all this strife, President Hoover promised that "prosperity was just around the corner." There was a lot of confusion among the experts as to what to do.

---

3   An eyewitness account.
4   A hobo is a migratory homeless vagabond, unlike tramps, who work only when they have to and bums, who don't work at all. Hoboes are workers who wander.

Prohibition, Bathtub Gin, Speakeasies

W e were a nation of law breakers. Prohibition was the law of the
land; the Eighteen**th** Amendment to the Constitution passed in
1920 banned the sale, transportation, and manufacture of alcohol in
America. Millions neither wanted nor respected the law. There was a
huge market for what was an illegal commodity. This situation ush-
ered in the heyday of the gangster era. Each major city had its gangster
element, but the most famous was Chicago with Al Capone. I have
heard it said that Capone was earning something like $60 million a
year from alcohol sales alone and that other rackets earned him several millions more. During this era the manufacture and distribution
of alcoholic beverages was also a lucrative cottage industry in which
many private citizens made a living. Prohibition gave rise to a whole
new lexicon in the American language as it referred to the beverage
industry, such colorful words as "speakeasy" or "blind pig" (an illegal
drinking establishment), "bootlegging" (illegal manufacturing and
selling of liquor, a term it is said was first used to describe the liquor
in boot tops when trading with the Indians), "bathtub gin" (any type
of homemade spirits made in amateur conditions), "moonshine,"
"white lightning," "mountain dew," "hooch" (Southern hill country terms for homemade liquor made back in the hills often by the
light of the moon), "jake" (a legal medicinal tonic of Jamaican ginger
and about 70 percent alcohol which during Prohibition was watered
down by the manufacturers with an industrial chemical which was
highly toxic to the spinal cord and caused paralysis in one or both
legs; the crippling effect was referred to as "jake leg"), "ridge runner"
(the drivers of souped-up automobiles who traveled the back roads

of the hill country delivering the moonshine. Their cars were made to out run law enforcement vehicles. The ridge runners' auto races with the law gave birth to the NASCAR races now so popular in the South). One of the more famous speakeasies was the Cotton Club in Harlem, a white-owned establishment for whites only. However, it featured many of the best black musicians including Duke Ellington, Cab Calloway, Louis Armstrong, Count Basie, and others.

The New Deal

Franklin Delano Roosevelt had campaigned for the presidency in 1932 on a Democratic platform promising a New Deal that included repeal of Prohibition, and upon his ascension to the presidency, it was repealed.

Roosevelt's New Deal was a series of economic programs. They were passed by congress during his first term. The programs were Roosevelt's responses to the Great Depression and focused on what historians refer to as the 3 Rs (relief, recovery, and reform)—that is, relief for the unemployed and the poor, recovery of the economy, and reform of the financial system to prevent a repeat Depression.

In Roosevelt's first term (1933–1936), poverty rates among senior citizens was more than 50 percent. More people were going to bed hungry than in any time in the country's history. The new president told the nation: "The only thing we have to fear is fear itself." A program of "social insurance" was proposed as an attempt to limit unforeseen and/or unprepared for dangers of old age, poverty, unemployment, and the burdens of widow(er)s with or without children. Right Wing opponents, however, labeled the proposal as socialism.

They loudly exclaimed, "We don't want the dole." The Social Security Act was signed into law in 1935. The first Social Security cards were issued in 1937, and the first benefit check was issued in 1940.

The 1930s were years of severe drought and severe dust storms and a hardscrabble existence on the western plains and the prairie lands of the Mississippi Valley, the areas referred to as the Dust Bowl. Millions of acres of farmland became useless because farmers didn't understand the value of rotating crops or contour plowing. "The dust got so bad," I heard tell, "that sometimes you couldn't see three feet in front you and it seeped through every crack in the house." Hundreds of thousands of people were forced to abandon their homes; many of these families, often known as Okies, since so many came from Oklahoma, migrated to California and other states where they found economic conditions a little better than those they had left. Now, owning no land, many became migrant workers who traveled from farm to farm to pick fruit at starvation wages. (These conditions are well depicted in John Steinbeck's *Grapes of Wrath*). The Depression and the dust storm era was lamented in song with such titles as "So Long, It's Been Good to Know Ya," "Nobody Knows Ya When You're Down and Out," and "Hey, Mister, Can You Spare a Dime?" The '30s were not all sad and bad; everyday life took place even though significantly adjusted in many cases.

My story starts with the first day I can remember; I was at the kitchen table. I saw the people and heard their voices and laughter. I was with all the family of my grandparent's home on East Moreno Street in Colorado Springs, Colorado. I only knew one of them, Mother. I was three years old. The household consisted of my grandfather Elza Armstrong Frazee (the undisputed head of the household), my grandmother Bertha Maude Dewald Frazee (whose love, kindness, and understanding, I learned later, bound us all to each other and made us a family), my uncle Walter "Walt" Frazee (my mother's eighteen-year-old brother who was a high school student), my half brother Kenny (eight years my senior) Mother, my sister, me, and a mongrel dog named Buddy, who belonged to Kenny. I didn't know all these people, but I felt secure and happy in this environment. I have no memory of living in Virginia, only stories of it as told by Mother. She related that while in the South, my sister and I had a "colored Mammy" to take care of us while she worked shifts at the hospital. "Mammy," she said, was more than a baby sitter; she was like a second mother who taught us manners as well as values. Even if I had known it, Mammy's name escapes me now. Mother told me I called her "Mama." I was told that I cried my heart out upon realizing I was being taken away from her. It was also told of my being given a "sugar tit," today's equivalent of the pacifier. It was a little sugar wrapped in a soft cloth and tied off with string for baby to suck on.

I now consider our having moved to the mountain area of Colorado Springs especially auspicious. The majesty of the mountains of the Pikes Peak Region has had a lasting influence on me spiritually, mentally, and physically. The region attracted worldwide attention in 1859, the peak year of the great Pikes Peak Gold Rush. It was estimated that the rush of fortune-seeking immigrants populated the region by more than one hundred thousand. Towns grew up where only bears and mountain sheep had roamed. Towns like Cripple Creek, which in 1930 was nearly a ghost town, was a city of fifty thousand during the boom years boasting two stage lines, two telegraph lines, two hotels, two dance halls, saloons, and whore houses—all the necessities for prospecting for gold. The nearby lusty gold camp towns of Victor and the silver camp of Leadville were booming just as Cripple Creek. All these towns were within the shadow of Pikes Peak. Fortunes were made and lost. The first millionaire prospector was Winfield Scott Stratton, who sold his Independence mine for 11 million dollars. Many prospectors sold their claims for a few hundred dollars, only to see the claim produce millions. Those who couldn't even sell their claims went home busted, saying they had "seen the elephant," meaning it was all too big, too unbeatable. The mountains around Cripple Creek were pock marked with prospect holes. Prostitution in the gold camps, though glamorized by some historians, was in truth a dark underside of Western life, attracting women who had no other way to earn a living. Hundreds participated, but only a few found a way out. The majority of Cripple Creek's three hundred prostitutes lived in shacks along Myers Avenue and Poverty Gulch, accepting all comers. Cripple Creek, in the 1950s, became a summer theater center. Hundreds of tourists have replaced the prospectors.

Victor's mines were the richest, but the mine owners and big spenders lived in Cripple Creek, which attracted the press and other writers due to its being close to the railroad from Colorado Springs. The great Independence mine of Stratton's was located near Victor, on Battle Mountain, so named for a multiday battle between the Utes and Arapahos in the mid-1800s over hunting territory on the mountain. The decreasing price of gold over the years caused reduced output of the mines. The final blow came during World War I, when miners left in great numbers to join the army. The mines shut down for good with the outbreak of World War II. There was no one left but old people living on pensions, sitting around stoves in the cafes on winter days talking of the fortunes to be made when the price of gold rises. In 1960 the nearby mountain sides were still being picked around by weekenders looking for the lost gold mines of local legends.

Leadville was the wildest, gaudiest, most raucous mining town in Colorado. During its heyday, Leadville produced more than $200 million in ore, mostly silver. But the 1893 silver crash closed most of the mines for good, throwing Leadville into a depression from which it never really recovered. By the turn of the century, houses were torn down for firewood. It was said, that dogs slept undisturbed in the middle of the street. The old mine shafts were used to operate stills during the Prohibition period, and Leadville became Colorado's bootlegger of illicit whiskey; in fact, it was the county's major source of income in the 1920s.

At East Moreno Street, Kenny and Betty would be off to school each morning with Buddy tagging along. Buddy, after walking them to school, would come back home and spend the day with me. Buddy and I were about the same size. He might have thought I was just another dog to play with. We would explore the neighborhood around the house, in the alley, and the vacant lot next door. The vacant lot was filled with all kinds of adventures. There were grasshoppers which spit chewing tobacco on you if you picked them up. There were butterflies, bumblebees, assorted flying and crawling insects, horny toads, flowers, and many exotic weeds. A wonder land for a four-year-old. For Buddy, this wonderful field provided infinite smells and interesting digging discoveries. This magical field provided unlimited adventures for us on a daily basis. A beautiful little oval-shaped ladybug sporting bright-orange wings with black polka dots landed on me. I watched her walk all over my forearm.

When she crossed over my elbow and was headed up my shirtsleeve, I chanted as Grandma had taught me:

> Lady bug, lady bug
> Fly away home.
> Your house is on fire,
> And your children will burn.

And she flew away home. It was magic. *How do they know what I'm saying?*

One day in the field, Betty and I were sailing tin-can lids when a lid that I had tossed sailed across the field and struck her in the forehead and stuck there. I took her by the hand and led her to the house. The blood was flowing from her head, and I was really scared, but Grandma removed the lid, washed the wound, and dabbed it with iodine as my sister screamed. I felt sick and sat down. Grandma then wrapped Betty's head with a clean rag from her rag bin and told us to stay inside and play for the rest of the day.

It was suppertime, and Buddy hadn't come home. Kenny went out looking for him around the neighborhood till it got dark. No Buddy. The next morning, as soon as I got up, I went downstairs barefoot in my pajamas and out the back door. I searched the backyard out by the henhouse, which was one of his favorite hangouts. I looked up and down the alley and then went around to the front and looked up and down the street. No Buddy.

"Jack! Get in here this instant."

Later in the day the man who lived on the other side of the vacant lot came up the walk carrying a limp, lifeless Buddy. I was sitting on the front porch steps.

"I found your dog. Is your grandmother home?"

He laid Buddy on the porch floor.

I sat on the floor and held Buddy's head and petted him. He didn't respond at all. I looked up at the man. "What's wrong with him?"

"I'm sorry, son. I don't know."

I ran into the house and back to the kitchen. No Grandma.

"GRANDMA!" I yelled.

She came downstairs.

"A man brought Buddy. He's on the porch!" I continued to scream.

She patted my head and walked out to the porch where the man was waiting.

"Mrs. Frazee, I found your dog in the vacant lot."

I sat down and held Buddy's head. Grandma and the man had some grown-up conversation, and as the man was leaving, I heard Grandma say, "Thank you," and the man say sadly, "I'm sorry."

"Will Buddy be okay, Grandma?"

She sat down next to me and put her arm around me. For the longest time, she didn't speak.

"Will he be okay?"

She moved closer to me and held me tightly. "No, Jack, Buddy is dead."

The tears I had been holding back rushed forward, and I couldn't stop sobbing. I tried to speak, but I couldn't.

I finally blubbered, "Why is he dead?"

I didn't hear her answer, nor did I want to. She took my hand and led me back into the house. Buddy was left on the porch. I avoided the porch for the rest of the afternoon. When Kenny got home from school, he buried Buddy in the vacant lot.

The next day I woke up with no thoughts of Buddy. His death didn't actually strike me until it was time for him to return from walking to school with Kenny. He was late, then he was later, then it struck me. I fought back the tears and went to the vacant lot to find his burial spot. I saw the mound of freshly upturned earth. I stood over the mound and released the tears. I dropped to my knees and sat down in the dirt, wanting to say something, but words wouldn't come. I just sobbed and cried for the longest time. Grandma called me to the house.

One of the big events in my life, while at the Moreno Street address, was when Kenny would bring home a big brown paper grocery bag filled with broken potato chips from the Golden Flake

Potato Chip Company. This was a luxury that didn't make the cut on Grandma's frugal Depression-era grocery list.

My next best friend at this time (after Buddy) was Phyliss Addison, the girl my age who lived next door. Phyliss was a pretty redhead with freckles with whom I argued as much as I played. We argued and called each other names mostly when we couldn't agree on what to play. She wanted to play games like "hop scotch" or play with dolls, and I wanted to play in the field or look for treasure in trash cans in the alley. Sometimes we could be very compatible when I agreed to be the "daddy" to her dolls or when she agreed to play in the field. When we moved away from Moreno Street (the rent had been raised to twelve dollars, which Grandpa thought was "goddamned robbery"), nine years passed before I saw Phyliss again.

In seventh grade I saw Phyliss in the South Junior High School corridor and knew her right off. I stopped her and, just to be sure, asked her if her name was Phyliss. She said yes. I then asked if she used to live on Moreno Street. She said yes, giving no indication that she recognized me. I told her my name and that we had been neighbors in our preschool years. She then very exuberantly exclaimed something like "Oh yes!" We then exchanged "remember when" stories and spoke of what we had been doing in the interim years.

She had gone on to Helen Hunt grade school in the old neighborhood where she still lived. I told her of my sojourn through the school system and neighborhoods of the city. We parted with each of us saying something like "See you later" and continued on to our respective classes. This was the first time I had ever reminisced with anyone whom I hadn't seen in years. I enjoyed it and savored the experience for a few days. We didn't play or argue together ever again.

Bobby, across the alley, I played with on occasion. I went to his house early one morning and was invited in by his mother.

"Bobby is still eating his breakfast, would you like to come in and wait?"

I followed her through the dining room where there was a bowl of fresh, real oranges sitting in the middle of the dining table. *These people are rich*, I thought. The only time we had oranges was in our Christmas stocking. In the kitchen Bobby sat at the table eating shredded wheat with banana slices and cinnamon toast. He was washing all this down with hot chocolate. *These people are really rich.* I had just come from a bowl of Post Toasties cornflakes.

Leaving my birth place in Virginia at such a young age, I have no memory of Lexington, the Shenandoah Valley, or the Appalachian Mountains. To me there was no better place to grow up than in the shadow of Pikes Peak. The Peak was named after Captain Zebulon Pike, who is credited with discovering it in 1806 while exploring the nation's newly acquired Louisiana Territory. Pike made an attempt to scale the mountain in November but gave up his ascent in waist-deep snow. The Pikes Peak region is somewhat pristine pine-blanketed mountains, valleys, canyons, streams, and rivers. It includes all areas whose people are within eyesight of Pikes Peak. One could see very far in that cool once clean air. Cripple Creek, Victor, Leadville, Rosemont, Divide, Cascade, Green Mountain Falls, Gold Field, and other mountain communities are all situated to view the dominate mighty 14,115-feet high peak. The Peak is composed of pink granite, and when not white with snow, it gives a pink glow when the sun's first morning rays hit it while the townsfolk are still in the pre-dawn semidarkness. The same sight is presented when the sun sets behind the mountains. "These high passes give you an eerie feeling," wrote famous newspaper war correspondent Ernie Pyle. He went on, "Because you come up out of summer heat and green vegetation and worldliness and suddenly you're driving along in another world, a world of vast treeless sweeps, and queer roadside marshes that seem out of place, and cold little lakes and pools and splotches of snow, and there's an indescribable kind of chill in the air even though it's summer and the sun is hot." He's describing the timberline elevation where trees don't grow, eleven thousand to twelve thousand feet above sea level.

Humming a lullaby, Grandma would rock me to sleep after lunch in my preschool days. When I woke up, I was in her bed snuggled in a big soft feather bed which was a comforter about twelve inches thick filled with goose down or probably chicken feathers in our case. It was placed on top of the mattress, and I would lie on it and sink down into the soft down, and with a blanket covering me, I was really warm. This was true of the feather bed even on the coldest nights. On a rainy day, she would sing,

> Rain, rain, go away;
> Come again another day,
> So Jack can go out and play.

If she had company at my nap time, she would just take me in to the bed room and tuck me in the bed. I liked these times because I could lie awake and hear the muffled voices and sounds moving around the house. I couldn't make out any words or identify any of the other sounds, but I felt warm and secure just hearing them while I was cozy in the feather bed. If it was raining, the sound of raindrops hitting the window and the rush of water down the gutter right outside the window was fun listening to. I would eventually drift off into dreamland.

In those days, if your home didn't have a coal-burning furnace in the basement with ducts and vents to the rooms, you had instead a centrally located cast iron wood and/or coal-burning heating stove. Ours was located in the living room. The dining room was seldom used since we took the majority of our meals at the kitchen table. The kitchen was heated by the coal-burning kitchen cook stove. The coal company delivered coal to our home by backing their dump truck up to the coal shoot door, which was in the foundation of the house. They raised the truck bed and dumped the coal into the coal shoot door which led to the coal bin in the basement.

Grandma gave me my moral sense. She provided the soft, warm, and forgiving affection I needed to balance the manly unemotional makeup of Grandpa's expression of love. I knew Grandma loved me, and I knew Grandpa liked me. Grandma gave me moral treasures such as the little ditty:

> Hearts, like doors, open with keys such as "Thank you, sir" and "If you please."

It was during this preschool period that I had the exiting experience of going to the neighborhood grocery with Grandma. This was my first experience with economics, finance, trade, American capitalism, and the free-enterprise system. I observed that Grandma gave some coins to the man at the grocery, and he bagged up some fresh vegetables (which I later learned were cucumbers, which we did not grow in our home garden) and gave them to her. But a greater revelation was that she gave him another coin, and he gave her some CANDY, which she gave to me. I was astonished. I had no idea where candy came from. Witnessing these transactions of the conversion of vegetables to coins and coins to candy gave rise in me creative entrepreneurial juices heretofore unknown to me. I knew that some vegetables just like the ones Grandma traded for were growing on vines in our neighbor's backyard. I set out on a quest. I picked two cucumbers from the neighbor's yard. (I had no concept of private property or the laws of trespass.) Since Grandma already had cucumbers, I went door to door offering to sell them. A lady down the street bought them for a penny a piece. I took my two pennies to the grocery store and bought some "penny candies" (five for a penny). Grandma saw me eating the candy and asked where it came from. I proudly told her of the whole entrepreneurial saga. My adventures into the world of capitalism were ended right then and there. Grandma lectured me about the property of others, the laws against trespassing, and the concept of thievery. She took me in hand, and we went next door, and she explained to the neighbor lady that the thief was apprehended and wished to apologize and make restitution. Grandma offered to pay the lady for the stolen produce, but the lady refused it.

"Tell the lady you're sorry, Jack."

I looked at my bare feet and mumbled, "I'm sorry."

A great amount of legal, economic, and moral knowledge was gained by that adventure.

Mother respected Grandpa, but being such a headstrong free spirit, she could only live under his authoritative rule of the household for brief periods. She soon left the Moreno Street household to be on her own. She went to work nursing at the Union Printer's Home, which provided a room for her. My brother and I remained with our grandparents. My sister went to live with some of Mother's friends. This sort of arrangement became typical in our lives. The first eleven years of my life were spent living here and there, usually with my grandparents, but sometimes with Mother or some friends of hers. At one time I stayed at the city-run day nursery. Some kids just spent the day there and were picked up by their parents at the end of the day, and some of us actually lived there day and night. Two things remain vivid in my memory of the day nursery. The matrons insisted that we all have a bowel movement before going to school. They would not let you flush the toilet until they had inspected. When my body couldn't hear nature's call, I would flush the toilet anyway and tell the matron I forgot I was not to flush. They considered this an act of insubordination and scolded me like my action had created very serious consequences for the institution. The other unforgettable memory is being taught a frightening prayer each night while kneeling on the floor beside our beds. The passage of the prayer, which scared me each night, was, "If I should die before I wake, I pray the Lord my soul to take." It meant to me there was a good chance I might not make it through the night. I didn't mind that something or someone would take my soul because I had no idea what a soul was, unless it had something to do with the sole of your shoes. I don't know any more about it today than I knew then.

The hub of the Pike's Peak region is Colorado Springs, seat of El Paso County.[5] The city rests on the alluvial plain of the eastern slope of the mountains, hugging up against Cheyenne Mountain. The Colorado Front Range is a major landform, extending for 185 miles north to south. Looking west, from town you could see the prominent peaks of Mount Rosa and Pike's Peak. Stretching as far as the eye could see, northwest and southwest is the mountainous Pike National Forest. Cheyenne Mountain to the immediate southwest is known to some only as the mountain deep, into which is the Aerospace Defense Command. The mountain was very much a part

---

[5] So called to give recognition to the Ute Indian's mountain pass rising just west of Manitou Springs, later found by Spanish explorers in the 1600s, thus El Paso, the Pass.

of what Colorado Springs was, just as was the Garden of the Gods, to the northwest—two especially prominent, naturally beautiful areas within a bike ride from downtown. I use the past tense here because I hear real estate developers have done their ugliness to both of these magnificent natural areas. I remember when the town boasted of its thirty thousand people. Now there are more than 450,000. What is Colorado Springs without the splendor of its surrounding natural beauty, just another commercial hub of ticky-tacky condominium projects? Thomas Wolf was right, "you can't go home again." To the east of the city, the vast rolling plains go forever—the land of wheat, cattle, sagebrush, cactus, yucca, tumble weed, wind, and dust. The zoo on Cheyenne Mountain was one of the best. The Will Rogers Shrine of the Sun, built in 1935 by Spencer Penrose on the side of the mountain, is a stone structure of Romanesque architecture standing one hundred feet tall, whose chimes sound the time each quarter hour. They can be heard in the town below when the atmosphere is right. The Garden of the Gods rock formations, the dramatic outstanding geologic features of the park, are ancient beds of sea-bottom sediment that were deposited horizontally but were pushed up vertically when the Rocky Mountains were uplifted by tectonic forces. I knew of one of the formations off the beaten path which contained sharks teeth. To me, walking among these towering natural red and white sand stone monuments, knowing that they once were sea beds and sandy beaches, was more than exciting. The white towers are of an alabaster like substance. I used to pick up chunks of it around the base to carve on.

One summer I spent living on a farm with the Rodd family. I think they agreed to take care of me for the summer as payment to my step-father, Dr. McCracken. (There was a lot of barter going on during the Depression.) The Rodd sons, Jake and Andy, were about my age. Mr. Rodd, a lean, raw-boned, weathered-looking, soft-spoken man, in bib overalls, was a poor, salt-of-the-earth dirt farmer, whose small acreage was out on the hardscrabble flat prairie land outside of the town of Calhan, about thirty miles east of Colorado Springs. Calhan was a small tank town founded as a water station for the railroad in the 1880s. Driving through, it smelled like cows and sagebrush. Mr. Rodd had a small dairy herd, some chickens, and a corn field, as well as a vegetable garden attended by Mrs. Rodd, who looked as if she had just stepped out of the American Gothic paint-ing, what with her hair pulled back tight to a bun in the back and her shapeless smock over her house dress made of floral-printed feed sack cloth. Mr. and Mrs. Rodd were kindly country folk, and they treated me like a son. He plowed with a mule and washed up in the stock tank.

We planted corn in the spring. We hoed weeds about every two to three weeks, and the rest of the grain's growing needs were left up to whatever nature gave up. I think the Rodd brothers liked having a city boy to teach the ways of the farm. They taught me how to ride their pony without bouncing up and down on the saddle by use of my thighs. We usually just rode using only the bridle and the saddle blanket. We swam in the big galvanized steel stock tank the cows and the horse drank from. The tank was supplied by a windmill which pumped water up from a well. I learned how to milk a cow after days of trial and error. At first I didn't position my hands in the right place on the teat, then I didn't move my fingers with the correct motion, and while I was trying to grasp all this, the cow would move and knock me off the stool and kick the milk pail. It was a glorious moment when on that day I saw the first dribbles of milk appear as a result of my effort, but I never was able to get the pull-squeeze action coordinated to constantly get a steady stream of milk. With no thanks to me, we did have all the milk we could drink.

Jake and Andy also introduced me to smoking corn silk. We smoked out in the cornfield out of sight of their parents. We some-times helped Mrs. Rodd weed her garden, and other times helping Mr. Rodd hoe weeds out of the corn. Other than these duties, we were free to roam wherever we wished. We sometimes would get up in the barn loft and jump off into hay stacked up below or go out in the hay field and climb up on the hay stack and slide down. About four thirty each evening, Mr. Rodd came in from the field, and the cows came in from the pasture. (I used to wonder how cows knew it was time to come in.) The cows came in single file following the same path day after day. They then gathered in the corral outside the barn, and we would each bring one in and put it in a stall and milk it. Then go get another, until the entire small herd had all been milked. The buckets used for milking were shined, new looking steel. We emptied our buckets into two five-gallon milk cans, each with two handles and a lid. The cans were stored in the cool root cellar until Mr. Rodd took it to market. The landscape around the farm was desolate, dry, and vast. There was not another farmhouse in sight. It was an event when a car drove by. They always honked and waved and left a trail of road dust that would eventually settle until the next car came. They all knew each other out there for miles around. If a car turned into the yard, it was a cause for a mini celebration. Mrs. Rodd would seat the visitors in the shade of the porch and give them lemonade and cookies. If Mr. Rodd wasn't too far out in the field, he would come in. Jake, Andy, and I came in at these times because we knew there would be refreshments. We sat on the steps and listened to the gossip and news. This was the rural telegraph. Farmers for miles around learned whose cow was sick and who was pregnant. A couple of times I heard them speculating on who the father might be. These visits also brought news of who was arrested for drunk driving, and of course, there were the births and deaths. These neighborly visits were usually motivated by the need to borrow or return tools. And they gave rise to lively conversation at the supper table.

"Do you really think he could be the father?"

"I don't know. That girl is a wild one."

And on another news bit:

"How many drunk-driving charges has he had?"

"Too many, I'll tell ya. They should take his license away from him."

"They took it away once, but he told the judge he would not be able to feed his children if he couldn't drive."

I delighted in all this new gossip. It was better than radio drama.

The Rodd farmhouse was old, and its clapboard siding was once painted white, but time and the elements had turned it gray. There was a front porch and a front door, both of which were used only when there was company. The bedrooms were tucked in under the roof rafters with about five-feet clearance at the peak. On the first floor was the living room, kitchen, and back porch called the "milk room," because that was where the milk separator was kept. This machine was where the powerful technology of centrifugal force had been harnessed to separate cream from milk. The living room boasted a Persian-style rug, a davenport, a rocker, an upholstered easy chair, a lamp table with a lamp, and a shiny black heating stove. A light bulb hung down from a wire leading up to a hole in the ceiling. The Rodd farm was one of the first properties to benefit from the newly established Rural Electrification Administration. Prior to this time, nine out of ten farms in America were without electricity. There was a horseshoe with the rounded part on the bottom nailed above the front door.

"What's the horseshoe for?" I asked.

"It's for good luck," Jake said.

Why's it upside down?

"So the luck won't run out the ends."

That made sense to me.

On Saturdays we took eggs to town for sale. This wonderful summer came to an end, and I had to leave the farm. I went back to Colorado Springs to live with Grandma and Grandpa. As much as I loved my grandparents, I really wished I could have stayed with the Rodd family.

I didn't like Larry, the only child of Ralph and Buelah Wilky, a family I once was placed with. Larry was a mama's boy, who would rather stay in the house with his mother than go outside and explore the neighborhood. Larry and I didn't have anything in common. His father worked at the Golden Cycle mill, and when he was home, he and I would do things together like yard work and tinkering around the garage. He taught me how to put new half soles and heels on my worn-out shoes. These were activities Larry's mom would not even allow him to do, even if he had wanted to. Larry and I had to sleep together and eat together. He nettled me with his dumb remarks and his constant whining. On the bright side, it was summer, so I didn't have to go to school with him.

There were times when Mrs. Wilky would take Larry and me down to Fountain to visit her parents. Fountain was a small one horse town about ten miles south of Colorado Springs. It was founded in the mid–nineteenth century as a railroad shipping station for local farmers and ranchers. "Fontaine qui Bouille," or "Boiling Fountain," was the name given by French explorers to the town's nearby namesake, Fountain Creek. Its Main Street was one short block of stores on the old roadway to Pueblo: US 87. This narrow highway was referred to locally as the Ribbon of Death because of the many auto accidents caused by motorists crashing into concrete bridges, which were narrower than the road. Mrs. Wilky's parents lived in an old Victorian home on a large town lot. While Larry stayed inside, I wandered around the big property and played with their dog. They had a big woodpile out in back behind the shed, which caused me some concern. Grandpa had an expression: "There's a Nigger in the woodpile somewhere." His attitude toward colored people was as patronizing and unenlightened as was most of his generation. However, even though I didn't know what he meant, nor could I make any sense of why anyone would be in a woodpile, still I was cautious about getting too close to that woodpile.

The meals served here were real big farm-like presentations of fried chicken or ham, mashed potatoes, gravy, biscuits, fresh-picked green beans, corn, and radishes. There were home-canned pickles and piccalilli, followed by big slabs of apple pie. As much as I liked going to Fountain, I still didn't like living with Larry Wilky. I felt that the situation at that place was too much for me, so I ran away and went to Grandma's. She let me stay, and I never went back there.

Down along Fountain Creek, there were truck gardens farmed by Italian families, as I remember. Two names come to mind: Cimino and Venetucci. From time to time my cousin Duane Inzer and I would find a snack of carrots, lettuce, or cucumbers to hold us over while playing in the creek. We approached the vegetable gardens crawling on the ground with the stealth of ninjas because we had heard that "Peg- Leg-Pete" Cimino was cruel to boys who helped themselves to his produce. I never laid eyes on Mr. Cimino, but the scary image of him in my mind was of pirate Long John Silver—eye patch, saber, and all. I could just picture him stomping me with his peg leg. This image didn't prevent me from liberating a bit of his garden treasure though; it only made me very cautious when doing so.

The annual Pikes Peak or Bust rodeo was the most celebrated day in town. There was a parade down Tejon Street, led by a celebrity Grand Marshall, usually chosen from among Hollywood stars of B westerns; Buck Jones, Tex Ritter, Johnny Mack Brown, Hoot Gibson and others. Following the Grand Marshal. There were hundreds of beautiful horses of all description—paints, some white with dark markings and some dark with white marks; muscular quarter horses, often used by mounted police; the spotted Appaloosas, bred by the Nez Perce tribe; Arabians, originally domesticated in the Middle East, proud walking, huge (eighteen hands high, or six feet); Clydesdales, brown with white manes and feather above their hooves, weighing over two thousand pounds; the golden palominos with ivory-colored mane and tail. There were Morgans and Pintos and ponies of all kinds, including tiny Shetlands ridden by small cowboys and cowgirls. Most riders (both men and women) and horses alike were all decked for show with silver concho bridles, saddles, belts, and chaps. Some wore buckskins, and most wore cowboy boots and hats, the Mexican vaquerros, resplendent in their elaborately stitched Charro suits, some black with white stitching and some white with white or black stitching; all wore sombreros with leather chin straps and brims broad enough to cast a shadow over their heads, necks, and shoulders. The Mexican saddles were elaborate in design. They weren't to herd cattle or chase mustangs. The saddles were elaborately tooled and engraved with silver. It was purely pride in horsemanship. Riding their favored brown-and-white pintos came the Native Americans wearing silver and turquoise adornments, riding bareback in buckskins, moccasins, and elaborate feathered war bonnets.

The parade included a stage coach robbery, square dancers with fiddle players, and Indian dances with tom-toms and chants. There were marching bands and baton twirling majorettes from the Colorado Springs High School and Colorado College. During and after the war, Camp Carson joined the parade with bands, drill teams, ski troops (all in white) tanks, artillery, troop carriers, jeeps, and such. The floats were many and varied. My favorite floats were the ones that had people on them that were throwing candy to the spectators. The Shriners, in their fezzes with tassels, rode their little motor scooters in intricate formations. Veterans of World War I were represented with a sizeable contingency. All this was followed by the street department crew with shovels and truck scooping up road apples. They always got a big round of applause from the spectators.

The Pikes Peak or Bust rodeo took place in the Penrose Stadium. There was bronc riding, bull riding, barrel racing, calf roping, bull-dogging, stunt riders, and clowns. An enacted battle between "settlers" in covered wagons and whooping "Indians" on horseback took place with the "settlers holding their own until the Indians gave up and rode off."

For the kids there was greased-pig chasing. The rodeo hosted future hall-of-fame rodeo cowboys like Casey Tibbs, Jim Shoulders, and Bill Linderman. For weeks leading up to Rodeo Day, the downtown merchants competed in decorating their windows and store fronts with a Western cowboy/frontier theme. There were first, second, and third ribbons given with lots of newspaper coverage with pictures. There was a beard-growing contest (in the '30s, beards were extremely rare). If a man didn't grow a beard at this time, he was ridiculed; some were even dunked in a horse trough of water. To some men the growing of a beard was welcome. It was something they always wanted to do but didn't have the moxie to buck 1930s convention. To others it was a pain in the ass, but they participated because everyone else was doing it. The herd instinct is strongly imbedded. Once the winners were announced, all beards vanished. Other than rodeo time, the dandies and ladies of fashion wore white from Decoration Day (last Monday in May, the unofficial beginning of summer) to Labor Day. The men put aside their felt fedoras, Stetsons, and wool caps for straw panama flat-top boaters, white shoes, and trousers and seer-sucker jackets. The ladies, not to be outdone, wore white skirts, blouses, and brown-and-white spectator shoes.

It seemed like about all adults and a lot of teenagers, both male and female, used tobacco of some kind: cigarettes, pipes, cigars, chewing tobacco, or snuff. Even the president openly smoked cigarettes with a holder. Camel cigarettes advertised that "more doctors smoke Camels than any other cigarette." Lucky Strike cigarettes ran a newspaper ad featuring a young couple in swimsuits, both smoking. The caption was, "Smoke a Lucky to feel your level best." We viewed movies wherein about all the sophisticated and unsophisticated actors smoked and enjoyed cocktails. The kids of this generation were being made to think that smoking and drinking were the proof of being grown up. A lot of us couldn't wait to imbibe.

I attended thirteen or fourteen different elementary schools. This was because my address was changed so often. Either we moved because, I guess, Grandpa found cheaper rent, or Mother moved me and my sister to live with her. There also was a scattering of foster homes and other addresses too many to be remembered. I think Mother felt that Grandma and Grandpa shouldn't bear the full responsibility of raising us since they had raised Kenny from birth. By attending all these different schools in different[6] neighborhoods, I was developing a perceptive awareness of new and different people, places, and things around me—lay of the land, so to speak.

Mother married again to Doctor Charles McCracken, whose small practice was in a second floor walk-up. He was a divorced recovering alcoholic who lived in a room behind his office. She was his nurse and lived there also. I didn't know him very well. I remember he had a false leg and a glass eye and was missing one hand. He lost the hand while chopping wood. The other parts were lost in World War I. Like many doctors of the day, he charged patient on a sliding scale, based on their ability to pay. Some could not pay at all, and some paid by barter with fruit and vegetables from their gardens.

Doctor once took me on his house rounds. (Doctors made house calls at that time. They treated people, not diseases.) I waited in the car while he went in the patient's house. He returned shortly, and we went to the next home. There were about four or five stops. While he was inside the homes, I was eating Hershey chocolate kisses from a white paper bag I found in his car. I had never even seen this candy before, but I knew chocolate when I saw it. A short time after

---

[6]   I think I may be the only person who ever flunked kindergarten.

he brought me home, I had an acute case of diarrhea right in my pants.

After Mother and Grandma cleaned me up, Mother inquired, "What have you been eating?"

When I told her about the kisses, she said to Grandma, words to the effect that the kisses acted as a laxative. I took that to mean that the kisses were not candy, and I avoided them the rest of my childhood. Dr. McCracken died in 1939. Mother inherited nothing from his estate. All moneys received from the sale of his practice and equipment went to his children. I was proud that my "father" was a doctor and I inherited a short-lived yearning to follow in his footsteps even though I hardly knew him. He did set a broken arm for me once though, and he was always pleasant to be around. I just didn't come in contact with him much.

My attendance at so many schools resulted in my always being the new kid, which in the culture of young boys of that time meant I had to establish where I was to fit in the pecking order of the male hierarchy of the present school. This was usually settled by a fight or two. Other times respect was achieved by demonstrated athletic ability. I did learn after more than a few schools that by "whistling past the grave yard," I could bluff by talking and walking with an air of fearlessness. This acquired skill served me well for many years even long into adulthood.

Construction Work and Kool-Aid

At one time my grandparents, Uncle Walt, Kenny, and I lived on the northeast corner of Platte Avenue and El Paso Street. This was during the construction of the Platte Avenue underpass, which resulted in the avenue going under the railroad tracks rather than crossing them. This was a large construction project which offered many hours of things to see and wonder about. I first saw the jackhammers tearing up the pavement and sidewalks, then the big yellow Caterpillars gouging and moving the earth into large mountains to then be lifted by the great steam shovel bucket on a boom, which then rotated around and dumped the earth into the waiting bed of an enormous dump truck to be hauled away to where I didn't know. "Gee haw," you could hear the mule drivers call out. Even though they had gasoline-driven earth-moving equipment, mule-pulling plows and scoops were also in use with a man walking behind two black mules with the reins tied together and pulled over one shoulder while his hands guided the scoop. I was mesmerized by all this activity. The mules were big and strong with muscles and ears bigger than horses. Their manes had been cut short, and they were wearing big collars with straps and strips of leather going everywhere. Sweat was dripping off their bodies by the gallon. I was also thrilled to watch the iron workers heat large steel bolts and nuts in a burner of hot coals sitting on the ground then with tongs toss them one at a time up to a worker balanced on a steel girder who caught it in a big metal funnel with a handle, extracted it with tongs, and then pounded it with a hand sledge into lined up holes in two girders in order to bolt them together.

When all this was going on, I was about age six doing my kindergarten encore at Columbia School, where I learned to play and sing "Pop Goes the Weasel," and I never forget the lyrics:

> It's raining, it's pouring;
> The old man is snoring.
> Bumped his head,
> And he went to bed,
> And he couldn't get up in the morning.

I don't know how I missed learning such deathless lyrics my first run at kindergarten. The subtle philosophic nuances were probably too deep for me at the time. For this poetic enlightenment alone, I've lived a life of gratitude for having had the second chance at kindergarten. We also sang "Polly Put the Kettle On," one of those songs whose lyrics keep popping up in your head even though you don't like the lyrics or the tune. Being a veteran kindergartner, I was a whiz at "London Bridge Is Falling Down." At eraser cleaning, I had no peers. I was a tall, scrawny kid, but I was wiry. After two stints at kindergarten, the folks in charge of Columbia School felt I had become worldly enough to grapple with the arduous curriculum of first grade. I didn't disappoint them. I got deep into first grade books: Dick and Jane, Little Black Sambo, and I found the story of Peter Rabbit and Farmer McGregor stirring.

Radio Event

June 22, 1937, Comiskey Park, Chicago
Joe Louis, KOs Jim Braddock in 8th round to become Heavyweight Champion of the World

There were celebrations in the streets of the colored neighborhoods all across the country. The first colored heavyweight champ since Jack Johnson was defeated by Jess Willard in 1915. The people's racial pride was uplifted even though bogged down in the depths of the Depression when most were living on relief. Louis stated that he didn't feel he was the champion until he could again meet Max Schmeling, the only man to ever knock him out.

The Platte Avenue construction project led me into the beverage business. I set up a Kool-Aid stand in the front yard. It consisted of a wooden box standing on end with a pitcher of Kool-Aid and three or four glasses. The price was a penny a glass. The construction workers almost always paid more. Some paid as much as a nickel. The glasses were not washed between customers use, but then neither was the dipper they used at their water bucket. The enterprise was quite successful. The earnings-to-equity ratio would make any corporation envious. Grandpa was not at all impressed with this entrepreneurial genius in his house. He ran over my bicycle, which he had promised me he would if I left it in the driveway one more time. I was devastated when I saw the mangled bike. It was totaled. I was too scared to go in the house. I stayed outside until Grandma called me to dinner. I walked in cautiously staying close to Grandma. At the dinner table, Grandpa didn't say a word about the bike. I didn't either. That was a lesson I learned; that Grandpa never pointed an empty gun. What he promised, he delivered.

In 1935 John L. Lewis of the United Mine Workers Union had been rejected for the last time in his bid to get the American Federation of Labor (AFL) to include industrial workers. The AFL is a coalition of unions of specific old-line crafts, like printers, carpenters, masons, and the like. They wanted nothing to do with workers without a craft or trade. Lewis then, along with his mine workers, put together a coalition of workers of various industries such as steel workers and auto workers. This new coalition became known as the Congress of Industrial Organizations. (CIO) The new organization grew in numbers, stature, and strength to a point that politicians campaigning for office energetically courted the CIO endorsement. The industrial workers were a significant factor in Roosevelt's reelection in 1936. The CIO was widely considered to be the most important progressive force in the country.

Cowboys Indians and Early Childhood Sex Education

One of my favorite pastimes was playing either cops and robbers or cowboys. I had a Dick Tracy cap gun and a set of two Gene Autry six shooters with holsters. We would chase each other around the sheds and garages in the alley shooting back and forth. When I had no caps for my gun, I sometimes would cut off and use the heads of kitchen matches, but this was too cumbersome for quick shooting gun play.

"Hey, I shot you. You're supposed to be dead."

"I shot you first."

"No, you didn't. I shot you first, you cheater."

This would usually end the game. A shot was purely vocal unless someone had some caps, which was rare. All opinions were based on auditory perception. I also spent time with the crystal set[7] Kenny had built for me. It fascinated me how this little device could produce radio programs. The signal was weak and often too scratchy with static to hear clearly, but it thrilled me to hear music, news reports, and plays on my own radio—the same programs that were being broadcast on the big consol radio in the living room that the family sat around listening to in the evening. I probably spent the most time in the activity of daydreaming and imagining. These pas-

---

[7]   [6] The crystal set is a very simple radio receiver. It needs no battery or power source. It is powered by radio waves from a long wire antenna. It is operated by scratching a "cat's whisker" across a crystal made of galena. The sound comes through earphones.

times pushed me into many characters and heroics of all kinds. I still maintain a goodly amount of talent in daydreaming and imagining.

Even the birds and the bees do it. And little boys too young to participate talk about it. While in discourse with Henry Biggs, a boy in my first grade class, he said, "The man puts his thing in the woman's behind."

I told him, "No, they don't. There's a hole in front where they put it. My sister told me, and she showed me hers."

How we got on this subject, I couldn't even guess. I didn't have an interest in this subject till much later. This misled boy had the possession-of-all-possessions, a Mickey Mouse wristwatch. He let me wear it once. We went in the house so I could show it to Grandma.

"That is very nice, now where did you get it?"

"It's Henry's. He let me wear it. Could I get one?"

"It looks expensive. When my ship comes in, we'll see about getting you one. But now I think you should give the watch back to Henry before you break it."

Colorado Springs Floods
The Grasshopper Plague

O n Memorial Day 1935, the *Gazette* reported that Colorado Springs had suffered its greatest-ever natural disaster when a series of thunderstorms dropped 7.5 inches of rain, causing the Monument and Fountain Creeks to swell and burst through their banks. All bridges across the creeks except the Bijou Street viaduct were destroyed, as well as many homes and businesses that lay within the flood plain. A good portion of the city lay in ruins. As many as eighteen people died in the flood.

"The destructive floodwaters from half a dozen cloudbursts swept through the city in all its fury shortly after noon. Though ample warning was given to most persons in the path of the oncoming waters, many failed to realize the danger and remained in their homes," the newspaper also reported. "Others did not receive warning before the onrushing water struck."

About a week after the flood, Grandpa and Grandma and I went for a drive to see the devastation. My four-year-old memory is pretty bare of any actual flood sightings on that trip. I do however, remember my grandparents talking about it. Grandpa would point out locations where a particular business once stood or where a person he knew once lived. The flood was a topic of conversation in our home for years to come. I began to believe I had actually witnessed it. I suppose it must have been the same with some folks in the post-diluvian period. A few years later while playing down by the creek, I did see some of the ruined collapsed and washed-out abandoned homes. I would guess this "greatest natural disaster" is unknown to the present residents of Colorado Springs.

As if the Depression, the dust storms, and the flood were not trial enough, El Paso County, Eastern Colorado, Western Kansas, and Oklahoma were visited by a grasshopper plague. Grandpa, being a foreman with the County Road Department, was working right in the heart of the problem areas. His truck would be covered with dead grasshoppers each night when he came home. He would get the garden hose out and wash grasshoppers out of the truck's front grill and radiator to prevent the motor from overheating. The insects even got down into the air intake vents and the carburetor. While Grandpa was cleaning the truck, he kept repeating, "Goddamn, goddamn, goddamn." His voice would alternate between rising into a great crescendo, first giving emphasis to "god" and the next time emphasizing "damn." He then would drop to a whisper and start all over again. I stayed out of his way and enjoyed watching the performance while repeating his words under my breath. I realized then why Grandma referred to him as the "Old Bull of the Woods." There were stories of swarms of grasshoppers descending on crop fields and eating the entire crop within hours. In the back of Grandpa's pickup truck, there were tubs of pesticide mixed with sorghum molasses used to combat the insects. I was afraid to eat sorghum molasses after that.

Boys Club, Caddying the Broadmoor

When I was about age seven or eight, Grandma gave Kenny ten cents to pay for me to go to the Boys Club for a month (Kenny was already a member). I went to the club almost every night from about 6:00 to 8:00 p.m.

Kenny had to take me there and bring me home. Like any big brother, I'm sure he looked forward to this duty. He got me signed up then went off on his own and told me to meet him back at the entrance when the club closed.

One of my favorite activities at the club was wood shop, where I built useful things like doorstops of wood and an ashtray made from cow horns. I also liked to watch old black and white silent movies with Charlie Chaplin or the Keystone Cops. I spent a lot of time at the club viewing pictures of faraway exotic places with the stereoscope, which was a devise you placed a card on that had two identical photos side by side and you held the scope up to your face and looked in the viewer and it gave you a three dimensional view of the photo. It seemed like magic to me. My favorite sport was boxing. We had tournaments where the winner of a bout would then take on a new opponent right after his win. Usually you were so tired from holding up your arms wearing sixteen-ounce gloves during the first bout, that you were lucky to win the second bout. If you went beyond the third bout, you were an exceptional athlete. I never did. It seemed to me that the poorer kids went to the Boys Club, and the rich kids went to the YMCA.

Duane was my best friend during these years, even though we sometimes lived too far apart to be able to get together very often, but when we did, a world of adventure always ensued. The summer of 1942, Duane and I caddied at the Broadmoor Golf Club as had Uncle Walt and Kenny before me. I was ten years old, and Duane was eleven. We were the youngest caddies on the course and were barely able to carry the golf bags even though the bags of that era were not nearly as heavy as today's bags. They were often made of a stiff canvas trimmed with leather, but when filled with golf clubs, they were pretty heavy for a ten-year-old.

After my first day caddying, I went home with a very sore and blistered shoulder where the golf bag strap had rubbed. I had carried two eighteen-hole loops that day. Mother sewed shoulder pads into my shirt. The pads worked well. Caddies at the club were paid a caddy fee of one dollar per eighteen-hole loop and if you impressed the golfer in some manner such as helping his score by being knowledgeable as to the terrain of the course and which club to suggest etc. At ten years old, I didn't get any inquiries as to how to play the course, but there were other ways to help your golfer, which I learned from the older caddies: carry some balls in your pocket, and drop one in an advantageous spot when your golfer's ball was in extreme rough, then identify the placed ball as his/hers. Another way to help was to step on the opponent's ball so it would sink into the soil and be very difficult to hit.

A caddy might be tipped as much as one dollar, but the average was fifty cents. I once carried "doubles," meaning that I carried the bags of two golfers at the same time. This was done when there was a shortage of caddies. This was a heavy load, but it paid well. Each golfer paid me two dollars. I once carried for a golfer, a doctor, who had only one club (a two iron) in his bag. He used it both as a driver off the tee and as a putter on the green and every club in between. Obviously he didn't need a caddie or a bag, but both were required by club rules. There was one old guy caddying (maybe fiftyish) whose name was something like John Batist. He was a shaggy, long-haired old guy who kept to himself pretty much. When he did feel like conversing, he demonstrated a great amount of knowledge about the

Broadmoor golf course. The guys would often ask his advice. (There were rumors that he had once been a pro golfer.) He took an interest in us neophytes and helped us learn the trade. He taught us the use of each club, how to carry the bag, and all the gentlemanly protocols of the game. We all called him "John the Baptist." He didn't preach or anything. We just called him that because his name sounded like that. One of the caddies made up a little song about him, sung to the tune of Battle Hymn of the Republic. I can only remember that it began with, "They put John the Baptist in the concentration camp." He didn't seem to mind.

We also earned money by shagging balls on the driving range. We would take a wire basket and go out on the driving range and be the target of the driving golfer. Each ball driven would have to be retrieved and placed in the basket and then be ready for the next drive. Sometimes the next drive would come while you were retrieving the previously driven ball. You had to be very watchful and duck the balls coming at you. "You stupid shit head!" I would yell when a driven ball came close to hitting me. Being two hundred yards away, of course the golfer couldn't hear me. The retrieved basket of balls was returned to the caddy shack where they were counted to see if any were missing. If the count was good, I got paid. If not, I was told to return to the range and retrieve the missing balls. There was the option of just going without the shagging fee. I never exercised the option.

While we hung out around the caddy shack waiting for a loop, we would lag pennies, arm wrestle, drink Cokes, or play rock-pa-per-scissors. On a whim, the older guys might decide to initiate a few younger new caddies. On one occasion they made two brothers fight each other while they stood around them with belts withdrawn and whipped the fighters if they thought they were faking it. It was ugly and scary. The boys were both crying, and one had a bloody nose. I couldn't stand to watch any more of it. Duane and I were thinking the same thing; we were afraid they might make us fight. Without speaking of our fear, we decided to leave. We slowly backed away so as not to be noticed by any of the sadistic older guys. We eased around the corner of the shack where we couldn't be seen, turned, and ran as fast as we could until we ran out of breath. We hitched a ride and went home. That was the last time we caddied, and the summer wasn't half over. We went back to collecting and selling scrap metal.

The Big Wheel, Scrap Peddlers, and Funny Papers

Duane and I invented what became known as the Big Wheel Tricycle. We didn't know we had invented something that would become such a popular toy. We just took the front wheel, the seat, and handlebars off an old tricycle, turned the tricycle upside down, remounted the wheel where the handlebars had been, and mounted the handlebars where the wheel had been. We used the rear-axle step to sit on. Today this idea is manifested in a mass-produced plastic vehicle selling in the millions and is no more than a tricycle turned upside down. Many years later while living in Park Forest, Illinois, I made these same conversions with the tricycles belonging to my sons, Dan and Geoff. They had outgrown them. Several neighborhood kids came around and asked if I would do the same to their tricycles. Fearing that perhaps their parents would not approve of my tearing apart their child's toy, I told them, "You ask your mom and dad if it's OK and have them come see me." Nobody came. The kids probably explained it in such a way to their parents that understandably it appeared that this crazy man in the neighborhood was going to totally destroy the kid's tricycle.

Duane and I did, however, demonstrate certain entrepreneurial skills in that we collected scrap iron from the city dump and hauled it in a wagon and sold it to the scrap yard. We did this when in need of movie money. In that time a Saturday matinee at the movie theatre would often be a double feature with a cartoon, a short subject film (a film not long enough to be considered a feature film, known as shorts), and a news reel of the week's current events dominated by events of the war in Europe. Pictures of the war always featured Adolf Hitler with his silly-looking little square patch of hair under his nose and Benito Mussolini, who looked like a uniformed peacock buffoon. Our favorite shows were cowboy shows with Buck Jones, Lash Larue, Tom Mix, and Gene Autry. There were futuristic space pilots Buck Rogers and Flash Gordon flying in space ships in the year 2040. We saw all the tough-guy movies too with stars the likes of James Cagney, George Raft, Edward G. Robinson, and Humphrey Bogart. Gangsters in those days didn't pack "heat" or carry a "piece." They packed a "rod," a "roscoe," or a "gat." All this entertainment was for eleven cents. We usually watched it all a second time before leaving. The Tomkins Theater on Nevada Avenue had drawings for bags of groceries on Saturday night. This was a big draw for Depression-struggling families.

After Grandpa was finished with the newspaper, I would read all the "funny papers." There was Dick Tracy, Superman, Popeye, Little Orphan Annie, Li'l Abner, Tarzan, and many others. My favorite of all, which only appeared in the Sunday paper, was Prince Valiant, which was a continuous story adventure during the days of King Arthur. I didn't know it at the time, but Edward, Duke of Windsor, had called Prince Valiant the "greatest contribution to English literature in the past hundred years." I liked the elaborate, detailed pictures of the strip, which created fantasies, in my young head, of living in the days of chivalry battling the powers of evil so as to win the favor of the fair maiden. I made a wooden sword and rode one of Grandpa's saw horses off into battle (the same horse I rode as a cowboy).

Treasure Hunting at the City Dump

Before there was land fill for municipal waste, each town had an area on the outskirts of the city limits for the city dump, where all trash was hauled and periodically burned. Colorado Springs distinguished trash from garbage. Garbage was waste food. Trash was all other refuse. Each household had a garbage can and a trash can. The city picked up the trash and the Babcock hog farm trucks picked up the garbage to feed the hogs. In addition, each home had an ash pit. The ash pit was an igloo-shaped structure about five feet high, made of brick and mortar, and coated with a cement plaster. It had an opening at the top for loading and for smoke to escape and an opening at the bottom for cleaning out when it got full. This structure was used for burnable trash and for ashes from the coal furnace and kitchen stove. A private trash hauler was hired to empty and haul away the ashes when it was filled.

The city dump was a treasure trove for Duane and me. We found broken items we could either repair or alter to something useful to us beyond its original intended use, such as a broken-down baby carriage which still had four wheels. This find and a couple pieces of scrap boards and bailing wire would miraculously be transformed into a magnificent and very utilitarian vehicle in which to haul scrap metal to market or race down a hill. The prisoners always waved at us as we pulled our scrap-loaded makeshift lorries by the county jail on South Cascade Avenue. I imagined these were hardened bank robbers, murderers, and high-jackers, not drunks, petty thieves, and nuisances.

Grandma Names Two Mountains, Throwing Bricks at Pigeons Skydiving, and Smoking Driftwood

T he dump was across the street from the cemetery. (I find humor in the fact that these two resting places for dead people on one side of the street and dead stuff on the other were in such close proximity.) Not all my toys came from the dump. I had a few other favorite things which occupied my time, like my Lincoln logs which were a Christmas gift. A short walk beyond the dump there were two hills side by side where we coasted all sorts of wheeled contraptions. These hills were known to us as Mount Washington and Mount Lincoln. Family legend had it that they had been named by Grandma. However, we might have been the only family who knew their names.

Down the hill from Grandma's mountains by East Las Vegas Street, which had been the old road to Pueblo, was an old abandoned brick factory. The brick yard had all grown up in weeds. There were loose and broken bricks strewn all over, some half buried in the ground. The wooden buildings, long absent of paint, were leaning over or had already fallen except for one big warehouse building which had all the windows either broken or missing. Duane and I would go in this dilapidated building and throw brick chards at the pigeons that roosted up in the rafters. Our aim was no good. We never hit one.

Radio Event
June 22, 1938

Joe Louis, having suffered his only knockout defeat at the hands of the German Max Schmeling in their 1936 bout, flattened the thought-to-be Nazi in two minutes, four seconds of the first round. This sold-out event at Yankee Stadium drew gate receipts of a few thousand over a million dollars [over seventeen million in 2016 dollars]. It was attended by the rich and the famous of many walks of life as well as the little guy who spent part of the rent money for a ticket. In the minds of the people, this was the real championship fight to prove for all whether the American Negro or the German Nazi earned the right to be called boxing's heavyweight champion of the world. In America, to some, "colored" pride was at stake. ("If Joe loses, colored people lose.") To some, National pride was on the line and sadly to say to some, White pride was at risk. In Germany, It was said that Hitler ordered German radio to go off the air once the outcome was known.

Pandemonium broke out filling the streets of Harlem, the Black Bottom of Detroit, Chicago's Southside, Mill Creek at St. Louis, Eighteenth Street in Kansas City, and many other African American neighborhoods across the country. The people were proud and loud and together doing their thing. Celebrations went on all night long. To some it was a time to thank the Lord. Some wanted Joe Louis for President. A few incidents of lawlessness and violence were reported and required the police to keep order, but by and large, it was a joyous outpouring of Black pride and solidarity like none the country had ever experienced before. On that night everybody was somebody.

I accidentally might have been one of the first skydivers. I made a parachute by tying the four corners of an old bedsheet with four lengths of hemp twine I then tied the four loose ends to my belt loops, two in front and two in back. There was a telephone pole next to the ally on one side and Grandpa's garden on the other. Using the climbing spikes attached to the pole, I climbed up about halfway. I faced the garden side which would make a softer landing than the hard packed gravel of the alley. I centered my parasheet over my head so it would catch the air and not snag on one of the climbing spikes and leave me dangling on the pole but, instead, float me down gently to the garden. Without further ado, I leaped. The impact of crashing to the ground was so instant I didn't get to even feel the dive, let alone a gentle float. I went immediately from leap to pain everywhere—ankles, knees, hips. I rolled over in the dirt moaning. The landing jolted my jaw bone and my neck. I gathered up my sheet and limped slowly to the house greatly disappointed. Why didn't that work?

Duane and I played down by Fountain Creek where we smoked driftwood sticks as if they were cigars and cut willow branches which we turned into furniture by tying larger pieces together to frame a chair or table then weaving the thinner more pliable pieces into tabletop and chair seats. These adventures kept us well occupied and interested, and they didn't require money, of which we had none. We fished in the creek with our poles made of willow branches, string, and a hook made from a safety pin. The hooks were baited with night crawlers we had gathered in a coffee can the night before, or we might use a grasshopper. Regardless of the bait, we never caught any fish.

Our Unorganized Fun

Kids were allowed to dream, create, and use their imaginations in those days. We were not bombarded with organized activities and shuttled off to play T-Ball or little league baseball, football, soccer, or anything else organized by adults. There was no preschool. We all started kindergarten at age five, going half days in the morning. From first grade on we went full-time 9:00 a.m. to 3:30 p.m. Other than that we were free to devise any recreation we could think of. As boys, we did play baseball and football, but all we needed for baseball was a ball of any kind. It didn't have to be a Rawlings official major league ball. Our bat could be a tree limb, a board, or a broomstick. Our playing field was the nearest vacant lot, the alley, or the street. These venues also served as football stadia. Football required only that we had an object we could pass or run with; an old rolled-up towel or shirt served quite well. Girls played hop scotch, jax, and jump rope. Hop scotch required only a sidewalk and something that would make a mark on it; chalk was preferred, but a nail would suffice. Rope-jumping needed no more than something long enough that could be used as a rope. Jax and ball had to be bought at the dime store. Girls also played with dolls and created their own fantasies of motherhood and other grown-up female things. Swimming didn't require lessons at the YMCA, a pond, lake, or creek would do. Our water park was a garden sprinkler on the front lawn. There was a public pool at Monument Valley Park, but no organized lessons. We held track meets wherever we were. We would race from one end of the block to the other. Our trophy for winning was that we would not be called a "rotten egg." The loser of the race had exclusive use of that title until the next race where he would have his chance for redemption. Our lives were our own, uncluttered with adult organized activities.

Hobo Jungle

Aunt Pearl packed bologna sandwiches and dried apricots using empty one gallon syrup buckets, from the "relief commodities," as lunch pails. Duane and I would take our buckets down by the creek and sit on a washed up log and eat. On one such trip we walked down the railroad tracks a ways then went down the embankment into a stand of cottonwood trees by the creek. We came upon a group of men in a "hobo jungle."

"Hobo jungles" were commonplace in the Depression years. The "jungle" was a place for homeless men to rest while on the road outside of town. They were out-of-the-way places where the hobos could eat, sleep, and wash before jumping on the next freight train. The "jungles" ideally were located near a rail yard and a water source and where there would be dry fire wood and shade. It was better yet if there was a store nearby to buy a little food, and not so far away from town that the penniless men could not panhandle a few coins.

We were caught by surprise to find this group of men. At first we froze still in our tracks. I was too scared to even run. I guess Duane was also. I hoped we hadn't been seen, but once my eyes refocused through my fear, I realized they were all looking at us. They waved for us to come over. We moved toward them haltingly.

One of them said, "Come on over. We won't bite you."

The smell of coffee and wood burning was coming from a fire with a coffee pot suspended above it. They all smiled and said "Hi" or "Howdy" or some such friendly greeting.

A tall thin man, looking older than the rest, asked, "What's your names?"

"Duane," "Jack," we said in unison.

"Well hello, boys. How old are you?"

After we told him (I think we were about eight and nine), he said: "My boy's nine years old. I'm going to be home for his birthday."

We lost some of our fear with this news. This was a regular grown-up with a son and all. The younger one of the group asked where we were going. We told him we were going down by the creek.

"Well, have fun," one of them said.

We left feeling we had escaped from what could have been a terrible fate. We never returned to that spot again. The fear we had first felt in that place never really left us.

Hitchhiking and Riding on Dynamite

Duane and I once hitched a ride to Manitou with a man who had us sit in the back seat of his car. On the rear floor of which was several large cardboard boxes we had to climb over.

Once we got settled and he started up again, he said, "Be careful back there. Those boxes are filled with dynamite."

My heart jumped up in to my throat. I almost choked. I assume Duane had the same response. I looked in the rearview mirror. The man had a smirk on his face. He got a real kick out of scaring us to death. I don't know if there really were any explosives in that car or not, but I rode scared all the way to Manitou. Sometimes in the crowded slow-moving summer tourist traffic, we would just slide on to a rear bumper of a car and ride to Manitou. Cars didn't have side mirrors then, so it was easy to come from the rear side of the car without being seen, and we didn't weigh enough to be felt.

Toy Makers, Submariners, Thieves, and Chocolate

Kids in our circumstances used to hand-make a lot of our toys. We made scooters from scrap wood and a pair of roller skates. The skates were made to pull apart to adjust for size to fit your shoe. We would pull them completely apart and nail the front wheels onto the end of a board and the back wheels onto the other end. On the front end of the board was nailed another board at ninety degrees to hold the scooter handles. Another invention was the "Tin Can Shoe"; we would take used Columbine condensed milk cans, crush them with our foot, and hammer them around our shoes to walk around on the sidewalk clicking and clacking. It didn't take much to amuse us.

When the Inzers lived on the dirt road called East Costilla Street on the other side of where all the colored people lived, there was an old car top in the backyard which made Duane and me a perfect fort after we dug out under it so we could stand up and look out the window openings which long ago had been divested of their glass. That old car top was used as a race car with a pretend steering wheel. It was a surfacing submarine and a secret hideout. During this period we also built a one-hole golf course out in a hilly weed field. The green was a weed cleared patch of dirt with an old tomato can sunk in the ground for the hole. The first (and only), Tee was on a weed cleared hill top. We used a couple of golf clubs "borrowed" from Duane's older brother Frank. I don't remember which clubs we used, but they worked for us. Our biggest problem on the links was finding our ball after we knocked it into the tall weeds. We were okay with improving our lie on each stroke.

Duane and I used to go over and sit on the Sinton Dairy steps and dream up images of being grownups. In this fantasy world we rode horses, ate candy, ice cream, chocolate cake, fried chicken, and Coca Cola. We stayed up late and didn't have to take a bath or brush our teeth, comb our hair, or change our underwear. It was on these same dairy steps that Duane revealed to me one morning that he had a one dollar bill he had come across while rummaging through his father's pants pockets.

"We can buy candy with this."

"Are kids supposed to have those?"

"I don't know. We can ask at the store."

"What if they put us in jail?' I was scared.

"We can run and hide."

"You go ask at the store."

"You come with me."

"I'm not sure."

"Come on, don't be a sissy."

I gave in given that alterative.

There was a small neighborhood grocery right across the street where we had now and then bought penny candies and five-cent Popsicles. We browsed the candy counter for the longest time.

"What can I do for you, boys?

"We're looking," Duane forced out.

I had butterflies in my stomach. The man returned to his cash register. We continued to pretend to be making a choice.

Duane whispered, "What do you want?"

"I don't know."

Through the cloak of fear surrounding me I hadn't been able to even see the candy. A lifetime passed, and I was just ready to say, "Let's leave," when Duane picked up a candy bar and said, "Let's get this."

My knees were bucking uncontrollably when Duane put the candy bar on the counter and dug in his pants pocket and handed the dollar bill to the man.

"That'll be five cents out of a one-dollar bill," the man said.

The cash register rang, and the cash drawer opened. I hoped he wasn't going for his gun. He counted out some coins and put them in Duane's small hand. We left the store, and I didn't start breathing again till after we cleared the door and were on the sidewalk. We crossed the street and sat on the dairy steps.

It was not until then that I realized that Duane had selected a Hershey bar. We ate it, each eating one small section at a time. I finally settled my butterflies and greatly enjoyed the chocolate. We went back to the store and bought another one and went back across the street to the dairy steps and ate it. We repeated this routine a couple more times until we got sick, at which time we went back in the alley and heaved it all up, first me, then Duane. I think we only bought one chocolate bar at a time because we had never made a purchase larger than a nickel in our lives, nor did we at my age, about six years old and Duane age seven, know how many candy bars we could buy with a dollar. That grocer must have been one greedy guy to let us spend that kind of money during those hard Depression times when no kid had that kind of money to spend on candy. That $1.00 would be equal to $15.56 in 2010. That amount of money out of his father's pocket was obviously missed. Duane paid dearly.

East Moreno Street was on "Sinton Hill" just a couple of blocks from the Sinton dairy on South El Paso Street where in the course of a day Duane and I might go climb on the board fence and pet the milk wagon horses. Sometimes we would wrap up some sugar in newspaper and have the horses lick it out of our hands. We laughed with the sensation of the horses' tongue tickling the palm of our hands. We wiped the slobber off on our pants. Pants were good for wiping lots of things off the hands, just like fingernails were so good for collecting earth.

"Look at the thing on that one!" One of the most fun things at the corral was seeing a horse's erect "thing." Some were pink, and some were black, and they seemed to push them out and suck them back in. We had no idea what all this meant. I had the feeling that viewing this was sort of a forbidden experience, but it brought forth giggles to us anyway. Another funny spectacle was when they let go a stream of pee like someone had turned on a garden hose. And of course there was the thrill of watching them raise their tails and poop. We didn't know the term "road apple," at the time or I'm sure we would have been making and laughing at scat jokes for a long time.

Those Fascinating Trains

When we lived by the tracks on north El Paso Street, Duane and I used to put a penny on the railroad track, which was across the street, and wait for the train to come and run over it. After all the rail cars had passed, we would go retrieve a very larger, flatter, and illegible coin. We considered our end product a trophy of our ingenuity. We also liked to stand by the tracks and wave to the engineers and the firemen who were shoveling coal from the coal car to the engine's fire box. Passengers often waved to us, as did the Porters, cooks, and waiters who sometimes were standing in the stairways between the cars. On the freight trains, we waved at the trainmen in the bright-red end car, the caboose, which was a special car at the end of the train for an office, sleeping quarters, and kitchen. The caboose also had a small windowed projection on the roof called the cupola, where the crew sat in elevated chairs. From this perch they could observe the entire train. To me this looked like the greatest way in the world to live. Each time I saw a caboose or a passenger train go by, it engendered in me a longing to go to all the strange and exotic places I had heard of. I would daydream forever with fantasies of going to all these places.

We lived just three or four blocks down the tracks from the Santa Fe railroad station. We could hear the steam driven engines starting up to begin a run. The loud "chuhs" from steam escaping started very slowly and spaced far apart. As the engine began to get a head of steam, the "chuhs" sped up. When it went by our house, the big black eight-wheel engine with valves and hoses connected all over it and with white steam and black smoke billowing out of the stacks gave out a much louder and more rapid and rhythmic staccato, "chuh-chuh-chuh-chuh," which then gradually faded away as the engine traveled on. About this time the train whistle would sound down the track, warning drivers at the road intersections. (It is my understanding that Einstein gave birth to his theory of relativity while watching such a train.) I never tired of watching and/or listening to this orchestration and watching the different types of rail cars. Besides the passenger cars there were boxcars, flatbeds, gondolas, tank cars, and hoppers. At times a train would be parked right in front of our house while they were coupling and uncoupling cars. This looked dangerous. A trainman stood near the couplings while tons of steel rail cars slammed together at steel couplings. The trainman had to make sure the couplings were in the right position and that they securely locked. A hand or arm in the wrong place could wind up being lost forever.

From time to time the railroad Section Gangs would be working on the tracks replacing rails and/or ties. Sometimes the gangs would be made up of Mexicans, and other times, the gang would be all colored. *Gandy dancers* was the term used for these workers. I would always go watch them lift and place the creosote-soaked ties, which you could smell from a mile away. The most fun and most vivid in my memory was when the Negro gangs were lifting, placing, and aligning the heavy fifteen-feet, long steel rails, some weighing as much as six hundred pounds. In order to synchronize their efforts, they would chant in unison to perform each task. A chant would begin with a single "caller." Following his call, there was a response in unison by the others. The aligning of the rails was done with iron crowbar-looking tools called a gandy. This call and response method was used for driving the spikes also. There was rhythm and lyrics for each task that required coordination of effort. A chant would go something like this:

> Caller: "I don't know, but I've been told Mable's
> toes is mighty cold."
> "She's a sport, though."
> Response: "Huh."

"Give her a go."
"Huh."
"Then you'll know."
"Huh."
"Mable's toes cold."
"Huh."

With each "Huh," the men would push their gandy forward and align the heavy rail with the adjacent rail. The spike drivers followed with their big sledgehammer-looking tool driving those big iron spikes down into the wooden ties. I learned as a young man that these rhythmic, melodic chants were also used at times to convey coded messages to each other so as not be understood by the white foreman. I could have watched the gandy dancers all day long, but Grandma would eventually call me in for lunch or something. The rhythm of those chants would sound in my head for days, and I would respond, "Huh."

In bed at night I would hear that lonesome whistle and fall asleep, imagining traveling to far-off places. The rails in those days were the most popular means of distance travel. Passenger trains were equipped with dining cars featuring a variety of menu items served on linen tablecloths by black waiters in white jackets. There were sleeping cars, about twelve sleeping compartments sharing one restroom, and there were deluxe sleepers with private compartments, each with a sink and commode. The Club Car was the cocktail lounge of the train, furnished with a bar, bartender, and overstuffed lounge chairs and cocktail tables. The large windows presented a variety of views of towering mountains, flowing rivers, small towns, people, and more.

Floyd the Barber and Other Matters

M other took me to Floyd's Barbershop. Floyd was a friend of hers who had been her patient during her days of nursing at various small private tuberculosis sanitariums, which dotted the landscape of the Colorado Springs area in the 1930s. The barber, Floyd Miller, who always wore a starched white shirt and tie covered by a starched white cotton barber's jacket, was a middle-aged balding, somewhat-paunchy, affable person with a ready smile. I suspected he had a crush on Mother. Floyd would put a board across the barber chair arm rests and lift me up to sit on the board. (I was willowy and slim and not hard to lift.) He then secured a barber cape around my neck, which covered my whole body, even my shoes. It felt neat having my entire body completely hidden from sight, with only my head sticking out. It felt like being the invisible man on the radio show *The Shadow*. I enjoyed haircuts, which I didn't get very often. It was soothing and tingling feeling the buzzing electric clippers, the scissors, and the comb skim through my hair and tickle my scalp. After the clip, cut, and comb, from a bottle of witch hazel (which smelled really good), he would pour some on his hands and rub it on the back of my neck. I think witch hazel was to disinfect the scrapes on the neck caused by the barber's razor. He then took a big soft long bristled brush dipped in talcum powder and dusted my neck where he had just applied the witch hazel. Floyd then gave me a candy sucker and placed me on the floor with a "That's a good boy."

I didn't see Floyd during the war years as I was living at the Stratton Home (more about the home later), and the postwar years took me away from home more often than not, but when I returned home from serving in the navy, I had no barber, so I went to see Floyd. He hadn't seen me since I was eight or nine years old.

I said, "Floyd, I'm Jack Walker, Lucy McCracken's son."

He said, "Oh god, yes, Jack, I remember you. You weren't big enough to sit in the chair the last time I saw you."

He asked how Mother was getting along and said he hadn't seen her in some time either. He then proudly announced to the men in the shop, both barbers and patrons, "I used to cut this big six-footer's hair when he wasn't big enough to climb up in the chair."

I'm sure that announcement really excited them. I felt very self-conscious. I just wanted to get a haircut and get out of there. The next two times I went to Floyd's shop, he made the same announcement. I quit going to Floyd's Barbershop.

"If you don't eat, I'll put you in the nutrition camp," Grandma would threaten when I was picking around my dinner plate trying to avoid it altogether because the plate had been loaded with vegetables I didn't like (which included most vegetables). The nutrition camp was operated by the junior league so that the children of poor families would be fed.

When we lived down on Las Vegas Street, Kenny, in one of his charitable moments, gave me my first full-size bicycle. He was casting off this old bike and out of the kindness of his heart, gifted it to his little brother. I was thrilled. I had never been on a big bike before. It was a full-size bike with twenty-six-inch wheels.

I could barely climb up on it. The wheels had no tires, just wheel rims. No seat came with it, which didn't matter because the bike sat too tall for me to sit on anyway. Kenny held it up while I climbed on and got settled on the cross bar. He then gave me a running push barreling me down the sidewalk, which was in disrepair. At first I was thrilled and scared, then only scared. I didn't know how to stop the bike, and I was coming to a high curb, which dropped off about ten inches. I dropped off the curb and landed sideways on the street and fell off the bike skinning up my leg and elbow. When I got up, I looked back to Kenny for help. He was gone. I don't think I ever mastered that bike, but I was proud to own it.

Once in a while Kenny would let me come out to his pigeon coop in the backyard and let me hold one. They were homing pigeons that would fly right back to the coop if Kenny took them somewhere. Kenny knew each one by name. I used to wonder how he knew their names. Did they tell him? Once when he was gone, I went out to the coop and asked a pigeon its name. It ignored me as if I hadn't even spoken. Behind the coop was the alley which ran parallel to the railroad tracks. Somehow the rails fascinated me. I would climb up the track embankment and put my ear to a steel rail and hear it sing like a harp string. You could also hear when a train was near, by the rhythmic clicking.

Grandma saw me on the track and yelled, "JACK, GET OFF THOSE TRACKS! COME HERE RIGHT NOW!"

I scurried off stumbling down the embankment and rushed toward her. After she scolded me and went back in the house, I sat on the back porch and wondered how she knew I was up there. I thought I was well hidden from view behind the pigeon coop.

Later that afternoon I asked her how she knew I was on the tracks.

She said, "One of the chickens told me."

I went outside to the chicken pen and gave a hard look at each bird in there to see if I could find the tattler. They all looked innocent. I never trusted chickens after that. It was about this time that Kenny was caught burglarizing a downtown store and was made to serve time in the reform school at Buena Vista. There were other boys with him, but they got away, and Kenny wouldn't squeal on them. I remember hearing the names of two of them; cousin Frank Inzer and Earl Sullivan, who was to grow up and serve as El Paso County Sheriff.

One vivid memory I have of living on the west side was eating sour kraut by the handful pulled from a barrel on a shady side of the house. Grandpa just brought the barrel of kraut home one day, and since Grandma wouldn't let him crowd it into the pantry or any other place in the house, he did the next best thing and put it under the eaves out by the back porch. The barrel was right near the cardboard box hideout I climbed into to eat my bread and ketchup or mayonnaise sandwiches and Grandma's ice-box cookies. The kraut was a welcome addition to my menu. Grandma was unaware of my hideout dining activity.

In 1935 President Roosevelt refused to speak out in favor of an antilynching bill being proposed in Congress. He argued that white voters in the South would never forgive him if he supported the bill and he would lose the next election. The bill was defeated by Southern opposition.

Boys and girls alike were in love with Shirley Temple, child movie star and number one box office draw for several years. She was a beautiful girl with curly ringlets who could act, sing, and dance. There were all kinds of merchandise sold based on her image, including dolls, dishes, and clothing. We would sit around and just imagine what her life was like—a big mansion with servants, swimming pool, ponies, and the one thing we were sure of was that she must have her own soda fountain. I only saw one of her movies, *The Little Colonel*, a movie she made with famous colored dancer Bill "Bojangles" Robinson. I can still see vividly their famous staircase dance.

My cousins, the Inzers, at one time were living in an old rundown farmhouse on the outskirts Southeast of town. It was a fun place for me to spend a week end with Duane and all his brothers and sisters (there were six kids in all). When staying with them, I slept in a bed with three cousins, two of us at each end of the bed. There was no electricity in their house. They lighted their house with kerosene lamps. I thought this was really exciting and fun. Their water was drawn from a hand pump over a well outside. I thought this was a great invention, even more so than the kerosene lamp. Baths were taken by carrying water from the pump in a bucket to the kitchen, where it would be heated in a kettle on the coal-fired kitchen stove then poured into a large tin wash tub on the floor near the stove. It took several trips with the bucket, and the bath water was merely tepid at best. A tub of bath water was used for several consecutive baths before emptying. It was obviously best to be first to get the warmest and cleanest water.

The Inzers received "commodities," as we called them, which was food distributed under the Department of Agriculture's Surplus

Commodities Act as part of President Roosevelt's New Deal. The thing I especially remember eating from the "commodities" was dried apricots. I had never eaten dried fruit before, and to me, it was a real delicacy. I wished we had "commodities." I didn't know at the time that a family had to be really destitute in order to get them. The Inzers were certainly destitute.

Grandpa said, "They have nothing that can be stolen or sold."

People on "relief" were not happy with their circumstances. By and large they were ashamed. They would all work and pay their own way if only they had a job—any job.

Playing "hide-and-seek" with the Inzer kids, in the neighboring full-grown cornfield was endless fun. The acres of cornstalks being about six feet tall, row on row about three feet apart and throwing shadows made for great hiding, sometimes so great we would get lost in the field and wander around blindly trying to find our way out of the maze of stalks. By yelling back and forth, we would eventually find each other and a way out.

"Ash bombs" were made from a couple of handsful of ashes from the ash pile out back. The ashes were wrapped in newspaper. We chose up sides and played war by throwing the bombs at the enemy. Whatever they hit, the paper would give way to an explosion of ashes.

Another war game was conducted with "rubber guns" as the weapons of choice. The rubber gun was made from scrap wood, a clothespin, and a rubber missile cut from a discarded tire inner tube. We also made high stilts. They were leaned against the sloping roof of the back porch. We then climbed up the gutter drain pipe to the roof and shoved off on the stilts. After a few spills, we finally got pretty adept at keeping our balance while stilting five feet up from the ground.

Pitching horse shoes was another diversion we played from time to time. When there was a family gathering at the Inzer place, we kids took turns grinding the homemade ice-cream maker. It was hard work, but it was worth it.

But the greatest attraction on this old homestead was what I thought was one of man's greatest ideas, the outhouse—the privy.

This unusual edifice was foreign to me, having always lived with indoor plumbing, but it was quite common in the more rural areas of the day. It was a closet-size wooden shed like building with a plank floor out away from the house which effectively served as a toilet. It had a sloping roof to run off rain and snow. It had a door in front with a peephole cut in it so you could peek in to see if it was in use, also for ventilation. Inside there was an enclosed wooden bench with two round holes cut in the top for sitting over to do your business. The holes were cut in two sizes, an adult size about like the opening in a standard toilet seat and a smaller size for children. The edge of the holes were rounded off and sanded for comfort. Beneath the bench, there was no floor. It opened up to a deep hand dug pit to receive the patron's offerings. When nearly filled after a few years' use, a new pit was dug nearby and the shed moved to the new pit. The old pit was then filled up with some of the dirt dug up from the new pit. For toilet paper, there was usually an old Sears and Roebuck, or other, catalog, which also provided reading material for the contributors. The outhouse was such an institution of early American culture that it was even immortalized in poem by the celebrated humorist William "Bill" Rutherford (nom de plume, Pot Barnhouse) 1871–1935 in his book *Pot Shots*:

> Then in great and glorious phrases he proceeds
> to eulogize
> On the virtues of the back house and the tears
> are in his eyes
> As he spreads the glory round it tells how it has
> been maligned
> When in aiding man's discomfort nothing's ever
> been so kind."

Rutherford further waxes:

> I'm not castin' no reflections on the little house
> behind

And to its many virtues may my eyes be never
blind
'Twas a place for meditation and the wiminfolk's
retreat
And it wasn't so uncomfortable when rounded
off the seat."

In 1940 Mother, Betty, Uncle Walt, Kenny, Grandma, Grandpa, and I were all living together again[8]on West Pikes Peak Avenue, an old but comfortable house. With the exception of Betty, I thought all these people were the same age. They were the grown-ups, to obey. Not until I was about ten did I realize there were different generations to my family. The house was large and sat on a lot sizeable enough for Grandpa to have a good-sized garden and Grandma her chickens. It had a full attic, where all kinds of household items and clothing were kept in trunks and boxes. The attic was a great place for exploring on rainy days. Once I found an old rain coat in an old trunk of clothing. I went downstairs and got a pair of scissors and cut the bottom of the coat and the sleeves to fit my eight-year-old frame. I was so proud of my design creation that I went downstairs to show it off to Grandma and Mother. They both gasped in horror at what I had done to Uncle Walt's raincoat.

Once they recovered, they began to laugh at the sight of this very large garment wrapped around me about twice and tied with the belt that then hung down and dragged on the floor. (I forgot to custom-cut the belt.) After the laughter wore off, they scolded me and took the coat. I have no further knowledge of the mitigation of that situation with Uncle Walt. It was never mentioned to me again.

Uncle Walt used a hair oil to make his wavy hair shiny. I tried some on my hair. I used entirely too much and came out of the bathroom with oily slicked-down hair and oil running down the side of my head. This garnered another round of shock, laughter, and scolding from Grandma.

---

[8]   Kenny later joined the navy and was aboard ship in Honolulu, Hawaii.

On summer evenings the kids in the neighborhood would gather in the middle of the street to play tin can nerky, known in other locales as kick the can. We also played hide-and-seek until called in by our parents, who had been enjoying the cool evening air on their front porches. Evenings were always cool near the mountains regardless of how hot it got during the day. Faded but still fragrant in my memory of that west side house is the smell of burning leaves in our backyard in autumn and the perfume of the springtime lilac blossoms in the front yard.

One of Mother's boyfriends, a traveling salesman named Carol, came to town each summer. Carol was a tall, good-looking guy, probably about Mother's age, early thirties. He had curly blond hair, and he dressed well, suit and tie. He seemed to take a genuine liking to Betty and me. We liked him.

One summer evening he took us all to the carnival which had arrived in town about two days earlier. You could always tell when the carnival was in town by seeing the beams of the large spotlights crisscrossing in the night sky. As I remember, it was a pleasantly warm evening with a cool breeze present. I had never been to a carnival before. It was purely magical. The sights, smells, and sounds transported me on a flying carpet to a land of total joy and excitement.

"Step right up!" barked the men in the straw hats and colorful vests.

The concessions of the midway were a cornucopia of color with large elaborate letters on signs inviting us to play games of chance and skill like Spill the Milk, where you threw a ball at some standing wooden milk bottles.

Carol gave us some change and said, "Go play the games. Maybe you'll win something."

We never did. There was Dart Balloons, Bean Bag Toss, and the Hammer Striker to demonstrate your strength, and many more. You could win prizes like stuffed teddy bears and cupie dolls. You were invited to indulge in cotton candy, hot dogs, corn dogs, hamburgers, lemonade, and taffy apples. The food smells were as delicious as the foods. Betty and I gorged at Carol's expense. The carnival had so many people—from newborns to toothless, all had smiles and laughter even in those hard times. There was calliope music coming from somewhere through loud speakers. Colorful banners, tents, and awnings flapped in the evening breeze, making a snapping sound. There were rides of all kinds: the carousel with its elaborately painted horses, the loop-o-plane, which let you dangle high up in the air upside down, bumper cars, the Pendulum, which swung you back and forth like a pendulum. My favorite was the tilt-a-whirl, which was a ride where you sat in a car on a circular track mounted on a revolving deck that tilted up and down and went round and round. And up and down. And, of course, there was a Ferris wheel.

We kids had a taunt when someone had told our parents about something we shouldn't have been doing.

> Tattle tale, tattle tale
> Hanging on a bull's tail
> When the bull begins to pee,
> You will have a cup of tea.

Another ugly thing in our repertoire was to refer to kids that had to wear eyeglasses as "four eyes" or extra thick glasses were referred to as "Coke bottle" glasses. "You're going to get in Dutch" was an expression warning someone who had broken a rule, broken a valuable object, or engaged in some other wrong doing. If a big guy called you a bad name, or made an ugly face at you, your defense was this:

> Sticks and stones can break my bones.
> But names and faces won't hurt me.

Of course this wasn't the way you actually felt, because bad names and ugly faces did hurt. If a little guy was careless enough to offend you in this way, you would, as a matter of course, punch them square in the nose.

When we moved to the west side, I entered the Washington Grade School. At recess about the second day at Washington, a boy I didn't know came up to me at the drinking fountain and asked, "Have you ever fought?"

Thinking that all boys my age had fought, I thought I didn't hear him correctly, so not really knowing what was asked, I figured I would err on the side of caution, and answered no.

He then pushed me and said, "Then you must be a sissy."

The next thing I remember seeing was my fist slamming against his nose. He fell backward and dropped to the ground, howling loudly. His nose was bleeding all over his mouth. My hand felt like it was broken. The recess teacher, hearing his cries, came over and helped him up then looked at me.

"Go to the principal's office," she ordered.

She then took him inside. I told my story to the principal. She sent me to my classroom. I never heard more about it. The battered boy, whom I'll call Billy W., and I became friends for the remainder of my stay at Washington. Some years later we met while playing interschool junior high basketball. He was still living on the west side and played for West Junior. I played for South Junior. I reminded Billy of our grade school bout. He didn't remember.

Grandpa was working for the county when we moved to the west side so times were pretty good, so good that he ordered a telephone to be installed. The man from Mountain States Telephone and Telegraph (MTST&T) came to the house and hooked up the black Bakelite devise (no dial, no touch tone) provided by the company. There was a phone line already running from the house out to a telephone pole in the alley. He showed Grandma how to use it; you picked up the headset from its cradle and placed one end of it to your ear and the other end down by your mouth. There was no dial-tone to listen for. A voice on the other end said, "Number please." You gave her the four-digit phone number of the party you wished to call, and she connected you with them. If you wanted to call "long distance" (to another city), you asked for the long-distance operator and gave her the number you wished to call. "Just a moment please," she would say. There would be a delay while she made the connection for you. The farther the distance of the call, the longer would be the delay. Long-distance was much more expensive than local calls. You only made these calls when it was absolutely necessary. We had a "party line," which didn't cost as much as a private line. A party line meant you shared the phone line with one or more other parties. The disadvantage of this was that you might pick up your phone to call and you would hear a conversation taking place. Telephone etiquette called for you to then hang up and try again later. You can see how this could be troublesome if the other parties are long winded and you need to make an urgent call. Sometimes you had to just interrupt their call and ask if you could have the line. Some nosy people listened in on the other party's conversation.

In the school Christmas pageant, I played one of the three wise men and had to walk down the filled auditorium center aisle singing solo "Myrrh is mine, its bitter perfume," etc. A teacher was playing the tune on a tinny piano, and I was scared to death. I was told later by the teacher in charge, who was very disgusted, that no one could hear me. Walking home with Grandma, she said she was proud of me. At recess we used to play marbles for "keeps" I had a "steely" for a shooter. It sometimes was outlawed because, when shot, it had an impact on marbles in the ring that caused almost all of them to be blown out of the ring, which meant I got to keep them. I wasn't the only one with a steel-ball bearing shooter in my arsenal. There were others. I also had an oversize, beautiful, multicolored agate shooter, which sometimes was voted out for the same reason.

Grown-up's language didn't make sense to me sometimes. Grandma would say that someone was getting on their "high horse"; under my questioning, she would then tell me the person didn't have a horse. She often told me, "You're getting 'too big for your britches.'" I once overheard Uncle Walt telling Grandma that a good friend of his had gotten "fired." They went on to talk about him getting another job while I was waiting to hear how the man was doing after being burned.

Aunt Helen married Denverite Andrew Earthman (Uncle Andy), whose mother was Italian and had taught Helen how to cook Italian. Helen introduced us to the most delicious meal I had ever eaten: Italian spaghetti with a sausage tomato sauce topped with Parmesan cheese, then we grated right at the table. I didn't know this cheese even existed. This exotic dish became my favorite food from then on. Aunt Helen's young sister in law, Eileen, would someday marry Uncle Walt and serve for our delight, Italian spaghetti that had no equal.

While we all were living together on the west side, Mother took a job with a state run child care center in Manitou Springs. Mother, Betty, and I moved to Manitou Springs. We had to move because during the Depression years, there could only be one public payrollee in a household, and as Grandpa at the time was an employee of the county road department, Mother had to move to hold her job.

Manitou

Manitou Springs, shortened to "Manitou" by locals, was a small tourist town settled in a forested box canyon at the foot of Ute Pass on the way to Pikes Peak. The three-mile drive on Highway 24 from Colorado Springs to Manitou was laden with tourist courts, cabins, and lodges, all advertising with large gaudy colorful signs proclaiming the merits of being a guest at their location. Some advertised a private bath in each unit. Some advertised daily linen changes. Some advertised a radio in each unit at no extra cost, and some could rightfully only advertise their price, as they provided none of the fore mentioned amenities. Regardless of their ads, they were all filled to capacity with the soaring population of summer tourists.

Mother rented a small house on Deerpath Street. A path is about all it was too. The street was a gravel road leading steeply up the mountain side from the main drag. The house was on a corner lot, and our front door sat about twelve feet higher than the road. But if you went on up and around the corner to High Street, our back door was lower than the street. We had a coal-fired cook stove which I, at age nine, as the nominal "man of the house," kept fired up when needed. The bathroom was right off the kitchen, which used to ruin my appetite if someone used the toilet when we were eating. A large central room housed a coal-fired heating stove. The black cast iron stove sat on four claw-foot legs in the middle of the room. It had an ornate nickel plated dome head and a fire door with mica section windows which permitted some light from the bright embers. A tin flu rose up out of the top through the ceiling which went on up through, and helped heat, the upstairs bedroom where we all slept.

Mother and Betty shared a double bed, and I had a fold-up canvas army cot of World War I vintage.

During the summer Manitou was as alive as Las Vegas and, with the exception of the roller rink, as dead as a cadaver in the winter. Manitou Avenue in downtown Manitou was replete with arcades and curio shops. There was a carnival-like atmosphere about the downtown area with the smells of cotton candy, popcorn, and fudge. There were games of chance and games of skill in which you could win prizes. Several stores were owned by Japanese Americans who offered all sorts of gifts and curios from the Orient as well as souvenirs of the Pikes Peak Region. These stores all had the exotic aroma of incense and were mysteriously scary to a boy whose only information about Orientals was provided by Hollywood in the persons of characters like the evil Fu Man Chu and the wise but mystical distant Charlie Chan. The businesses were open till late at night, and the tourists thronged to them day and night.

There was a large roller rink on the avenue which was crowded every night. The rink was a large wooden building with a domed roof. The floor was hardwood as smooth as a dance floor. The lighting would range from bright to dark with rotating colors. Music was broadcast through speakers connected to a record player operated by who may have been the first disk jockeys. Big-band swing music was played, and before a new song, the floor manager would announce what the next formation would be: "couples skate," "triples skate," backward skate," "free skate," and for the more advanced skaters, there was "dance skate," both figure and free style. I worked there for a short time as one of about six skate boys. The rink customers who didn't bring their own roller skates would come in and find a seat which they had to step up into chairs like a shoe shine parlor. A sign on the wall behind the chairs warned: No Socks, No Skates. The skaters told us what size shoe skate they wanted and we would go back to the skate room where large bins stored skates by size; women's sizes on one side and men's on the other. We found the size and returned to put the skates on their feet and lace it up. We worked on tips only and it paid well, but we were run ragged from about five in the evening till nine or after. Some of the smelly feet I had to work with made me sometimes wonder if it was worth it. We skate boys wore skates because we were called upon to go onto the skate floor to push large dust mops every so often and to pick up fallen objects and debris of all kinds. We were like roller rink Zambonis. Some of the best tippers, even though they had little money, were the guys from the CCC Camps nearby. There was a camp about four miles west of Manitou and one at Woodland Park which was just a few miles up Ute Pass and a camp at Monument, a few miles north of Colorado Springs.

The CCC (Civilian Conservation Corps) was born of the New Deal. The corps's purpose was to conserve our natural resources and to provide jobs and training for our young men. They were engaged in such activities as building roadways, studying, and working at soil conservation, building, and operating fish hatcheries and reintroducing wildlife to depleted areas. They lived a military-like camp life and wore army-looking khaki uniforms and supported their families by earning thirty dollars monthly. A twenty-five-dollar allotment was sent to their home. When World War II broke out in 1941, it was a relatively uncomplicated transition for these young guys to be inducted into the army.

The town pretty much closed down to the tourist trade in September. The arcades, candy shops, and curio shops all closed up. Only basic-needs businesses remained open. The winter snows piled up in storefront doorways, and snowdrifts blocked the passageways to the courtyards within the arcade malls. The tourist courts on the highway remained open as long as possible with signs proclaiming discount rates; they eventually succumbed to the inevitable, and new signs were erected announcing their opening day in the spring. The only fall and winter recreational action for locals as well as outsiders was the roller rink, and the bars, which were oblivious to the seasons.

Manitou was famous for its mineral springs which had a natural carbonation as well as several healthy minerals. In the summer tourists would come year after year from sweltering crowded cities in all parts of the country to enjoy the spring water and the natural beauty as well as the cool dry air of the region. Colorado Springs attracted large numbers of tubercular sufferers in the early years and was known as the Saratoga of the West. The springs of Manitou were said to have been sacred to Native Americans who considered the eruption of bubbles in the mineral water to be the breath of the Great Spirit. Offerings of beads and fetishes were left in gratitude. "Manitou water" made great lemonade.

Lying at the foot of the front range of the Pike National Forest in the shadow of Pikes Peak, Manitou was built on mountain sides on each side of the canyon. There wasn't a natural piece of level ground in the whole town. Tourists also came to visit the natural caverns nearby up in Williams canyon. The Apaches migrating through the area around 1000 AD told of where the Great Spirit of the Wind resided. This would later become known as the Cave of the Winds. It was easy to sneak into as there were a couple of small openings available if you were willing to hike around the mountain to the opposite side of the tourist entrance and crawl on your belly through a tight tunnel. Manitou boasted of its Anasazi cliff dwellings which were taken from a collapsed Anasazi site near Cortez in Southwest Colorado and reassembled at their present site just north of Manitou in the "Garden of the Gods." In a ravine just north and west of the Garden of the Gods was Glen Eyrie, the magnificent thirty-eight-thousand-square-foot castle built by Colorado Springs founder General Palmer. I was told it was guarded and that no one could enter to see it. Duane and I verified that the property was gated and locked. We hiked up and around some foothills and ravines and came onto the property from behind. We just wanted to see the castle we had heard so much about. We sat on a big granite boulder and looked down on a great stone castle and carriage house that I imagined must have looked not much different from the castle in which King Arthur resided.

Since 1891, the Manitou and Pikes Peak Railway, the world's highest cog railroad, carried thousands of excited ogling tourists on a three-hour alpine trip through stands of pine and aspen trees before ascending above the tree line to the 14,110-foot summit of Pikes Peak. Along the way it was not uncommon to see bighorn sheep, deer, and other wildlife. At the summit looking east out over the vast plains of eastern Colorado, it was said that one could see as far as Kansas, some 150 miles distant. The stay at the summit was limited to about thirty minutes because most people from the "flat lands," begin to feel the effects of high altitude which may be light headedness, nausea, and shortness of breath due to the oxygen-rare atmosphere. Some of them were just not accustomed to breathing air they couldn't see.

It was from the summit of the Peak the summer of 1893 that Katharine Lee Bates, a Colorado College English teacher, jotted down the first draft notes of "America the Beautiful."

In addition to the Pikes Peak Railway, there was the Mt. Manitou Incline, a cable car cog rail rising to the top of Mount Manitou (elevation 9,429 feet). It was built in 1907 to aid in the building of a hydroelectric plant and its water line. At completion of construction, the rail was converted for passenger use and became known as the "Mount Manitou Scenic Incline Railway," with brochures proclaiming "Scenic splendors unfolded are unrivaled anywhere in the world."[9]

The incline was lit up at night. You could see the lights trailing up the mountain for miles away. Once, in my teens, a tourist girl I met at the Acacia Park square dance[10] asked me what the lights were. I told her it was an ancient Indian ritual of worship of the mountain god and that the Indians were carrying torches as they chanted while trekking up the mountain. She wanted to go see it, but I had to tell her it would be dangerous as they didn't allow outsiders to even come near. Somehow in my youthful ignorance, I thought a good story like that would make me more attractive to her. She was thrilled by the story but not necessarily by me.

My best friend while living in Manitou Springs was Oscar Holloway, the only colored boy in that town. ("Black" was considered derogatory back then.) Oscar lived across the street and would come over to play in our clubhouse, which was actually an old dilapidated shed in the backyard. The club membership of three was made

---

[9]   Mat Carpenter, *Friends of the Peak Newsletters*, Fall 2000, Fall and Spring 2001.
[10]   I didn't square dance, and neither did most of the tourists. They came to see the Western-costumed dancers and listen to the dance caller call out the dance moves. I was there to meet the tourist girls.

up of my sister, Oscar, and me. Our meetings would be conducted by going to the club house, finding something to sit on, and eat chocolate cake which my sister had baked. That was our idea of a meeting. Most meetings I've attended in my adult life achieved about the same results as our clubhouse meetings. (The only significant difference being that doughnuts and sweet rolls have replaced my sister's chocolate cake.)

Oscar's folks had a jukebox with some of the greatest music I had ever heard. I later in life learned that these were "race records," which was music by colored artists who, because they were colored, could not get their recordings heard on standard radio broadcasts: Louis Armstrong, Duke Ellington, Fats Waller, Cab Calloway, and others. The music was mostly blues and jazz. Sitting on the back stoop at Oscar's on an evening his parents had a party—listening to the music from within as we ate fried chicken and potato salad his mother had served—and looking at the thousands of stars in the sky (as can only be seen in the clear mountain skies of the west) was one of the most memorable activities of my stay in Manitou.

During that same period, I also befriended two Native American twin brothers named Jay and Jan Campbell. They were being raised by their grandfather, who looked just like the face on the nickel. He had dark leather like wrinkled brown skin, and he wore his hair in two long braids and wore silver and turquoise jewelry. I thought he was about the neatest-looking grandpa I had ever seen. The brothers were hard to tell apart. They looked alike; their voices were the same, and they dressed alike. I learned over time that their body language and hand gestures were different. The three of us played hooky together one day and were playing down by the creek when the town marshal, Dave Banks (who, in the absence of a truancy officer, drove around looking for kids skipping school, I guess) caught us and hauled us back to the school. We had to sit in the principal's office for the rest of the day and were given notes to take home to our parents. I didn't think Mother would be interested in the note, so I didn't bother her with it.

While walking by the Manitou Springs Public School one evening when the Boy Scouts were meeting inside, I saw several bicycles parked around the flag pole. I hooked one of the bikes to the flag rope and pulled it to the top of the pole. I didn't stick around to see what took place when the bike was missed. I could only fantasize. I don't know why I did this. I guess it was one of those times when I asked myself, "What if?" It was a challenge with no good end to it. I was never a real fan of practical jokes. I did, however, have a dislike for the Boy Scouts. I thought they were dummies because they had to wear those dumb uniforms. Maybe I resented them because I couldn't afford to buy the uniform. (Self-analysis is always suspect.)

"Second prize goes to Jack Walker—the Hobo," announced the lady at the park costume contest.

Betty did the creative cosmetics to make me look like a clown hobo with a sad face and a red nose like Emmett Kelly, the famous circus clown. She smeared coal dust on my face to look like an unshaven bum. With some light-colored makeup of Mother's, she marked an oversize, sad, downturned mouth. This was topped off with a bright red lip-sticked nose. I wore an old pair of Betty's slacks which were way too big. We held them up with a rope over the shoulder tied front and back at the belt loops. For authenticity, we put real mud splotches on the pants and my old torn shirt. An old rumpled felt hat of Mother's found in the attic gave the makeover a complete appearance. Mother was waiting downstairs for us. She was literally in tears of laughter at the sight. I went to the front of the pavilion to receive my reward. The park lady shook my hand and handed me a small box, which I opened to find a fountain pen. I unscrewed the pen and discovered a little rubber bladder inside. I pulled on it, and it came loose.

"OUCH!" I blurted.

The park lady had slapped my hand, and I dropped box, pen, and bladder.

"Why did you tear it apart?' she bellowed while I was kneeling to pick up my prize.

Mother angrily spoke up, "He was only curious to see how it works. Don't you ever strike my son!"

She took my hand and almost dragged me away, even before they served the ice cream and cake. Adult priorities were hard to comprehend.

The organist was producing some resounding music as we filed in and sat in the hard wooden pews. The Manitou Church was just down from us on Pawnee Street. I decided I would go see what "churchgoing" was like. I told Mother at Sunday breakfast what I had planned.

She said, "Be sure to wash behind your ears."

I put on my school shirt and pants and my new Mexican huaraches, which were hugely popular at the time. I watered down my hair and combed it. Water was still dripping off my head when I went out the door. This was going to be new, and I was in high spirits walking over there. I was one of the stragglers going in, so I missed the pastor's greeting at the door. I cautiously walked in and slid in to an empty pew which was nearest the door. The organ music stopped, and the pastor stepped up to the podium and began to speak. I didn't understand what he was talking about. I had never been inside a church. As the pastor's voice droned on, I looked all around with amazement at this wonder of a structure with its incredibly high ceiling and enormous color filled widows of stained glass sections the sun was shining through and reflecting a rainbow on the opposite wall. Every so often I joined everyone in standing to sing songs from the books that were in racks on the backs of the pews in front of us. I lip-synced through the singing and sat down in unison with the rest of the congregation, only to be called at intervals to stand up and sing a couple more times. Then came the passing of the plate, a wooden dish in which each person put dollar bills or coins and passed it on to their neighbor. I had neither bills nor coins, so I passed. We stood again and bowed our heads while the pastor prayed. The organ started up again, and people started to leave. I slipped out of my pew, out the door, down the steps, and was away without speaking to anyone. I never returned, and I never forgot.

Manitou Springs had a large dance hall pavilion called Hiawatha Gardens. In the summer we kids would hang around outside in the gardens surrounding the pavilion and listen to the live band music.

These big dance bands like Paul Whitman, Lawrence Welk, as well as the race records at Oscar's house, were the beginning of my music appreciation. To this day my favorite music is swing, jazz, and blues.

One day while hiking alone in the mountains around Manitou, I discovered some half-buried, broken Indian clay pottery in a gully washout. I took a chard of it to school to show my teacher. I let her borrow it to get it authenticated. I didn't hear from her for several weeks. When I did hear from her, she told me she was going to keep the pottery piece for the school. She then asked if I would lead a class field trip to the site of the find. I agreed. But since she had not returned my pottery piece, I led the class to a spot far away from my find. They were all disappointed that they didn't find pottery, but my secret was safe. I later returned and dug up a few more pieces and gave them to Grandma.

One lazy fall day while living in Manitou Springs, my cousin Duane came to visit. We had run out of ideas of things to do until we came up with the idea of putting my dog, Ralph, inside the neighbor's chicken pen so we could watch him chase chickens all over the place. We cut an opening in the fence and put Ralph in. He did not disappoint us. He chased chickens all over the place, and we laughed our heads off watching chickens running, hopping, flying, and loudly squawking all over the pen. But to our surprise, he caught one of them and returned to the fence opening wagging his tail with it in his mouth. We let him out and wired the fence back in place. I opened the dog's jaws. The poor chicken dropped lifeless to the ground. Not readily knowing what to do with a dead chicken, we came up with the idea of eating it. I went in the house to get some kitchen matches, then we went down to the creek, built a fire, plucked, and eviscerated the chicken with my pocket knife and roasted it over the fire. I can still taste that chicken. It was delicious even though the skin was burnt black and the meat a bit rare. (Remember these were times of the Great Depression when food was scarce to those without funds.) Today I often refer to any exceptionally good-tasting food as "as good as stolen chicken."

I didn't get away with this chicken rustling caper. I was found out by some means and had to go before a justice of the peace.[11] Mother washed me up good, put a clean shirt on me, and marched me off to court. I confessed and was fined and directed to make restitution of a combined amount totaling $5.00 (equivalent to $76.87 in 2010 dollars). This was a greatly overpriced chicken. The plaintiff set the price and said that the confiscated bird was his prize hen. I told the judge I didn't have $5.00 (I'm sure he knew a nine-year-old chicken rustler wouldn't have that kind of money). The city attorney, who was the prosecutor in this case, said he would pay the $5.00 in exchange for my coming to work for him after school each day. Mother thought that was a much more lenient arrangement than paying the $5.00, so they all agreed to indenture me to the lawyer.

After school for almost the entire school year, I spent two hours (before going to my chores at home) at the attorney's home raking leaves, shoveling snow, hauling trash, washing windows, dusting, cleaning the basement, running errands, etc. I was truly indentured but felt enslaved.

I think he got his money's worth. I wonder if I have a rap sheet of record in the Manitou Springs Hall of Justice.

Mother owned an old car during our stay in Manitou. (She had never owned a car prior to that to my memory.) I had to put hot water in the car's radiator on cold winter mornings. Permanent antifreeze had not been developed yet. The antifreeze of the day was alcohol based and would evaporate in the course of a day's driving. It was too expensive. We couldn't leave the water in the radiator overnight, or it would freeze, so it would have to be drained each night by the petcock valve at the bottom of the radiator. Sometimes I would forget to close the valve before adding the hot water, and it would run out. I would have to trudge back to the house through the snow to heat another kettle of water.

---

[11]   An elected official who dispensed justice in small towns and rural areas who could not afford a salaried judge. They were paid by the fees and fines they collected.

To support the food budget, Mother would sometimes bring home fresh fruit which she had taken from the day care cellar where she was employed. Also at this time, Mother told Betty and me that for us to get by, we would have to discipline ourselves to a regimen of limiting our meals. She said we would have a good breakfast, skip lunch, and then have a good dinner. On winter evenings we would make popcorn in an iron skillet on the kitchen stove and listen to radio shows. Mother's favorite show was the *Lanny Ross Show*. Ross was a popular singer of Mother's generation. His theme song was "Moonlight and Roses." Betty and I liked all the mystery shows. Mother often couldn't pay the rent on time, and when the landlord came calling, she sent me to answer the doorbell and tell him that she wasn't home. In later years my mother would deny these things. She was ashamed, but Betty and I knew she did her best under truly adverse conditions for a single mom, and she never lost the love of her children.

Grandma (Bertha Maud Frazee)

G randma was short and kind of chubby (she had a very warm and comfortable and comforting lap). She was a wonderful, loving, warm, kind, gentle, and magical person. She rarely raised her voice, and I never heard her say an unkind word about anyone. She had a smile and a kind word for all, whether they be family members, friends, or strangers. All of us in the family went to Grandma when seeking wisdom and understanding. We were never disappointed. She had a soft, gentle voice. She raised it to speak to Grandpa because he was hard of hearing. Something about her manner put people at ease. You just felt good in her presence. Her harshest word came loudly out of her mouth when she had some accident in the kitchen such as spilling something on the floor. On that rare occasion, her reaction was "Oh shite."

On lesser occasions the response was "Oh shistle pot." Grandma was a living encyclopedia of Poor Richard's Almanac and other homilies. She often counseled me with such pearls as, "Little strokes fell great oaks," "God helps them that help themselves," and "Cleanliness is next to godliness." When she heard of someone with a chronic problem, she would say, "Everyone has a cross to bear." There were many more. She never was at a loss for words of wisdom.

She sometimes would tell me when I had just come in from outside, "You look like the wreck of the Hesperus."[12] I would then get

---

[12] "Wreck of the Hesperus," a narrative poem by Henry Wadsworth Longfellow, about a fateful wreck of an ocean schooner during a storm at sea, published in 1842.

a thorough scrubbing. Toward me she was very affectionate, but not spoiling. She was primarily concerned with my character, whereas Grandpa was mainly interested in my future occupational abilities. I feel the three primary adults in my life at that time each contributed significantly to the better side of who I became. Grandma gave me a soft heart. Grandpa gave me a strong resolve, and Uncle Walt gave me a desire for class.

"I'm a universalist," Grandma responded when conversation went to religion. This was not referring to any established religious denomination. It meant she felt herself to be a creature of the universe like all other living things. We didn't attend church, mosque, or temple. Clergy came rarely into our lives only for marriages and funerals, and that was only because it would show consideration for the feelings of extended family, friends, and others who might attend these events. The Frazees didn't feel the need for religious adornment or a show of dignity for their neighbors. They just didn't fit the Victorian image of their era: that of an emphasis on refinement, morality, and general straight-laced behavior.

"Spitting is a nasty habit," she would say about Grandpa's chewing tobacco habit. She would not allow it in her house. He could chew in the house if he wished, but he must go outside to spit. He chose to abstain from chewing while at home. She normally was the dutiful wife and mother, but she sometimes would draw the line, and Grandpa, undisputed head of the household, would not protest much. She knew when to light his fire and when to douse it. She did all things with great economy. The two of them must have had some affection for each other, but it was only demonstrated to the rest of the family on the rarest occasion. They were sort of complementary opposites.

"These didoes of yours are going to get you in hot water," she would admonish when I had done something she considered mischievous.

She also used the word "dido" to mean knickknack or any trifling thing. Or she might say, "You're getting too big for your britches."

For women in the '30s, the frivolous clothing fashions of the '20s had given away to more austere and thrifty garments. Grandma, not a person to "gild the lilly," or to be a slave to the fashion of any decade, continued to dress as she had always dressed. For her daily household work, she wore house dresses and an apron, both of which were often made from colorful feed or flour sacks. "Repair, reuse, make do, and don't throw away," was a motto during the Depression years. Actually, the feed sacks came in some very bright and pretty printed patterns, usually floral. Feed sacks were intentionally made attractive to increase feed sales, and since most women of the day did a lot of their own sewing, and most families raised chickens; the picturesque sacks that held the feed for their chickens were a real inducement to buy. The only problem with using feed sacks for dress making was that if you ran out of fabric, it was difficult to find the same pattern the next time you needed feed.

Grandma made most of her own clothes, and a lot of the clothes worn by the rest of the family, by use of her Singer sewing machine, which sat in the dining room. This was a magical machine. I never got tired of watching her use it. It was amazing to me how Grandma took a lot of shapeless cloth, worked it in and out and around that machine, and it came out as a very wearable professionally tailored looking piece of clothing. The sewing machine was a solid oak cabinet with a lid on top which when opened lifted the sewing machine from below the surface of the cabinet. The lid then folded out to make a table to place the fabric to be sewn. The cabinet had two levels of drawers on each side to hold thread, bobbins, scissors, and such. It sat on a black enameled molded iron frame of open grillwork design. The frame housed a foot treadle which when rocked back and forth by Grandma's foot would turn a pulley with a belt drive up to a pulley on the sewing machine, thereby providing the power for the devise. This well used old machine had nicks and scratches from many moves and many garments. It was lovingly treated with 3-IN-ONE oil after each use. Grandma also embroidered dish towels, pillowcases, and handkerchiefs, and she crocheted doilies on those rare occasions when her hands had nothing better to do. The doilies were placed on the arms and the back of the davenport and the overstuffed chairs, on tabletops and any other surface where one could be placed or held with a pin. Her dresser drawers and closets held handmade crocheted and perfumed sachets.

Grandma's "dress up" dresses were lower calf length and of a dark solid-blue or black color and made of a finer more expensive cloth than feed sacks. She probably had no more than two such garments. They had lace collars that could be detached for laundering, thus saving wear and tear on the dress. When dressing up to go out, she always put on her corset, which reduced her waistline some. It was a very uncomfortable-looking garment. (I once wandered into Grandma's bedroom and saw her in the corset and her "bloomers" with her hair down. I was startled and for a moment didn't know who she was. I was uncomfortable with that scene.) Grandma dressed and groomed before the "looking glass" on her dresser. Her shoes were black lace-up oxfords with conservatively moderate high wide heels. She had a pair for work and a pair for dress (the former had once been the latter). A hat of some kind was always worn when leaving the house. Grandma's dress hats were usually short brimmed or had no brim. If brimmed, they had a ribbon around the crown and a bow in front. The brimless hats which perched on her head and were held in place by hair pins sometimes had a veil which hung down over the eyes. Out in the garden she wore a plain muslin sun bonnet with ties to make a bow under her chin. The bonnet had a four-to-five-inch brim to fully shade her face from the damaging rays of the sun. Her hose were of a tan (flesh) colored, opaque cotton fabric. The fashion stockings of the day were made of silk but were very expensive. Nylon stockings didn't come into being until 1939. Though nylon lacked the prestige of silk, it promised sheer, affordable elegance for the masses. Ladies stockings of the day had seams up the back and were always a subject of concern as to whether the seams were straight. She called her underpants "bloomers," which I thought was a funny word. I used to see them blowing in the wind on the clothesline on laundry day. They were pink and looked like they must have been about knee length. Grandma always emitted a nice, musky fragrance of face powder. She rarely used perfume. Rouge, Pond's cold cream, and lipstick adorned her dresser. After giving each of them the taste test, I gave my endorsement to the cold cream. She curled her hair in the kitchen using aluminum rollers and a curling iron heated on the kitchen stove. Mother and Grandma gave each other home permanents. The smell of the solution they used always drove me out of the house. They would walk around in curlers for the rest of the day looking silly to me.

A whiff of the aromas from Grandma's kitchen was always enticing. I especially remember the smell of pinto beans cooking with salt pork and herbs, mixed with the smell of corn bread baking in the oven. She had specific days for such activities as baking, laundry, sewing, and shopping. I looked forward with longing to baking day. On this eventful day the heaven sent aromas of fresh bread, cinnamon rolls, soda biscuits (which I used to poke a finger in and pour Karo syrup in the resulting hole), and sweet-smelling pies and cakes. (I always got the first slab of pie or wedge of cake because I was always in the kitchen on baking day.) This day was special also because I got to lick the bowl and big mixing spoon which still had the leavings of the sweet cake dough on them. Grandma always had leftover pie dough which she cut in strips, sugared, baked, and gave to me. The bread dough was in a tub rising with a dish towel over it. She would dump it onto the bread board and knead it, punch it, flip it over, and knead it again. Then she shaped it into the bread pans, and into the oven it went. It wasn't long before the delicious smell filled the house. I carried my lunch to school and felt deprived because my sandwich was made with homemade bread, cut somewhat irregular by Grandma. I thought the kids who had bakery presliced, store-bought bread were so very privileged. We also had delicious homemade syrup for our pancakes made from sugar, boiling water, and vanilla extract. If Grandma was out of some ingredient she would substitute and say, "A nod is as good as a wink to a blind horse."

"Think of the poor starving Armenians," I heard that refrain each time I told Grandma I didn't want to eat something she had served, like boiled turnips, wilted lettuce,[13] or liver, to name a few. I

---

[13] A mixture of hot bacon grease, sugar, and vinegar poured over leaf lettuce.

didn't know who the poor Armenians were.[14] For the longest time, I thought it might be the poor Mexican family who lived down the street. I didn't know their name.

Going into a pout one day at supper, I said, "I wish there never was liver."

"If wishes were horses, beggars would ride," she said.

If I was rambunctious, she often cautioned, "Hold your horses, young man."

Grandma created all these marvelous meals on a large, black cast-iron coal-fired kitchen cooking stove. (There was such a stove in every house in which we lived.) It could be fueled with hard coal, soft coal, wood, coke, or even corncobs. The stove was about four feet wide and around twenty-eight inches deep. It was made of foundry molded iron and trimmed-in shiny ornate nickel plate. It had a main top surface about thirty inches high, which was a good-working height for Grandma. She wasn't much over five foot tall as were most women of her generation. Sitting about twenty-six inches above the main top was the warming closet of steel which was heated by the radiant heat of the stove's flu. The closet shelf could be closed off by a front roll-back into the top of the closet. Grandma did most of her daily cooking on the main top, which had four round openings with iron lids, which could be removed with a lifting tool to expose the burning coal embers in the fire box below. By placing a pot over an opening, Grandma produced more heat on the pot; otherwise, the pot of cooking food could sit on the surface of the lidded hole and cook at a lesser degree of heat. When the stove was fired up, the kitchen became unbearably hot to the unaccustomed. At times, if a lengthy dinner was being prepared, the kitchen stove would heat the entire house. Sometimes the stove top would cast a red glow from the heat. There was always a large tea kettle of water sitting on the stove ever ready for any culinary use to which Grandma wished to put it. The ashes from the burned coal dropped down to a pit which had a

---

[14] During World War I, the Armenian people, living in what is now Eastern Turkey, were forced by the Turks to relocate. They were forced to march to the Syrian Desert and to Mesopotamia (Iraq). Many died from starvation.

hinged door to open for clean out. The ashes were scooped out and put in a nearby bucket to be taken out to the ash pit by the alley in back of the lot. Stove black paste was applied weekly which gave her stove a shiny luster like it was brand new. To the side of the stove was the ever present coffee can of bacon drippings used for frying. It was especially tasty in the making of flour gravy. The kitchen stove was the very heart of our home, and Grandma made it so.

There was no question but that Grandma was totally in control of this kitchen behemoth. She worked it like a symphony conductor and produced fabulous taste delights and comfort for her family. Her cook stove was like Grandma's pet: it seemed to lovingly do, and without ever questioning, Grandma's bidding. In the unstable world of the Great Depression, and the war, Grandma's kitchen was a warm, safe, and good place to be. She would put a whole chicken in a boiling pot before plucking and singing it free of feathers. She put up canned peaches, green beans, beets, piccalilli, and jellies in mason jars and sealed each jar with paraffin wax (which was fun to chew). The jars were stored on shelves in the cellar, to be eaten during the winter, when fresh fruit and vegetables were not readily available. Also, they were too costly due to shipping from warmer climates. (An orange and a banana were the rarest, most exotic of all foods in our house.) The kitchen pantry was a place for flour and sugar bins below a counter and shelves and cabinets above. All the commercially canned and dry food goods were stored here along with the large bread box. This was my favorite snack hangout. There were crackers, leftover biscuits, jelly, and my favorite of all, Hershey's Cocoa. I would spoon some cocoa into a glass of cold water along with enough sugar to make it interesting. The cocoa didn't mix well with cold water. In drinking this concoction, I must have conned myself into believing it was really good, because I did it often and usually left some mess behind. My home-cut bread slices ran from too thick at the top of the cut down to too thin at the bottom, but they were a delight to eat when slathered with ketchup or mayonnaise. Grandma often made "poor man's tea" for me in the winter. This "tea" was hot water, sugar, and some condensed milk. Dish "worshing" was done with a "dish rag," which was just that: a rag cut from a discarded garment that was too-many-times patched.

"Dear Ralph, would you please give Jack the items I've listed and charge it to me until Friday? Thank you." I would take this note and list to the neighborhood grocery. Ralph, the grocer, would fill the order, lick his pencil point, and list the items in the little pocket receipt book he kept in his apron bib pocket. He put the carbon copy in the bag. "You're all set, young man." And I was on my way. Most of our grocery shopping was done in this manner, a few items at a time.

Grandma taught me how to make a string rope with an empty thread spool with four small nails at the corners of one end of the spool. You threaded string in, out, and around the nails, and a rope came out the other end of the spool. I know she told me stories of her childhood, and early life, but all I can remember is that as a young teenage woman she was warned by her mother not to associate with those Frazee boys, as they were a "wild bunch." What if she had listened? Stories about her children were told to entertain me also. One I remember is the story about Walter (she never called her son Walt, and I was surprised to find out that my grown-up Uncle Walt was Grandma's boy). The story was that Walter, as a youngster, asked when they were going to eat supper.

Grandma's sister Minnie was visiting at the time, so she told him, "We'll eat as soon as Aunt Minnie leaves"

Walter then crawled under the dining room table and hidden by the overhanging table cloth, he, in his best eerie, ghostly voice, began repeating slowly, "Go home. Go home. Go home."

Minnie got a kick out of it, but she did go home.

Whenever I would ask for something that was too costly, Grandma would promise to get it for me, "When my ship comes in."

I would tell my friends about my Grandma's ship and all the good stuff I was going to get when it docked. I don't know where I thought it would dock. The lady that Grandma was, she rarely ever talked about herself. She thought that bringing attention to one's self was unbecoming.

If something unpleasant had happened and couldn't be recti-
fied, she would say, "That's water under the bridge."

After my bath, Grandma wouldn't let me put my same clothes
on. She laid out fresh laundered, and often mended, shirt, pants,
socks, and underwear, and quoted Jesus, "You don't put new wine in
old bottles."

"She doesn't know who the father is." Bertha Maud wasn't above
a little juicy gossip.

When I was nearby where she was exchanging scandalous gossip
with someone, she would caution, with her finger at her lips while
rolling her eyes toward me, "Little pitchers have big ears."

All these philosophic sayings and clichés used by Grandma and
Grandpa must be where I acquired my strong penchant for philosophic phrases.

Laundry day had its own array of smells of bleach, Mrs. Stewart's
bluing and homemade lye soap. No fancy cooking on this day,
just beans and corn bread. In the category of labor-saving devices,
Grandma treasured her Maytag electric, wringer washing machine
more even than her sewing machine. The alternative to her Maytag
was the back-breaking scrub board and the painfully tiring hand
wringing. She cleaned it and oiled the motor after each day's use. She
then put it away covered by a bedsheet until next week. Laundry day
began with a gathering and sorting of all things needing washing,
clothing (she always had to argue with Grandpa to change his long
underwear), sheets, pillowcases, dish towels, bath towels, and wash-
cloths. These items were all laid out on the kitchen floor in separate
piles according to some system. Grandma then brought the washing
machine in from the back porch. (This task took place on the porch
during the summer.) With a bucket, she filled the washer with warm
water, and using a paring knife, she cut and dropped, into the water,
shavings from one of her homemade bars of lye soap (in better times
she used store-bought Oxydoll laundry detergent as advertised on
the *Ma Perkins* radio soap opera: her favorite). She washed the more
delicate things first, and saved the water for the progressively dirty or
heavier items. Grandpa's overalls were always last. A fill of water was
used about three times before changing. After the washing machine

agitator had run long enough for the load to be clean, Grandma ran each item through the wringers and dropped them into a waiting bushel basket. Next the washed items were put in a tub of cold rinse water in which a few drops of "Mrs. Stewart's Bluing" had been added. The bluing was to make whites whiter and colors more colorful. It was also used on mosquito bites and to detect plumbing leaks. In the winter, the washing machine was drained into the bathtub. In the summer, it drained out into the backyard from the back porch. The laundry was hung out to dry on the clothesline unless it was unbearably cold, at which time it would be draped on anything in the house that would hold it. When she was ready to iron, she first sprinkled the garments by hand, with water, and rolled them up and placed them in a basket to dampen evenly.

In the fifteen years I knew Grandma, she always had a singing canary caged in the dining room. She would give it feed and water and some kind of bone thing attached to the cage. Daily she would remove the soiled newspaper at the bottom of the cage and replace it with a fresh one. The bird would sing, and Grandma would talk to it like it was human. The bird had a name, but it's lost in the waves of time to me.

The only time I remember experiencing Grandma's ire was when I was about eight years old. She and Grandpa were playing cribbage with some visiting family members, and I interrupted her game to ask if I could play with her bread board. She said "okay", without asking how I intended to use it as she was eager to get back to her card game. I went to the kitchen, got the bread board, placed it on the floor, propped it up against the wall, went to the knife drawer, and pulled out a large kitchen knife. I went to the opposite side of the kitchen from the bread board and aimed, pulled the knife back, holding on to it at the forward end of the blade like I had seen a knife thrower do in a movie, and with all my eight-year-old might, threw the knife at the board. The knife missed its target, hit the floor, bounced up over the bread board, ricocheted off the wall, and landed with a loud metal-to-metal crash bang on top of the kitchen stove.

In an instant I heard Grandma scream, "JACK!"

She was in the kitchen before I could even sort out in my mind what had gone wrong with my plan.

Still in a loud voice like I had never heard her use she said, "WHAT IN THE WORLD DID YOU DO?"

The loud tone of her voice frightened me to tears. In between sobs, I was able to tell her what I had done. She took a deep breath and exhaled. Her normally infinite tolerance for my behavior had reached the limit. She calmly told me to go sit quietly in the living room until she said I could leave. I did, and she didn't excuse me until the company left. It seemed like hours. Like I said, this was the only time I can remember her being upset with me. She wasn't even upset the time she intercepted some secret code messages that Duane and I were sending to each other, wherein we were exercising some of our newly acquired risqué and exciting vocabulary. The particular message that got her attention was the one which coded out: c-o-c-k-s-u-c-k-e-r. She quietly had Duane and me sit down on the sofa and asked us if we knew what this word meant. We had a hazy remote idea, but innocently, we shook our heads no. Grandma then proceeded to explain that this word referred to "old men in the crazy house who suck each other's thing." We assured her that in light of this revelation, we would never use this word again.

She said, "If I see or hear any more words like this, I'm going to wash your mouths out with soap."

We were excused and greatly relieved. Luckily, she hadn't discovered our total code vocabulary.

My grandparents moved often. They had eight different addresses during the first ten years of my life. They never left Colorado Springs, and the moves were always to a rental house. We lived on the north side, the west side, the east side, and the south side. Why they moved so often, I don't know. I don't remember actually moving. I only remember I lived in these places.

Grandma once said, "Every time we move, Jack gets sick."

Maybe it traumatized me. I don't know.

"We're going to clean you up and go to the show [movie]." These words were so joyful to hear that I didn't even mind being scrubbed behind the ears in preparation for this adventure.

With her hat perched on her head, her apron and house dress put aside in deference to her "dress-up" dress, and with purse in hand, we were out the door and headed downtown. We walked down El Paso Street along the railroad tracks to the Bijou Street underpass, where we turned and walked under the tracks. The graffiti art on the walls of the underpass were ignored by Grandma, but I tried to take it all in. I didn't know then, but years later I realized this was my first experience with porn. I just enjoyed seeing drawings and words on a wall. Even today I enjoy seeing skillful art that I don't necessarily understand, like the tag art on railroad boxcars.

Continuing on along the broken and heaved-up topography of the sidewalk on Bijou Street, we viewed all the pre–World War I bungalows with their attic dormers and clapboard siding. Some were in need of paint and some not. There were flower gardens, dandelions, rock gardens, fishponds, picket fences with broken gates wrought-iron fences, and decaying stone walls. There were well-kept lawns and also yards of weeds. Bijou Street had seen less painful times. Reaching the broad Nevada Avenue, the highway running north to Denver and south to Pueblo, we turned and walked past the Davis Sweet Shop, a high school hangout, and the Law Undertakers with a long black hearse parked in the drive. There was the mouthwatering aroma of hot roasted peanuts and popcorn as we walked by Sutak's Peanuts, a little hole-in the-wall place opening on to the sidewalk whose facade was covered with peanuts-in-the-shell.

We turned the corner onto Pikes Peak Avenue. We were now in the middle of downtown, on the Times Square of Colorado Springs. There were four theaters on two city blocks. The Ute Theatre marquee read, Wm. Powel, Myrna Loy, The Thin Man.

Grandma paid for tickets, which she gave to a man in uniform standing in the lobby. He tore them in half and returned a half. A uniformed usher had a few words with Grandma and with a flashlight led us down the aisle and stopped at a row of seats near the center. Two people in the row stood up and let us through to our seats. Before the main feature, there were some commercials, a newsreel showing an ocean liner burning, President Roosevelt speaking, a reporter announcing that bank robbers Bonny and Clyde were killed and that John Dillinger had shot his way out of a police trap. Next on the bill was a Pete Smith Specialties short subject film, on what, I can't recall. Then came the long awaited for cartoon, *Popeye the Sailor Man.*

> I'm Popeye the Sailor Man.
> I'm strong to the "Finich."
> 'Cause I eats me Spinach.
> I'm Popeye the Sailor Man.

I squirmed through the feature till the lights came on and everyone got up to leave. We walked home the same way we came. Grandma also took me downtown shopping. We would go to the big Kress "five and dime" store on North Tejon Street. There were hundreds of things to look at all piled in big bins to sort through—items like shoes, clothes, combs, dishes, thread, needles, clothespins, tooth powder, and more. They also had toys and candy-like sugar-coated candy orange slices and sugary-filled cone-shaped chocolates. Across the street was Woolworth's dime store, which had a lunch counter, where, if Grandma was flush, we would eat lunch. I always ordered a club sandwich and a Coke. These were rare and memorable occasions.

We always had a big Christmas tree that Grandpa had cut down and made a wood stand for. Grandma retrieved boxes of ornaments and lights from the attic, and she and I would decorate. I liked to throw the tinsel on. After that, I lost interest in the tree until the lights went on and gifts were placed under it. I began snooping around under the beds, in the closets and the pantry bins about two weeks before Christmas, looking for gifts. Usually, to no avail. I once found a new Mackinaw winter coat under Grandma's bed. One Christmas Grandma gave everyone (except me) a practical gift.

She gave Kenny a light bulb, Uncle Walt a broom, and Grandpa a potato masher. I was laughing at Kenny's light bulb when Grandma, seeing the disappointment on their faces, spoke, "These are the kinds of gifts all of you give me each year. I thought maybe you would like the same."

When Grandma opened her gifts, she proved her point. Kenny gave her two hot pads, Uncle Walt's gift was a Sunbeam Coffee Master coffee pot. Grandpa gave his wife a set of three kitchen knives. That was the year I got my Red Rider six shooters with holsters.

Grandma's Cinder Garden was a magical thing to behold. She mixed salt, food coloring, Mrs. Stewart's bluing, and ammonia and slowly poured these ingredients over a plate of cinders gathered from the railroad track. The salt crystallized into what looked like multi-colored coral formations. She always made a fresh one each fall. She called this our winter flower garden. There was a big old painted tractor tire planter in the front yard on El Paso Street. Grandma gave the old tire a fresh coat of paint in the spring, changing the color each year, from white to green, to orange to blue. After pulling up all the remains of last year's crop, she opened several packets of her Ferry-Morse seeds and spread new flower seeds. The old tire became filled with flowers of every kind. All of Grandma's activities were fun to watch, both in the house and out. I laughed as I watched her put bloomers on a big fat hen that had lost most all of her feathers. I don't know if covering this nude chicken's body was in the interest of vanity or to maybe prevent sun burn.

When I stayed home sick from school, Grandma made me a bed by putting two overstuffed chairs together, and we would listen to the soap operas on the radio, *Ma Perkins, One Man's Family, Our Gal Sunday, Lorenzo Jones and His Wife Belle*, and more. Only when I was sick did Grandma let me play with the little porcelain figurines she kept in a box on her bedroom dresser. There were porcelain people and animals. These were playthings from her childhood, and she cherished them dearly. The illnesses which prevented me from going to school were sometimes imagined, sometimes faked, and sometimes real. My most common complaints were headache, stomachache, and for-real laryngitis brought on by the croup. I seemed to have a proclivity for attracting the croup viral infection, which left me with no voice but with a barking cough. Mustard plaster—a paste made of flour, dry mustard, and water—was wrapped in one of Grandma's flour sack tea towels. This poultice was put on my chest to drive out the congestion. The plaster was hot like it was burning my skin, but it was felt that this was the best remedy. I guess it worked because I did eventually get back to school and my skin didn't burn. No matter the illness, Grandma made it fun to stay home.

Grandma's hands never rested from dawn to bedtime. She cooked, canned, sewed, mended, laundered, scrubbed floors, dusted furniture, washed windows, washed dishes with a "dish rag," and scrubbed toilets, sinks, and bathtub. In addition to all this, she nursed us all back to health with home remedies of all kinds. She was the emergency room and intensive care unit all in one. Even at rest while listening to the radio, she was darning socks, shelling peas, cutting patches for quilts, or peeling apples with her paring knife, which she wielded with the precision of a surgeon's scalpel. She toiled like an indentured servant giving loving care to all of us. Grandma was a first responder and caregiver before there were such designations. She was the ideal example of "Woman's work is never done." Once in a while she would relax on the sofa and thumb through the Sears and Roebuck mail order catalog, which she called the Wish Book. I don't think she ever ordered anything from it, but she enjoyed browsing through all the many items they offered. On the rarest of times, she would splurge on a *Ladies Home Journal*. She also liked reading Uncle Walt's *Saturday Evening Post* with its Norman Rockwell art on the cover.

I loved her deeply, and she loved me—that's about as much as I really knew of her. Her death left a vast irreparable crater in the Frazee family.

Elza Armstrong Frazee (Grandpa) (EA) 1871–1958

T he strongest influence on my life during my formative years was
my grandfather, Elza Armstrong Frazee, who was born just six
years after Lincoln's assassination. I called him Grandpa until I was
in my twenties, at which time I stopped and didn't address him with
any name but referred to him as EA, as did the rest of the adult family
members. Most of the first ten years of my life I spent living with my
grandparents. Grandpa made me feel safe, whereas Grandma made
me feel loved. One of my fondest memories of Grandpa, is, he took
me to the Knob Hill livestock auctions, Saturdays on the east side of
town. I don't think the auction barn was actually within the city limits. From the appearance of the Knob Hill area structures, there was
no building code in effect, and many of the streets were not paved.
Attending these auctions was a wonderful adventure for a young boy.
Besides seeing horses, cattle, and pigs up close and being mesmerized by the auctioneer's chant, we would also have lunch there. The
always crowded lunch counter at the auction served extra large fresh
handmade hamburger creations with lettuce, sliced tomato, onion,
pickle, and mustard. The big hamburgers were unwieldy for my
small hands, but I really gobbled them up. After the last bite, I had
to use several paper napkins to wipe up the ketchup dripping down
my shirt and my arms. This delightful repast was washed down with
a bottle of Pepsi Cola (Pepsi Cola came in a twelve-ounce bottle and
was touted as "Twice as much for a nickel too, Pepsi Cola is the drink

for you."[15] Grandpa drank draft beer, which was served in a tall narrow pilsner glass that the waitress had scraped off the excess head of foam. The savory smells of onions and hamburgers cooking on the grill were mouthwatering. It was exciting being among the crowd of people of every kind, young, old, male, female, fat, skinny, tall, and short, all talking and laughing. I was glad to be a part of it.

The auction site was also a place where people could bring used furniture and other items they wished to sell. It was like today's flea market. Grandpa would buy broken and/or scarred furniture. He would repair and/or refinish them and return to the auction with the repaired and renewed items to resell them at a small profit.

When I was not much taller than Grandpa's boots, he would sometimes use me as a bootjack by sitting in a chair and having me straddle his outstretched leg facing his foot and holding on to the heel of his boot. He would then place his other foot on my butt. "Hold on tight," he would say and shove me across the room holding the extracted boot. We would then repeat this procedure on the other boot.

Watching Grandpa shave was one of my favorite forms of entertainment. First he would remove his shirt and hand it to me. I was sitting up on the wooden lid of the old toilet which had a high wall tank and a pull chain. Next he unbuttoned the top two buttons of his long underwear. He then draped a towel loosely underneath his chin with each end pulled up over the shoulders. This was followed with pulling his straight edge razor and his shaving mug with brush from the medicine cabinet above the bathroom sink. He placed them on the flat rim of the sink. From its snap-together leather case, he removed the razor and slapped it back and forth on the leather strap hanging from the wall. This sharpened an already very sharp blade. Placing the now sharpened razor on the sink rim, he ran a small amount of hot water into the mug containing soap pieces of leftover bath soap. The brush in the mug was wallowed around to form thick frothy suds, which he then brushed on to his face forming what looked to me to be a white beard. I never failed to laugh at this phase

---

[15]   Coca Cola was bottled in six-ounce bottles.

of the operation. The razor was then moved deftly over his face, neck, and chin with the precision of a surgeon. Some froth would drop on to the draped towel. After each stroke of the razor, he shook off the suds from the blade into the sink and made the next stroke. When all areas had been visited by the razor, a washcloth removed any suds remaining. If the razor had gotten too cozy with the skin at any point where bleeding occurred, a small piece of toilet paper was placed over the injury to stem the flow. All items were then returned to their places, and the show was over. I would climb down from my vantage point on the toilet seat where I had been sitting enjoying the show. Watching Uncle Walt wasn't as much fun. He used a modern Gillete double-edged blade, safety razor, and never nicked his face and only took half the time. When I laughed at his sudsy beard, he flipped soap suds at me until I giggled and ran out of the room. He shut the door and locked it.

Grandpa's friends and associates knew him as Cap. He got this nickname when he was a county road gang foreman informally referred to as crew captain.[16] His nieces and nephews referred to him as Uncle El with the exception of one nephew, Hezekiah "Hezzie" Frazee, who called him Uncle Doc, prompted by the fact that Grandpa some years previous had saved his life while they were in the forest gathering firewood. Hezzie received a serious cut on his neck from a sharp tree limb. He was a hemophiliac and was bleeding profusely. While Hezzie held a rag over the gash, Grandpa and his brother John, Hezzie's father, built a fire and heated a tire iron to red hot. Grandpa then used the hot iron to cauterize the wound by searing the flesh and thereby stopping the bleeding—thus, Uncle Doc.

Grandpa rarely called me by name. He always referred to me as boy. There were times while living with my grandparents that I actually thought boy was my name. I knew it wasn't sweetheart, honey, or dear, as Grandma usually called me. From time to time though, each of them would use the name Jack.

---

[16]   One of his crew members painted a poem on his black metal lunch bucket: "If this bucket should get lost, please return it to its boss, Cap Frazee."

Elza Frazee had been a carpenter, surveyor, farmer, and teacher as well as other occupations in between. (At age seventy-one, he hired out as a carpenter to work on the construction of Camp Carson.) He would let me help him in his workshop. The shop was in the rear of the garage at 1608 N, Corona Street. The main part of the garage had a dirt floor. There was a wall between the shop, and the garage with a door. The shop was elevated and wood floored. Another door also led out to the backyard. The shop had a window giving good natural light. There was a large sturdy wooden workbench with legs the size of an elephant's, which Grandpa had built. Attached to the bench was a big steel vice. Tool chests were lined up around the perimeter of the room, and more tools hung from hooks on the walls. All acquired over the years when times were better. There was a small wood-burning heating stove which we would fire up in the winter. I relished the times we were in the shop with the fire going while outside maybe it was snowing. Grandpa let me do minor sawing, sanding, and painting on items he had picked up at the auction. He taught me how to sharpen handsaws with a file and hone a knife and ax blade. He gave me skills with the level, the brace and bit, wood planes, and whetstone. The framing square was the most fun of all. With it you could measure and cut stringers for stair steps, and you could figure angle cuts for rafters. He taught me how "rise" and "run" relate. To determine if a ninety-degree angle was true, he showed me the "three four five rule."[17] He taught me many things in that shop. Not all of it carpentry. From him I learned about life's challenges with such unforgettable sayings as, "There never was a horse that couldn't be rode, and there never was a cowboy who couldn't be thrown." His advice about fear was just to remember that "they might kill you but they won't eat you." This was like a Zen koan. I'm still searching for the wisdom in this. He taught me as a carpenter to "measure twice and cut once" and "Don't force it, let the tool do the work." He gave

---

[17]   In determining a true right angle without a carpenter's square, measure three units such as feet or inches from the corner on one side and mark it. Measure four corresponding units from the corner on the other side and mark it. The distance between the two marks should be five units to be a true ninety-degree right angle.

me a pocketknife and admonished, "Always cut away from yourself." My first knife-cutting project was on a plug of his chewing tobacco, which had been left on a bench in his shop. It tasted terrible, but this didn't deter me from performing this most grown-up and manly of all activities. It also didn't deter me from experiencing the most painful intestinal upheaval of my life. I threw up out in the back-yard and went and sat on the back steps with my head in my hands until I felt good enough to go inside and lie down unnoticed on the "Davenport." I dared not tell Grandma of this adventure, for fear of having further pain administered. His advice about threatening or bluffing was, "Never point an empty gun." When I had grown to maturity, he gave me advice on my sex life, "Never play around with the help or where you work." No one in our family ever had any "help" to play around with, so I was safe on that front.

From EA Frazee I got my liberal philosophy. He glorified the working man and vilified the plutocrats and the rich. It was a long time before I discovered that some rich can be nice. He taught man-ners also.

When we shared a drink of water from the canvas water bag hanging off the side of his car, he said, "When you share a drink from this canteen or a dipper or a bottle, always wipe it off before you pass it on to the next man. If you don't have a handkerchief, use your hand."

From time to time, he would help me with my arithmetic homework, which he called "ciphering," or "sums." (This help was not by request.) His input wasn't always helpful. He sometimes left me with answers only a surveyor could understand. He had surveyed in the Oklahoma territory. I discovered that my arithmetic teacher was not a surveyor and didn't' know that you could measure by rods, chains, initial points, and baselines.

Early on Grandpa owned an old Maxwell automobile which was a real experience to get started. He had to first make sure the car was on level ground so it wouldn't roll away when he put the trans-mission in neutral. He then set the spark by adjusting a lever on the steering column. Next he pulled the throttle lever out all the way. After these adjustments were made, he was then ready to crank it up. From under the front seat, he pulled out a hand crank and came around to the front of the car and inserted the crank into an opening just below the radiator and turned it clockwise and pulled the crank out quickly. The engine would cough and belch and die. Grandpa repeated with the crank as many times as it took. After about three unsuccessful cranks, he would add a few "goddamns" to the crank, and it would eventually start. He then hurried around to the steering column and readjusted the spark and the throttle. When the crank kicked back and hit his arm or wrist, he not only "goddamned" it, he stood up and kicked the car.

Grandpa smoked a pipe, chewed tobacco, and rolled his own cigarettes with his large rough hands. His cigarette tobacco of choice was Bull Durham, which was packed in a small cotton pocket-size bag with a drawstring. At the end of the drawstring, there was a paper tag with a picture of a bull. This dangled outside his shirt pocket for easy access. Rolling cigarettes to a tight, neat, evenly packed, and well-shaped cigarette is a real art, requiring many hours of practice, experimentation, and failures before ultimate success. (I know this firsthand.)

He used to say, "I can roll a cigarette with one hand while riding a wild mustang in a Wyoming windstorm."

Grandpa sometimes treated himself to a pack of "tailor made" cigarettes. He had no preference for brands. He sent me to the grocery with fifteen cents and a note reading, "Give the boy a pack of cigarettes." At the cigarette display shelves, I had my choice of brands; some of which were Camels, Lucky Strike, Chesterfield, Kools (a menthol-flavored brand I learned the hard way not to buy), Pall Mall, an extra-long cigarette, Old Gold, Wings and Spud.

Grandpa's chewing tobacco was "Days Work" plug cut. The plug was a solid, molasses-flavored, hard bar about the size of a deck of cards from which he cut a bite size chaw with his ever-present bone-handled pocketknife. That knife was used for a countless number of things: whittling, apple peeling, and fingernail trimming, to mention a few. Whittling on a piece of wood was to him what twiddling thumbs might be to someone else. It was a time passer.

Grandpa and Uncle Walt hunted jack rabbits out east of town. We ate rabbit about as often as chicken. Grandpa not only hunted rabbit, he also raised them in a hutch in the backyard. The hunters would usually bring back a few rabbits and sometimes some rattle snake rattles they had taken off snakes they had killed. They skinned and eviscerated the rabbits and left the rest up to Grandma. Grandpa had cut the foot off a rabbit and offered it to me.

"Here, boy, this will bring you good luck."

I stepped back and held my hands behind me. I couldn't bring myself to touch the hideous thing. He coaxed for a minute or two before he gave up and took the foot away. We also raised chickens for eggs and for eating. It was a gruesome sight, seeing a chicken either getting its head chopped off or its neck rung. The headless chicken would continue to hop around for a minute or two before collapsing.

If Grandpa liked persons, places, or things, he canonized them. On the other hand, if he disliked them, he demonized them. This characteristic came to be known, in the family, as "Frazeeing." It is a characteristic still demonstrated in his male progeny in the twenty-first century. I laugh when I hear the trendy phrase "man cave" used by today's realtors. I can just imagine explaining to Grandpa the concept of a place in the home where the man of the house can do as he pleases. I can imagine he would say, "Hell, boy, this whole damned house is my cave." (Not really.) I noticed one evening that he had left his pick and shovel leaning against the garage door.

"Grandpa someone might steal them," I said.

"Boy, those are the tools of hard manual labor, and no thief is going to steal such tools."

I guess in those hard-up days, things were stolen for personal use, not for resale.

Often Grandpa would grumble about the windows being covered by curtains. I heard him say more than once, "A man builds a house and puts openings in the walls [windows] to let in light and women come along and hang rags [curtains, drapes, etc.] over the opening." The contents of his wallet were well guarded. Grandma would only tell him the prices she paid for groceries and other household necessities when she had to, in order to get him to come up off the money. He sometimes, but not always, was very reluctant to part with the contents of his wallet. I realize now that he wasn't just recalcitrant; he was just trying to hold on to as much cash as he could during these extraordinarily hard times. Another stumbling stone for Grandma was that he had no idea what anything cost. As a carpenter during the Depression years, he wasn't always employed. Only after he got the job as road gang "ramrod" did he make a steady modest-but-adequate wage, which made us relatively well off.

Grandpa held a prejudice against all things and people he didn't understand, as did most of his generation, and as many do today.

"Let me see your 'Nigger shooter,'" Grandpa said of my "beanie" (sling shot).

Grandma interrupted that conversation with, "That's a terrible word, and, Jack, I never want to hear you say it."

In this respect Grandpa was a man of his generation who actually thought Negroes were an inferior race. Perhaps Grandma did also but felt they deserved as much kindness as anyone else.

My grandparents would have some friends over to play cards. Their game was pitch. I don't know how it's played, but I used to hear

Grandpa loudly exclaim, "High-Low-Jack and the Game." He was a noisy card player. During these card games, they drank beer and put the empty bottles back in the case in the kitchen. Unbeknownst to all, I would drain a small amount of beer left in the bottles into one bottle and drink it. I didn't have to acquire a taste, I liked it right off. I could never beat Grandpa in a game of dominoes or checkers because he would change the rules in the middle of the game.

In my grandparents' house, it seems that about every meal had something served that had been fried in either salt pork grease or lard. Even the shortening used in my grandma's home-baked bread was lard. We ate fried potatoes almost daily and fried chicken at least once a week. Even with this diet and Grandpa's habit of smoking a pipe, cigarettes, cigars, and chewing tobacco, he lived in good health to age eighty seven. His years didn't show as it does to most.

As far back as I can remember, there was always talk about politics at our oil-cloth-covered kitchen table. Of course the conversation was dominated by Grandpa. His favorite targets were the "goddamned Republicans" and Adolph Hitler, who he said "should be tied to a piss anthill." When World War II came to America, I learned who Adolph Hitler was. But it was much later that I found out what a "goddamned Republican was."

One morning Grandpa unsnapped and dug into his coin purse and gave me some money and said, "Go buy some breakfast food." This meant cereal. We always ate cornflakes, which came in a large box, but on this trip my orders were not specific as to type of cereal, so I, having always wanted to try Grape Nuts because the name sounded so inviting to my taste buds (I loved grapes, and I loved nuts), bought them. Grape Nuts came in a much smaller box than cornflakes, even though they weighed about the same. When Grandpa saw this small box of cereal and saw that it cost about the same as the large box of cornflakes, he exploded with, "God awmighty, boy. A fool can see that you don't pay the same price for a box less than half the size of a regular box." He sent me back to the store to make the exchange.

Long Horn cheese was a favorite of his. He bought it by the pound. The cheese was displayed in the meat counter case. It looked like a large, round pale-orange log wrapped in cheesecloth.

The butcher would cut off as much as you wanted and hand you a pie-shaped slice wrapped in white butcher's paper and tied with string. Its strong, sharp taste and low price made it attractive to Grandpa. I liked the less sharp American cheese, which came in a woodbox that could be made into any number of fun things. My tastes today lean more to the sharper. Maybe the taste buds dull with age. Going through a produce department, Grandpa would sample apples, grapes, radishes, carrots, and other finger foods all in one walk through. If he picked up an apple, to taste, he would give me a bite too. He might or might not have bought any of it. I really don't know what his intentions were.

Grandma made "Johnnie Cake" for him, a flat corn meal bread she flavored with Black Strap sorghum molasses. Aside from the molasses, this was an early Native American bread made with corn and water. Salt was added later. He must have picked up a taste for this bread down in the Cherokee territory. None of the rest of the family cared for this culinary creation.

Grandpa couldn't hear well. We all had to raise our voices to be heard. Grandma made all his phone calls. Once he took Grandma and me to a movie. The feature had been running for about fifteen minutes when he said, "We are leaving. I can't hear a damned thing."

We left. As time went on, he was only able to hear lower male voices. He could hear Grandma only if she yelled extra loud. Often she had Uncle Walt transmit for her. Grandpa, like many hard-of-hearing people, often faked as if he heard someone. Sometimes he would just smile and nod. I understand his problem well. My own hearing, even though enhanced by hearing aids of a technology unknown in Grandpa's day, leaves a lot to be desired, and it gets tiresome asking people to repeat themselves. I try to fake it sometimes also.

Some of Grandpa's expressions were colorful as well as meaningful. I had become bilingual just by my conversations with him and by listening to him converse with others. Even though his language was verified English, as was mine, they were different, the difference being cultural background and the wide gap of being two generations apart. When he was feeling bad, he was "feelin' poorly," or "I'm off my feed" (I'm sure this is a rural expression used in reference to live-stock that were giving the impression that they "felt poorly" and were not eating). When asked by some old friend, he hadn't seen for some time, how he was doing, his tongue-in-cheek response was often, "I'm able to sit up and take nourishment." Or he might say, "Fair to middlin'." Scattered throughout his vocabulary were such words as *cattywompus* (meaning "crooked, lopsided, askew, out of alignment") and *antigoglin* (meaning the same as *cattywompus*). These are words from his surveyor days. He used words of land measurement not used by many others, such as "rod" (16 feet), "chain" (sixty-six feet, or twenty-two yards).

"From hell to breakfast" meant he would do something for a long time. "I'd as leave" meant he would rather. If someone was lively, they were "full of piss and vinegar." If something was almost, it was "pert near," or if someone was cheated, they had been "skinned." When he thought a situation didn't appear quite right or legal, he would say, "There's a nigger in the woodpile somewhere." Relatives were referred to as "kin." When meeting an old friend after a long absence, his greeting would go something like, "Why, you old horse thief, I thought they would have hanged you by now."

He often threatened me with, "I'll beat the dog water out of you, boy," or, "I'll take you out to the woodshed." Another threat was, "I'll take my belt to you."

He never once even raised a hand at me.

"Boy, you look like you've been rode hard and put up wet." This meant I looked pretty messy to him. The word *customary* was short-ened to "custom." *Mite* meant "somewhat," or a "small amount." His swearing and tongue lashing had no equal. "You're still wet behind the ears,"[18] he would say when he thought I was too young to do something. If I procrastinated or was slow to respond to his call for action, he would say, "Open the gate, boy. You can't ride 'em in the chute."

---

[18]   This expression originally referred to newborn calves whose birth fluid had all dried up except in the area behind their ears.

Grandpa's luggage was either a "satchel" or a "grip." "The grip" was also a flu or pneumonia illness. "Victuals," pronounced "vittles," was all food served at mealtime. An unusually long time was a "coon's age." If things were as they should be, they were "up to snuff." If something was going to lead to disaster, it was "Katy, bar the door." If he thought he needed to leave right away, he would say, "I better hightail it out of here." If he thought someone was weak-willed, they were referred to as having no "gumption." It's no wonder I had trouble with English vocabulary in school. At school they were trying to teach me Standard English, and at home, I was learning frontier Frazee, and "I'll Billy-be-damned" if that wasn't a challenge.

"Boy, come along. We'll go see some bears."

I was excited about seeing bears. I had only seen them in pictures. I ran and jumped into the car.

"Go put some shoes on. If you step on a rusty nail, you'll wind up with lockjaw."

That sounded bad. After I retrieved my shoes, we drove out to Prospect Lake and slowly cruised around the lake. I kept looking out the windows for the bears. It was a hot day, and the lake's shores were crowded with people in bathing suits sunning and swimming. Grandpa parked the car. "We'll get out here." We left the car and I followed him on a walk along the perimeter of the beach. I grew more and more excited in anticipation of seeing the bears.

He stopped and said, "Well, let's go home."

Shock, I asked, "Where are the bears?"

"Everyone out here is as BARE as the law allows."

I was mad at him for the rest of the day.

Conversation with him was lively and interesting regardless of the subject.

The old beige-colored fedora hat that Grandpa wore had a wide brim that was loosely rolled up on the sides. The sweat band had seen many hours of moisture. It was browned with age and truly lived up to its name. The hat was creased down the crown and "pinched" in the front on both sides. This hat was part of who he was. He wore it with his work clothes as well as his dress suit. When he was really excited about something, he would pull his hat off and slap it on his thigh with one motion exclaiming something like, "Hot damn!" He rarely took that hat off outside the house. I think some people would not have recognized him without it. The hat was not to cover baldness. He had thick and course hair cut in a flat-top-style like a Prussian soldier.

He walked tall with long strides and head held high with the bearing of a general. He always spoke with authority and decisiveness and had no small amount of confidence and competence. This is not "Frazeeing." This is a boy's perception which didn't change with age. My relationship with him as a boy was good. He sometimes was stern and sometimes warm and loving in his way. The masculine element of my personality was forged in those first years of my life by this giant of a man.

His only suit was black, three piece and wool, worn to funerals and weddings. His dress boots were of the English riding style with tops that rose to the knee. They were always highly polished. He wore them inside the trousers. Grandpa owned two or three neck-ties and several solid-colored gabardine shirts. I don't think I ever saw him wear a white shirt. The finishing jewel to his dress attire was the floral-engraved gold pocket watch and chain. The shiny gold chain looped from his left vest pocket, where the watch lay, over to the right pocket where there was a buttonhole feature with which to connect it.

Grandpa's underwear was a one-piece Union Suit with a button flap opening in the rear. He had to be coaxed out of it by Grandma for laundering. He wore it summer and winter, day and night. His carpenter overalls, which he wore over his work pants, hung on the back porch and smelled of fresh cut pine. They were never washed.

E. A. Frazee took up a lot of space, not because of his size (6 feet tall, 190 pounds) but because of his powerful, all-pervading presence and thunder-booming, vibrating voice. He was in charge wherever he was. He was not offensive. He just seemed to command respect. He was fair, reasonably honest, and tough as iron. He was John Wayne before there was a John Wayne. Grandpa was not an affectionate per-son. The only time he hugged me was just before leaving on a trip to California to visit some relatives.

My aunt Helen shoving me toward him said, "Go kiss Grandpa goodbye."

He picked me up and hugged me. I could feel his bristly face scratching mine. I didn't like that experience. His favorite hangout was a bar and grill down on South Tejon Street called George's. He would take me in, set me up on a barstool, and order me a Pepsi and a beer for himself. The place smelled of stale beer and fried onions. While he kibitzed with the bar patrons, all of whom knew him as Cap, I would watch the pool players. It was fun watching the numbered balls, each a different color, roll around the table and carom off the side cushions and sometimes drop in a corner pocket. When the balls collided with each other, there was a loud click, then they rolled on off in their separate directions.

Sometimes, out in the shop, Grandpa would sit down on a saw horse, put a new load of tobacco in his pipe, let me light it with a kitchen match, draw on it a couple of times to make sure it was lit, blow out a cloud of smoke, and tell me stories from his boyhood all the way up to and including the present. I loved these stories and the aroma of his pipe. The stories of his life seemed like a novel to me. One of these stories he told time after time was of the time he was with the county road department and some of his Republican superiors were talking badly about Democrat governor Ed Johnson. Grandpa figured that since WPA funds administered by the State were used to subsidize the road project, they had no right to condemn a good Democrat. "I wrote a letter to Ed Johnson and told him he ought to get down here and straighten these old boys out." He said the governor came to our house and thanked him and then fired the culprits and "made me the ramrod of the road gang." I don't know if I really remember the governor's visit or if I've just heard it so often it's imbedded. He told me of the Ludlow massacre of 1914 where in Ludlow, Colorado, John D. Rockefeller, owner of the Colorado Fuel and Iron company, hired thugs who, along with the Colorado National Guardsmen, used machine guns against striking mine workers. They killed men, women, and even children in the tent city of the miners. I'm still not at all sure whether Grandpa was at

Ludlow or if he was just pointing out the nature of rich Republicans. Grandpa could spin colorful yarns with the best.

"The Frazees came here with Lafayette to help George Washington with the revolution," was one he told often.

He told me of surveying the townships six miles square in the Oklahoma territory so the land could be parceled out sixteen parcels to a section. "There were hostile Indians in the territory, so sometimes to expedite the survey, we measured the land by wrapping a rolled piece of canvas around the wagon wheel of the buckboard and counted the bumps of the revolving wagon wheel."

He told me that each township was supposed to set aside one section for public schools. Another good story was about the time he held up the paymaster at the mine at gun point because the mine owners wouldn't pay the miners. He didn't let facts get in the way of a good story. True or not, these were spellbinding good times with him sharing Frazee household mythology.

He took good care of his tools. He never borrowed a tool, and he never loaned one. He cut and planed joints by hand. All blades were put away sharpened for the next use. God forbid, I would leave a tool out. He expertly made me a crossbow one summer morning, using a young cherry tree growing in the backyard for the bow. I was overjoyed with the gun. It would shoot an arrow straight clear across the yard.

When I proudly showed it to Grandma and told her the origin of the bow, she said, "WHAT?"

I told her again. She pulled off her apron and made for the back door. I followed. She went into Grandpa's shop and slammed the door behind her. Her voice was raised and carried through the walls indistinctly. I went to the front yard. The two of them were noticeably not very talkative for a few days following.

I used to go down in the cellar with him while he scooped coal into the furnace. The cellar had a musty smell of coal dust and dampness. It was dimly lit down there by one lonely little yellowish light bulb hanging from the ceiling. Spiders found it suited to their tastes. Their webs were in every corner, ceiling and floor alike. The shadows were long and dark. It was kinda scary. I dreaded going down there alone when Grandma sent me to fetch a jar of peaches.

I was elated when Grandpa was rained out at work because he returned with a full lunch bucket which I would take to the back porch and eat the bologna sandwiches and pie and taste the coffee. This was my own private picnic. I don't think the lunch was missed because, I'm sure, Grandpa put it out of his mind, and maybe Grandma assumed he had eaten it.

"It's a damned shame a man lets himself get in this condition," EA (as I referred to him later on) was not at peace with old age.

He blamed himself for letting arthritis invade his joints in his eighties. Right up to the time he drew his last breath, he "did not go gentle into that good night."[19] In his heart he just knew he was going to soon get up from that hospital bed and go home.

At breakfast I was intrigued by the coffee ritual Grandpa and Uncle Walt went through each morning. They used cream (condensed milk) in their coffee. (Grandpa said he liked his coffee "the color of a new saddle"). After pouring the cream in, they would pour some coffee into their saucers to cool off. They then drank from the saucer while the coffee in the cup cooled off. They then placed the cup on the emptied saucer and drank from it. The coffee was very hot because the water used was boiling hot fresh from the percolator heated on the cook stove.

When EA quit working altogether at about age seventy-three, he drew the Colorado Old Age Pension. Social Security did not take effect until 1937, and even if he could have qualified for the minimum benefit, it would not have been equal to the Colorado benefit which attracted older people from all over the country. The Colorado Old Age Pension was established in 1936 by amendment to the State Constitution. Older people used to flock to Colorado, establish the five-year-residency requirement, and draw the pension.

One of EA's periodic actions was to get angry with some right-wing editorial in the *Gazette-Telegraph* and tell the paperboy not to deliver "that rag" any more. (He was a New Deal Democrat, who

---

[19] "Do Not Go Gentle into That Good Night," poem by Dylan Thomas.

never used the word "Republican" without the prefix "goddamned.")
After a week or two would pass with no newspaper, he would catch
the paperboy and ask him why he had not been delivering the paper.
The boy's answer fell on deaf ears. EA would then forgive the boy and
tell him to remember to deliver the paper. He was good till next time
an editorial went awry.

EA organized big family picnics. All the immediate family,
extended family, and old friends who had migrated from Oklahoma
would come. Walt would usually be the one who went to Cheyenne
Canyon early in the morning to pick a good picnic site and hold it
till the others arrived. There were people at these events that I had no
idea who they were or how or if they were related. At these events I
used to enjoy sitting and listening to the adults tell stories about the
Oklahoma days. I grew up hearing about such towns as Woodward,
Enid, and Alva. "John was over in Dewey County at that time." Like
a lot of people from a rural background they would often use only a
county as someone's address.

I took off by myself at these outings and went for hikes up the
stream and among the tall pines of the valleys and mountain sides of
the canyon. These picnics in the canyon were my first exposure to
real natural habitat. It was a wonderland. The ice-cold crystal-clear
water of the stream was fed by the snow melt-off high up in the
Rockies. Its rushing turbulence flowed over and around the rocks
and boulders in its path. It had over centuries worn them down,
rounded them off, and made them smooth. Once in a while I would
see a rainbow trout speeding by upstream showing its iridescent colors. The water was swift, cold, pure, and sweet. I would put my face
down in it and drink like I imagined the Indians and mountain men
of earlier times had done. I suppose acid rain has now made the
waters of the mountain streams toxic. Way up high in the pines, I
would listen to the wind.

A jay might sound its warning call high up in the branches. I
usually saw chipmunks and squirrels scurrying about. This whole
environment was magical to me. It was on these brief hikes that my
intimate reverent feeling for the majestic Rocky Mountains was con-
ceived, which is deep in my being to this day.

The Cheyenne Canyon picnic sites had concrete tables and benches and a stone outhouse as well as a fire pit for cooking. The WPA built these sites.[20]

In 1893, at the age of twenty-two, EA made the run for free homestead land in the Cimarron strip of what is now the state of Oklahoma. The territory of Cimarron (also called the Cherokee Strip, known today as the Panhandle of Oklahoma) was settled in the early 1800s by cattle ranchers, many of whom were squatters. To protect their claims, they attempted, in 1887, to create a separate territorial government. After subsequent efforts toward this end failed in the US Congress, Cimarron became part of the Oklahoma Territory in 1890. On September 16, 1893, the Strip, which had up to this time been designated as land belonging to the Indians, was opened up for white settlement. The parcels of land were to be determined by a "land rush" of individuals racing across the territory by horseback, wagons, trains, bicycles, and on foot to claim a quarter section of land which had been previously surveyed and marked. There were only forty-two thousand parcels available, and there were over one hundred thousand individuals participating in the race.

I think EA's run resulted in a valid homestead claim. He did subsequently locate and raise a family in the Oklahoma Territory. In addition to farming his homestead, he taught school in a one-room rural schoolhouse which I was told had nine Frazees in the class. Family legend had it that the people of the area took up a collection and sent him up to the nearest college up in Winfield, Kansas. For how long, I don't know. In the late 1920s, he surrendered to the unforgiving soil and climate for farming in the desolate territory.

---

[20] The Works Progress Administration (WPA) was a relief measure established in 1935 by President Roosevelt's executive order. It offered work to the unemployed on an unprecedented scale by spending money on a wide variety of programs.

Kid Stuff

One dark Halloween night when I was about six or seven, while out for "handouts" (we were too realistic to call it trick or treat), I got separated from my sister and the older kids who were supposed to look after me. I wandered lost into a gas station in tears and told the men I was lost. To soothe me, they gave me a candy bar. I wasn't scared anymore. I was in the company of grown-ups. Up to this point in my life, grown-ups had always been able to solve the problems that scared me. One of the men questioned me, "Where do you live?"

"With my grandma."

"What's her name?"

"Grandma."

"What street do you live on?"

"I don't know."

"What's Grandma's last name?"

"Frazee."

He pulled out a "telephone book" and started to thumb through it.

"Can you spell 'Frazee' for me?"

"No."

He sounded the name to himself and started thumbing the pages. He found the name and made a call. He hung up and said, "Come on, I'll give you a ride home." We got in his pickup truck, and we went home. The good man walked me to the door and delivered me to Grandma.

Another Halloween when I was a little older, I was out on the street early and alone for "handouts." One of the first doorbells I rang brought forth a nice little old lady. She looked frail and pale.

"Handouts," I said softly so as not to scare her.

She turned around and with both hands picked up a big brown paper bag bulging with something. She handed me the bag. It was heavy, so I put it down on the porch floor. As I started to open it, she said, "You look like a nice boy. I want you to take this bag of candy and share it with your little friends so I won't have to come to the door for each one. Will you do that?"

"Yes, ma'am."

I couldn't find any little friends, so I had to lug that whole bag of candy home.

Those rare times when we lived together, my sister and I dreamed up many things to do together. In the winter we made ice cream from snow, pet milk, sugar, and cocoa. Probably our favorite game was "'tend like" (pretend like). We would create scenarios to act out and cast ourselves in starring roles as adults. As our stories unwound, we would create additional acts to keep the story going. We sometimes, but rarely, argued over casting roles, dialogue, or storyline. We would play this until we could no longer come up with more plots. Betty's paper dolls made up a good cast for storylines. I used to enjoy designing outfits for them with paper, scissors, and crayons. Summer evenings we would sit out on the grass and listen to crickets, look at the stars, and chase fireflies. I made a ring toss game out of an old scrap board, a few nails, and some of Grandma's rubber canning jar gaskets. Grandma also furnished the title materials for "Drop the Clothespin in the Milk Bottle." None of these activities could take the place of my Lincoln logs though.

The decade of the 1930s was characterized not only by the Great Depression, but by many other factors such as the rise of Adolf Hitler and the Nazi Party in Germany and the German army's invasion of Czechoslovakia and Poland, the disastrous explosion of the *Hindenburg* dirigible, the heyday of notorious bank robbers like John Dillinger, Baby Face Nelson, and Bonny Parker and Clyde Barrow, who were considered by some as folk heroes because they were robbing the banks which had foreclosed on so many farms and homes. Aldous Huxley wrote *Brave New World*, a science fiction novel depicting a twenty-fifth century where art and personal relations were controlled by technology. Sinclair Lewis was awarded the Nobel Prize for literature. John Steinbeck wrote *Grapes of Wrath*, Ernest Hemingway wrote *For Whom the Bell Tolls*, Bela Lugosi starred in *Dracula*, and Boris Karloff turned in a superb performance as the monster in *Frankenstein*. *King Kong* brought to the screen the latest in special effects. *Gone with the Wind* was released in 1939. In China, Mao Tse-Tung's tattered army of eighty-six thousand made the legendary Long March of five thousand miles to avoid the pincer movement of the Nationalist forces of Chiang Kai-shek. The Volkswagen made its debut. Italy conquered Ethiopia. Spanish Civil War began. African American Jesse Owens with four gold medals was the star performer at the 1936 Olympic Games in Berlin at a time when Hitler's "Master Race" professed "White Supremacy" in all things.

Walt Disney's *Snow White and the Seven Dwarfs*, the first full featured animated film, was released in 1937. Major League baseball consisted of eight National League teams and eight in the American League. The great New York Yankee Babe Ruth (a season high sixty home runs) was winding down his career as fellow Yankee great, Joe "Joltin Joe, Yankee Clipper" Dimaggio (hit safely in fifty-six straight games) was beginning his climb to fame. Joe Louis became world heavyweight boxing champion in 1937. Superman was created in 1932 and first appeared in *Detective Comics* in 1938. Albert Einstein immigrated to the United States due to the rise to power of the anti-Semitic Adolph Hitler and the Nazi Party in Germany.

This was also the golden age of jazz and the big swing bands. The big swing bands were as popular as Hollywood movies, and often theatre owners would pair the two on the same bill. Big-band coast-to-coast radio broadcasts were popular during the 1930s and 1940s. These broadcasts were live coming from famous ball rooms and clubs all over the country. Each band had its own theme song with which they opened each performance. There were such renowned musician/band leaders as Glen Miller, Tommy Dorsey, Harry James, and Benny Goodman. The most popular singer of the time was Bing

Crosby, whose theme song was "Deep Purple." A sampling of popular songs of the decade were "Begin the Beguine," "Red Sails in the Sunset," "I got Plenty of Nuthin'," and "Just One of Those Things." You can't talk about music and musicians of the '30s without mentioning the "Dust Bowl Balladeer," Woody Guthry, the most influential American folk musician of the twentieth century. Guthry's "Goodbye, It's Been Good to Know Yuh," a sad ballad about dust bowl farmers, "packin' up and gittin' out." And you can't talk about Woody Guthry without talking about his "This Land Is Your Land," written in 1940, which is a patriotic ballad about America belonging to us, the people.

George Gershwin's "Porgy and Bess" and "The Petrified Forest" by Robert Sherwood were playing on Broadway. Movies were a major distraction during the hardships of the '30s. Hollywood met the challenge with such great performances as *Mutiny on the Bounty*, *A Midsummer Night's Dream*, *The Story of Louis Pasteur*, and all the Shirley Temple movies.

I have a warm memory of listening to the big-band broadcasts late at night when I was about five years old. At that age I didn't actually stay up that late, but I shared a bed with my twenty-year-old uncle Walt, who was out late most evenings and came home, got in bed, and turned the radio on quietly. I would wake up and then fall asleep listening to the music while resting my head on his outstretched arm.

For music, we also had an RCA "Victrola," a wind-up disc record player and cabinet. It was made of a dark cherrywood, which had a turntable under the top hinged lid and two cabinet doors below to store records. We had three Edison one-sided records; there was one of marches by the United States Marine Corps Band, led by John Philip Sousa. Enrico Caruso was Grandpa's favorite. He played it so loud you could hear it upstairs behind the closed door of the bathroom. Grandma especially liked the Johann Strauss waltzes. The labels on the records all depicted a dog listening to a wind-up gramophone, with the wording, "His master's voice."

Today whenever I hear "Stars and Stripes Forever," "O Sole Mio," or "The Blue Danube Waltz," I picture my grandparents winding up the old Victrola.

Even though Grandma and Grandpa always lived in rented houses and moved from place to place; each house was made a home of familiar homey items. Each room of the new house was arranged as much as possible like it was in the last house. Whenever we moved to a new address, the first thing Grandma did was hang the lace curtains on the windows. It was a respectable status symbol for her. "I don't want the neighbors to think we're common."

We sometimes painted over gaudy floral wallpaper with calcimine paint, a cheap colored powder substance that we mixed with water. Next, the faded Persian-like carpets were unrolled, displaying their complex paisley patterns. One of my fun jobs was to beat these carpets; carpet beaters were the primary means of removing dirt and dust. When Grandma wanted the carpets cleaned in the spring, Grandpa rolled them up and draped them over the clothes line in the backyard. I was given the carpet beater, a tennis-racket-looking tool made of rattan reed. With this implement I literally beat the dust out of the carpets.

A large oak table dominated the dining room. It had five legs with casters. The fifth leg supported the middle of the table when extension boards were inserted. When not extended, the tabletop was about four feet square. It could be extended in eight inch increments by pulling apart and inserting boards. It would extend up to twelve feet long to accommodate a large crowd of people or a quilt in progress. There was always a wooden rocking chair in the living room which had a carved floral design in the back panel and bent-wood arm rests supported by slat spindles. The chair seat was woven cane. The living room also housed two well-worn upholstered arm chairs and a "Davenport" (sofa) (divan) (couch).

I remember, when living at 1608 North Corona Street, Grandma and Grandpa's bed room was furnished with an oak bedstead. The headboard was decorated with heavy scrolled molding. Resting on wooden slats was coil springs and a mattress topped with a featherbed. There was an oak dresser with wide drawers and an oval-shaped "looking glass" which could be tilted up and down. The other bedrooms were not so lavishly appointed. They housed iron or brass bedsteads, chest of drawers of painted pinewood.

Even though the electric refrigerator was invented in 1876, most of us in the early 1930s used an Ice box to store perishable foods. Commonly ice boxes were made of wood. They had hollow walls that were lined with tin or zinc and packed with insulating materials such as cork, sawdust, or straw. A large block of ice was held in a tray or compartment near the top of the box. Cold air circulated down and around storage compartments in the lower section. A drip pan was placed under the box and had to be emptied at least daily. The melted block of ice was replenished by the ice man. In the summer when the ice man was making deliveries in the neighborhood we kids would wait for him to take a block of ice into a house and then we would get in the back of the ice truck and get big hand size pieces of ice to suck on.

Milk was delivered daily to homes. Some houses had a milk chute opening right into the house while most just had a box on the porch. The milk was delivered in glass quart bottles with paper lids. It was not homogenized, so you could see the cream on top had separated from the milk which you could either mix it back into the milk or pour it off to be used in your coffee. In the winter we kids would go bring the milk in only to find that it had frozen and pushed up and popped the lid off and the frozen cream was sticking up above the bottle rim. This was truly an ice-cream treat. Our first electric refrigerator was a Frigidaire. In later years the name fridge came to mean any refrigerator of any make.

"Where do you turn the light off in the refrigerator?" I asked Uncle Walt.

"There's a little man inside who turns it off."

I opened the refrigerator door to see the little man. "I don't see a little man."

"You have to be fast to see him."

I opened the door real fast. "I still don't see him."

"You're not fast enough."

I tried again.

"Aw, there's no little man in there."

"Yes, there is. His name is Yehudi."

"Yaw hoo dee," I laughed. Now I knew he was joking.

Grandma came in the room.

"Mother, tell Jack there's a little man named Yehudi who turns the light off in the refrigerator."

"Yes, that' true, Jack."

With that confirmation, I was back to believing. Over time I tried to surprise the little guy, several times, but to no avail. At what point in my life I let go of this spoof, I don't know.

Before the supermarket, each neighborhood had a small grocery store. These stores were usually "mom and pop" operations and there was one within walking distance of nearly every home. Moms could send their kids to the store with a list and the grocer would fill it or you could call the list in and the grocer would deliver it. The grocer knew all the kids in the neighborhood and their parents. If a kid came in the store and attempted to buy an extraordinary amount of candy, let's say a half a dollar's worth, the grocer would call the child's mother to confirm such a purchase. These grocers would also give credit and "put it on the cuff"[21] to neighbors who needed it. And many did.

Other than the newspapers, radio was the media of the day. Daytime radio was dominated by "soap opera" dramas. The prime-time broadcasts featured a mix of popular programming such as comedy, musical variety, romance, and mystery plays, classical music concerts, news, sidewalk interviews, and sports. We were entertained by such programs as *Amos & Andy* (a sitcom about two African Americans played by two white men), Jack Benny, Burns, and Allen, and kids programs such as *The Lone Ranger*, *Little Orphan Annie*, and *Dick Tracy*. There were mystery programs like *Inner Sanctum* and *Suspense*. Our living rooms were also visited weekly with broadcasts

---

[21] This expression comes from the Victorian period when men wore detachable collars and cuffs which could be wiped clean with a wet cloth. They were made of celluloid, a synthetic plastic-like substance. Merchants often wrote reminder notes and figures on them during the workday and wiped them clean at the end of the day. The cuffs might have the names and amounts of credit extensions or reminders of any kind.

of President Roosevelt's famous "fireside chats" assuring us that this generation has a "rendezvous with destiny." The Hollywood gossip broadcasters were household names: Hedda Hopper, Louela Parsons, and Walter Winchel. Without the visuals of television, we were left to our own creative imagination as to how people, places, and things looked. It was often a disappointment to see a radio actor's picture in a magazine or newspaper. It seems funny now how we used to sit and look at the big, highly polished wood cabinet console radio just as people now look at television. We could see sound. The vivid pictures in our imaginations made it seem so real. Sound effects used in radio were the equivalent of today's special effects of television and movies.

There were such realistic manually made sound effects such as thunder, wind, rain, traffic, footsteps, creaking doors, gunshots, and of course, canned applause and laughter.

Segregation of the races was quite prevalent in America in the 1930s, demonstrated by Jim Crow Laws[22] of the South and a more subtle culture of segregation in the North. The laws of the South required such things as a poll tax in order to vote, separate entrances in public buildings, separate seating in almost any public venue, separate restrooms, drinking fountains, and separate schools. There were of course strictly enforced miscegenation laws. Author Harry Golden said of segregation, "It seems that the problem in mixing of the races is primarily in places where people are seated. The solution to this problem is to remove all seats in busses, trains, and other public places."

Colorado Springs was no exception to the practices of segregation. The two most popular swimming holes were Prospect Lake and the pool at Monument Valley Park. The lake had a white side and a colored side. On the white side there was a sandy beach, a tree-covered grassy picnic area with tables and a beach house with restrooms, showers, and a concession stand selling candy, chewing gum, potato

---

22   The phrase "Jim Crow" came from a song-and-dance caricature of blacks performed by a white actor Thomas D. Rice in blackface in 1832. As a result of Rice's fame, "Jim Crow" became a pejorative meaning "Negro."

chips, and cigarettes. On the colored side there was a shoreline of mud and weeds and an outhouse. The swimming pool at the park was whites only until Friday which was the day before the water was drained out for the weekly pool cleaning. Saturday the week started with a freshly scrubbed pool filled with fresh water, whites only. Whites could swim with the "coloreds" if they wished, but I don't recall ever seeing that happen. When Paul Gonzales and Buddy Jefferson and I went to the movies, the ushers would make us sit in the balcony. They didn't make Grandma and me sit in the balcony. I thought it was just because we were not chaperoned by an adult. It was years before I figured out that this only happened when I was with a black or Hispanic friend. I heard the theater balconies referred to as "Nigger heaven." The newspapers referred to African Americans as "Negro." Grandma, having contempt for bigotry, taught me to say "colored" and to look down on racists as "white trash." There were many pejorative epithets other than "nigger" used by whites, many of which are still used by today's ignorant bigots, such as "jig, shine, boogie, spade," and many others too numerous to mention. No minority escaped the prejudiced tagging. My so-called "Mexican" friends, who preferred to be called Spanish, were showered with such monikers as "spic, beaner, chili shitter," and others. Our Jim Crow laws in Colorado were unwritten. There were no "whites" and "colored" signs on drinking fountains. However, often seen behind the counter of cafes and diners was a sign which read, "We reserve the right to refuse service to anyone," and we whites and coloreds both knew who "anyone" was. Housing was segregated in the same subtle fashion; it was unwritten that the colored would confine themselves with "their kind" to the area south of downtown in the old Lowell School area on and around Weber and Wasatch Streets, and down by the Shooks Run creek, one of the oldest parts of Colorado Springs. Most, but not all, of the homes were small in-need-of-paint, ramshackle structures. A one block strip on the south side of West Colorado Avenue just before going over the viaduct was the colored business section. That's just the way it was in those days, and nobody questioned it, colored or white. It sounds stupid, but we didn't know that segregation was wrong.

The Jim Crow laws remained in effect until Congress passed the Civil Rights Act of 1964. Although there has been significant improvement in civil rights since 1964, there is still a plentiful amount of racism flowing through the minds of America.

I was too young to know the real meaning of the Depression. I had what I considered all the necessities of life. I had enough food, enough clothing, and a home full of loving family. I knew the hoboes on the boxcars were poor, but I still saw their station in life as romantic. I envied their being able to travel to far-off places on the trains and the open road. I don't know how Grandma would have taken it if I had said, "I want to be a hobo when I grow up." When Grandpa, Uncle Walt, and Mother were all working at the same time, we were relatively well off by 1930s standards. I had no idea how much suffering and hard times people were going through. Even when the Inzers came to live in our garage, I only saw that as "Now Duane and I can play together every day." My understanding of economics was centered on the penny or two in my pocket.

Depending on where you lived, young people in the 1930s dated and double-dated by going to movies, eating out, going to the drive-in for a root beer or ice cream, visiting friends, going to dances, going for a drive to "lover's lane" for a bit of "necking, petting, and whatever." It was said that some guys drove girls to these places and told them, "Either put out or get out." This resulted in mothers advising daughters to always have bus-fare to get home with.

We had no wonder drugs like antibiotics. Penicillin was not in wide use or supply until 1943 when the War Production Board drew up plans for mass distribution to Allied troops fighting in Europe. Diseases were treated with only home remedies. Scarlet fever, diphtheria, pneumonia, typhoid fever, and tuberculosis were often as not fatal. Infantile paralysis (polio) the infectious disease causing disabling paralysis of the muscles was without an effective treatment. Most of the victims were children. The world's most recognized victim was President Roosevelt, who founded the March of Dimes Foundation that would fund the development of a vaccine. An effective vaccine was not discovered until 1952 by Jonas Salk, who was hailed as a "miracle worker" when the vaccine's success was made public in 1955.

Other common viral diseases affecting children were mumps, measles, chicken pox, and diphtheria. All of which are now controlled by vaccines. The Health Department used to post large red quarantine signs on the doors of homes where a diseased victim lived. These signs were to isolate and restrict movement of the victim and to warn others not to enter. For fear of being infected, I used to hold my breath when walking by a quarantined house. Medical science and health care have both come a long way since then. In the '30s all allergies were classified "hay fever," and it was not uncommon to see older people without teeth or dentures. The most popular remedy for stomach ailments was baking soda.

There was a large staircase in the El Paso Street house which I had to climb alone when Grandma said, "Jack. It's time for bed."

There was a dim light at the bottom of the stairs, and at the top, it was scary dark. I knew there were evil, scary things in that darkness just waiting for me to come up so they could do all sorts of indescribable painful things to me. I would stand at the bottom of the stairs getting my nerve up one more time. My tried and true method to ward off these ugly, scary things was to stomp heavy on each step in order to create the sound of a big, strong man like Grandpa coming up the stairs instead of a little five-year-old. I knew that no monster would dare attempt to hurt Grandpa. As part of the illusion, I cleared my throat in a deep, low sort of grunt like Grandpa. My act would begin stomp one.

Stomp two. Stomp three. So far so good, then, "Be sure to turn the lights out. Do you hear me?" This required a response from a five-year-old boy. In order to get out of earshot of the monsters, I scurried back down the three steps and said, "Okay." I started back up stomping and grunting to the top, one step at a time. There were thirteen in all. At the top was a light switch. I walked down the hall to the room I shared with Kenny. I turned on the overhead light and walked back down the hall to turn off the hall light. Staying away from the bed, I put on my pajamas. I now had the logistic challenge of turning off the bedroom light and getting in the bed and pull the covers over my head before the monsters which had assembled under the bed could grab me. I had lots of successful experience with this mad dash, but it scared me anew every night. It seemed that after the dash to the bed, the monsters went away. They were not there in the light of morning.

More were added to the unemployment ranks when in 1933 a mechanical cotton picker was developed that could pick 2,500 pounds of cotton in a day, more that a field hand could pick in two weeks. For the poor, life insurance could be bought for pennies per week, and the agent would come around to collect it.

Grandpa took Kenny and me fishing at Prospect Lake early one spring morning. He rented a row boat and rowed over to the east side of the lake.

Grandpa said to me, "Stay seated. Don't stand up in the boat."

He and Kenny then baited there hooks with worms from a can of dirt and coffee grounds. A few minutes after, they had cast their lines and were not looking at me. I stood up. The boat rocked, and I fell backward over the side of the boat. My head was underwater. I could see through the murky water to the surface and see Kenny reach over the side of the boat get hold of me and pull me up out of the water. I was wet and cold, but not choking on water. I must have subconsciously known to hold my breath.

Grandpa said, "We better get the boy home before he catches his death of cold."

I'm sure Grandpa was disappointed. He didn't fish for sport. He fished for food. I'm equally sure that Grandma, after she was sure I was out of harm's way, was gratified that she didn't have to gut and scale a mess of fish.

I faintly remember in about 1939 people were talking about the disappearance of Amelia Earhart during an attempt to make a flight around the world in 1937. She disappeared over the Central Pacific Ocean somewhere near Howland Island and to this date, 2015, has never been found. There are still conflicting theories of where and how she vanished. It's not like she was inexperienced. She was an accomplished pilot who was the first woman to fly solo across the Atlantic Ocean. The best theory proffered, I believe, was that Howland Island was actually six miles east of the position plotted for her and that unbeknownst to her was that wind was probably causing the plane to drift westward off course and she just ran out of gas searching for the island.[23] The year 1937 is also the year the Golden Gate Bridge was opened.

Air travel in the 1930s was rare. However, sky writing was a popular form of advertising, and aircraft racing and acrobatics, including wing walking, were just as popular. I would lie down on the grass and watch the letters develop in the sky and try to guess at each letter what the word was going to be; first there might be a fancy flowing cursive capital *P* written in white smoke. The plane would then circle around and come back and release a matching *e*. I had seen this one several times before. I knew this was going to be Pepsi Cola, but I remained mesmerized to the finish and beyond until the words in the sky were dissipated by the winds.

There was mass hysteria: "Never in the history of the United States had such a wave of terror and panic swept the continent." This was said of the fallout from a 1938 radio drama spoof titled *War of the Worlds*, a show depicting news bulletins of an invasion from outer space, interrupting a scheduled music program. Many people tuning in late to the show thought it was for real. Telephone switchboard operators were swamped with calls to local police stations and to CBS. Newspapers reported that there were traffic jams because people were fleeing their homes. Toward the ending of the broadcast it was reported, "Five great machines" wading across the Hudson River, poison smoke drifting over New York, people diving into the East River like rats," others, "falling like flies." Many listeners sued CBS for "mental anguish" and "personal injury." All were dismissed except for one man claimed he spent his shoe money trying to escape. Orson Welles, producer of the show, insisted the man be paid. Some historians since have said that the newspapers and radio broadcasters exaggerated the panic and that actually very few listeners were fooled.

Colorado Springs was the home of three distinguished institutions: the Colorado School for the Deaf and Blind, the Union Printers Home, and Colorado College. The School for the Deaf and

---

[23] Since writing this a photograph was discovered in July 2017 which is believed to be of Amelia in custody of the Japanese in the Marshall Islands. It is theorized that she crash-landed in the Marshall Islands and eventually died in Japanese custody on the island of Saipan.

Blind, referred to locally as the D&B, was founded in 1874 in the Colorado Territory as the Colorado Institute for the Education of Mutes. The name was changed in 1893. People of the day used the descriptive term "deaf and dumb" for deaf people who couldn't articulate spoken language. In high school, I played football against the D&B. When the institute was built, out on Knob Hill, there were no streets at the time. There was a road going by which later came to be known as Institute Street.

The Union Printers Home, building was known as the Castle on the Hill. It was erected in 1892 by the International Typographical Union as a home and medical facility for the Union's sick and indigent members. Its location, east of town, was referred to as Union Hill, and the road going out to the hill was aptly named Union Boulevard. Mother nursed there for a time. Many of the patients were tubercular who had come for the mountain air cure. Mother made many lifetime friends among the cured who remained in Colorado Springs. She worked in a number of TB Sans and small private and large public medical facilities and made long-time friends all along the way.

Colorado College was founded before Colorado statehood was granted. A private institution, it was founded in 1874. The first thoughts of a college in the territory were in a proposition made in 1868 to the Ministerial Congregational Association of the Territory of Colorado by Rev. Edward P. Tenney, pastor of the Congregational Church of Central City. It was decided that, as the population of the territory was yet so small and the communication with the states yet so difficult, it was advisable to postpone action.

In 1873 Professor Thomas Nelson Haskell, MA (Yale), late of the University of Wisconsin, came to Denver in the interest of the health of his daughter. She died shortly after. In her memory, he sought to found a college where students in the East, finding their health giving away, could come and continue their education while recovering. He succeeded in getting the Congregational Association actively committed to the enterprise.

General Palmer's Colorado Springs Colony company had set aside what is now the College Square for a college. He sought worldwide for a denomination that would establish and maintain a college in Colorado Springs. The Jesuit Fathers considered Palmer's proposition and settled on Denver. A small group of Congregationalists, including Professor Haskell, met in the parlor of Frank Rouse on the corner of West Costilla Street and South Cascade Street. They arranged to recommend to the Congregational Association that Colorado College be located in Colorado Springs. Their report was accepted and rooms were secured in the second story of the Wanless Building, northwest corner of North Tejon Street and East Pikes Peak Street (presently the center of downtown Colorado Springs). Later a two-room frame building was erected and served as the first home of CC. The college closed its first term with forty students representing ten states. Subjects taught were math, physics, Latin, and Greek. Later on assaying, chemistry, metallurgy, geology, and mining were taught in afternoon and night classes. In 1880, the doors were opened to the Victorian-Gothic Cutler Hall, which is still in use on the college campus today (2015).[24]

> News Break
> September 23, 1939
> Sigmund Freud Dies
> The father of psychoanalysis has died in London
> at the age of 83.

---

[24]   Historical data is from Pioneer Days of Colorado College, James Huchison Kerr, first historian of Colorado College.

The World at War

News Break
June 15, 1940
Nazi Flag Raised over Versailles
German occupation of France now complete.

T he summer of 1940 Kenny sent us gifts from Hawaii: a pillowcase for Grandma with the lyrics of the "M-O-T-H-E R" song on it, a Hawaiian shirt for me, and a carved coconut head for Grandpa. His home port was in Pearl Harbor, Honolulu. He sent pictures of Hula dancers in grass skirts, surfers, and volcanoes. I wished I was Kenny, to be able to travel to exotic places like "Hawaya".

News Break
October 31, 1941
Mount Rushmore Monument is completed and ready for dedication.

This same year saw President Roosevelt reelected for an unprecedented third term. Germany invaded Denmark, Norway, Belgium, the Netherlands, France, Yugoslavia, and Greece.[25] America's first peacetime military draft was begun. Japan, Germany and Italy entered into a tripartite military alliance in order to create a New Order in

---

[25] The start of World War II is generally held to be on September 1, 1939, beginning with the German invasion of Poland; Britain and France declared war on Germany two days later.

Europe and in Asia. Winston Churchill became Prime Minister of Great Britain, *Pinocchio*, opens at Center Theatre in New York, six-hundred-miles-per-hour barrier is broken by an airplane built by Bell Aircraft, US debt reported at $43 billion, the forty-hour workweek and child labor laws established.

In the first eleven months of 1941, the news was dominated by the war being waged in Europe and the Japanese militaristic exertions throughout Southeast Asia. War did appear to be on the American horizon, but when and in what manner or degree was unknown. However, on December 7, 1941, the Imperial Japanese Navy conducted a surprise military air and sea attack on the United States naval fleet anchored and docked at Pearl Harbor, Hawaii. The attack came as a profound shock to the American people and led directly to the American entry into World War II in both the Pacific and European Theatres. Subsequent actions by the US[26] prompted the Fascist dictators, Hitler of Germany and Mussolini of Italy, to declare war on the US on December 11, which was reciprocated by the US on the same day. The attack on Pearl Harbor was intended to neutralize the US Pacific Fleet. President Roosevelt proclaimed December 7, 1941, "a date which will live in infamy."

News of the attack was broadcast to the American public via radio bulletins, with many popular Sunday afternoon entertainment programs being interrupted. As a ten-year-old, I didn't really know the significance of this news, but I was scared because everyone around me appeared scared. Kenny's ship was stationed at Pearl Harbor. Mother and my grandparents stayed glued to the radio to hear if Kenny's ship, the USS *Flusser*, was one of the ships sunk in the attack. His ship was never mentioned. I don't know how many days it took for us to get the news that his ship had been on maneuvers and was not involved in the attack. I'm sure the wait was almost unbearable to the grown-ups.

Early the morning after the attack, I was out in the backyard shed getting coal for our kitchen stove when an airplane flew over.

---

[26] Clandestine support of Britain in its war with Germany was replaced by active alliance.

It frightened me because I thought we were being attacked by the Japanese. I ran to the house as fast as I could. Mother calmed me down and assured me that all was okay in my world. I was not the only American who was scared. There existed a mass fear and hatred of the Japanese. It was hysterical to the point that President Roosevelt authorized the shameful removal of all Japanese people from the West Coast, whether citizens or not. They had to give up their homes as well as their businesses and relocate to internment camps in Arizona, Colorado, Wyoming, and Idaho.

> News Break
> February 22, 1942
> President Orders McArthur to Evacuate
> President Roosevelt ordered General McArthur to evacuate the Philippines. It is felt that defending against the Japanese invasion would be futile.

Camp Carson

Colorado Springs was selected as the site of an army camp. The Pikes Peak region had the primary inducements—miles of prairie and a climate which would permit year around training. The engineering crews, not having done a detailed demographic study of the site, ran into trouble early on when they discovered that the chosen site had a sizeable number of rattlesnakes. We heard that the engineers wanted to call off the survey saying the site was unsuitable for soldiers. Somebody taught them that rattlesnakes move out when man moves in. The engineers went back to work and gave a good report on the site.

The site selected was south of Colorado Springs adjacent to the Myron Stratton Home on the five-thousand acre Cheyenne Valley Ranch at a cost of a little over thirty six thousand dollars. The first building went up within a month of the survey. The camp was named for Kit Carson, pioneer, scout, hunter, soldier, and Indian agent in the Colorado Territory.

> News Break
> June 7, 1942
> Japanese Fleet Defeated at Midway
> After four days of savage fighting on the sea and
> in the air near Midway Island, Admiral Chester
> Nimitz has forced a badly beaten Japanese Navy
> to withdraw.

Lowell School and Leg Makeup

That Christmas Grandma, Mother, Betty, and I all made candy to send to Kenny. I stuffed dates with walnut halves and dipped them in powdered sugar. Grandma made fudge, Mother and Betty teamed up to pull taffy. Shortly after Christmas Mother, Betty, and I left Manitou Springs and returned to Colorado Springs. We lived in a two-room first floor apartment on South Nevada Avenue. We shared the bathroom upstairs with the couple on the second floor. Our living room accommodated a double bed which doubled as a sofa. Mother and Betty shared the bed. I had a cot in the second room which was the kitchen. There was one small cubbyhole clothes closet under the staircase, which Mother filled easily with her blouses, skirts, dresses, hats, and uniforms. Her uniforms as well as a couple of her dresses were nearly knee-high in the 1940s fashion. The rest of her skirts were mid-calf length in the 1930s style. Betty's few simple dresses didn't take up much space, and my pants, shirts, socks, and underwear were stowed in a cardboard box beneath my cot. Mother's dresses blouses and jackets all had shoulder pads just like men's suits. She had a few wide brimmed hats and a couple pillbox hats. She also wore high-waisted, wide-at-the-bottom slacks. Uncle Sam was asking all the women to hand in their nylons for the war effort. Mother, being as patriotic as the next person, rolled up all but two pair and dropped them in the collection box at the post office. She then turned to the popular leg cosmetics being offered by such famous names as Elizabeth Arden, Max Factor and Helena Rubinstein. Product names like Stockingless Cream, Leg Art, Leg Charm, and Liquid Stockings became known to all women. Although cosmetics were not rationed, there were shortages and the government urged conservation. With or without stockings or leg make-up, I was always proud of the way Mother looked.

Men's apparel of the 1940s ran mostly to the military uniform. The Zoot Suit was popular with some young civilians and gangster types with its long jacket, wide shoulders, pegged pants and wild stripes and colors. Older men mostly wore the traditional simple single breasted suit, white shirt with a wide tie or a bow tie. The shoes of choice were wingtips and Spectators. The Porkpie hat went with the Zoot Suit and the traditional fedora was worn by others.

By this time I had already been registered in eight different schools, so I went alone and registered myself in the Lowell school as a fourth grader. (I had attended this school once before, in kindergarten when I was in the day nursery.) I had a teacher at Lowell, Miss Brogie, who fifteen years earlier was one of Uncle Walt's teachers. It was about this time, Mother told Betty and me that she was trying to get us admitted to the Stratton Home, a home for children. She told us that the home had bicycles, a swimming pool, and other good things. It sounded good to me.

Billy Gates next door was a tap dancer. Billy was younger than me, and I thought him to be kind of a sissy, but we sometimes sat on the front stoop together. He didn't wrestle or prowl the ally trash cans for treasure or throw rocks at tin cans. Even with these failings, I accepted his invitation to go in his apartment and view his dance costumes. There were many colors of bloused satin shirts and shoes with metal taps on them.

"Show me a dance," I encouraged.

He put on his tap shoes and led me across worn carpets onto the kitchen's linoleum floor. I was amazed watching him dance while softly singing the familiar lilting phrases of "The Streets of New York": "East side, west side, all around the town. Tots play ring-around-rosie, London Bridge is falling down."

"How did you learn all that stuff?" I was truly amazed at his tapping toes keeping rhythm with his singing.

"I've been taking lessons for a long time." His stature rose in my evaluation system after that kitchen performance.

We didn't become close friends, but we did hang out more often after that.

I met another kid, about my age, in that neighborhood, Freddie Schmidt, who lived in a second-floor apartment above one of the stores over on Tejon Street. I don't know if the place even had a front door. We always went in by climbing some rickety, old wooden stairs off the alley. I remember Freddie as being a cartoonist who could draw Disney cartoon characters as well as Disney himself. Freddie could also imitate to a T the voice of Donald Duck. Now these were talents to flat out be appreciated, for sure. I went to my cot at night with mixed feelings, wishing I could tap dance or sound like Donald Duck, and on the other hand, I was glad that I knew two guys with these talents and they felt I was okay to pal around with.

Nevada Avenue was a busy thoroughfare with a center parking dividing the Southbound traffic from the Northbound. It was one of my favorite pastimes to take my bologna sandwich lunch outside and sit on the front stoop and wave at all the truck drivers. Sometimes they would give me a blast on their horn. Watching people walk by was fun also. The sidewalk was only about ten feet from our stoop. I remember vividly two old men used to come by and say "Hello" to me. They were identical twins. They dressed alike, and both wore Coke bottle eyeglasses, which made their eyes look twice as big, like an owl's. I had known twin kids before, but I had never seen old twins. To myself I nicknamed them the Owls.

The Lowell school had a hot lunch program, which I suppose all public schools had in those Depression years. The meals cost five cents and were meant to see that no child went hungry during these troubled economic times. Mother gave me a half dollar to pay for lunches every two weeks. On one occasion, I took the entire half dollar, and instead of giving it to the school, I went to Booth's cafe on Vermijo Street and bought a chicken fried steak dinner for lunch and spent the entire fifty cents on this one meal. In addition to the steak, there were mashed potatoes with gravy, vegetables, bread and butter, and a salad. I passed on dessert. It cost extra. This experience was a Depression kid's dream come true. The meal was heavenly and seemed so right in the doing. Later on it struck me that I now had no money for lunch for the next two weeks. What to do? The next day I went home for lunch. (Mother was at work.) I opened a can of beans and ate them and got rid of the can so Mother would not be aware of my raid on the sparse larder. However, in those hard times, a can of beans missing was glaring. Mother confronted me, and I confessed. She sat me down on the bed/sofa and pointed out to me how difficult it was for her to support us on her meager wages and how she depended on me to help her. She had me in tears. I felt ashamed even though she held me and forgave me. She then gave me lunch money to last until she got paid again. I took it straight to school the next morning.

As part of the government's child nutrition program, the school nurse gave us a form of questions to answer, one of which asked us to relate what we had for breakfast and dinner at home. A girl in my class answered with a description of uncommonly elaborate, expensive, and childish-sounding meals. This thin, pale girl was, by appearance of clothing and grooming, from an apparently very poor family. The school nurse was suspicious and visited the girl's home. I never knew the details, but I heard she found them living in absolute poverty with barely enough food to sustain life. I don't know how or why this condition existed, as there were any number of government programs to prevent it. I felt pretty sure that she and her family got help because I had heard that President Roosevelt had promised that no one would go hungry.

Mother joined the local chapter of the Woodmen of the World, a "fraternal benefit society." The organization was basically an insurance company that fostered and supported local fraternal chapters for its policy holders. What brought Mother to this organization, I don't know. Perhaps she was persuaded by the local leader of the group, Paul Adams, who fifteen years later was to become my stepfather. Betty and I were insured for $500, which made us members of the Youth Chapter. Mother belonged to the female auxiliary. The main body of the Woodmen of the World chapter was restricted to white males between the ages of fifteen and fifty-two. The three of us belonged to our respective drill teams. We practiced military-like marching drills using light weight axes with aluminum heads instead of rifles. We wore white shirts, dark pants, a red sash around our waist, and blue army-style garrison caps. It seemed like fun at the time. It all sounds kind of silly today.

The Home

Midsummer of 1942, Mother told us that I was accepted to the Stratton Home but that they didn't have an opening at that time for any more girls, which meant Betty couldn't go.

On the day I was to leave for the home, Mother packed my clothing in an old cosmetic case which used to hold hair brushes, combs, mirrors, lipstick, and other cosmetics. It had long ago been divested of these items and had seen such service as my treasure chest, doctor's bag, tool chest, spy kit, and temporary home to a variety of living things like toads, grasshoppers, and various bugs. But on this day it was luggage. The small make-do piece of luggage barely held the one pair of pants, three shirts, a sweater, and two pairs of socks. This, along with my winter coat and the clothes I had on, made up my entire wardrobe. Mother drove me to the home in Grandpa's old Dodge coupe. This old car had a rumble seat which was an uphol-stered seat which opened up from the rear deck where the trunk would normally be. Rumble seat passengers were essentially seated out in the elements.[27] We kids loved to ride back there. Grandpa had lost the front bumper and replaced it with a piece of cog railroad track, thus giving rise to Grandma calling the car Old Iron Sides.

On the way to the home, we stopped at the Kress dime store,[28] where Mother bought me a pair of underwear shorts. Driving on

---

[27] An *1899 Century Dictionary* describes a *rumble* as "a seat for servants in the rear of a carriage."

[28] It was a store of the day which sold a vast variety of items at low prices. They were sometimes referred to as five and dime or nickel and dime. They were somewhat akin to today's dollar stores.

toward the home, Mother pulled the car over to the side of the road and had me remove my pants and shorts, even though recently laundered, were rather worn and ragged. She had me change into the new shorts. We drove under the arched iron gates which had the sign in bold letters MYRON STRATTON HOME.

Winfield Scott Stratton, 1848–1902, a Colorado Springs dollar-a-day carpenter who for seventeen years prospected for gold in the summer, found on July 4, 1891, one of the richest gold lodes in the world. His Independence mine delivered Stratton one of the greatest fortunes of the time. When Stratton died in 1902, he left instructions in his will that nearly all his fortune was to be used to establish and maintain a "free home for poor persons who are physically unable by reason of old age, youth, sickness, or infirmity to earn a livelihood." He wanted it named in memory of his father, Myron Stratton. He selected the trustees who he wished to implement the will. The home, which opened in 1913, has operated continuously since that time and has served hundreds of kids and elders. The Stratton Home endowment has been preserved and increased; it now exceeds $100 million. It was Stratton's intent that those he helped be treated with dignity and be well cared for, including the opportunity to receive education and training to enable them to become self-sustaining and, for the elderly, to live in a caring environment.

We followed the signs and parked Old Iron Sides in front of a large white stucco building with a small sign above the door which read Office. All around us were great expanses of sloping lawns, with bushes, trees, and flowers. I was introduced to Miss Lloyd, the superintendent of the home. She was pleasant and warmly welcomed me to the home. Her manner was elegant and stately. The gray hair put up in a soft bun fit her perfectly. She was quite attractive in a queenly sort of way. The three of us walked up a grassy slope to Independence Hall.

"This is the younger boy's building."

We met Mrs. McCarthy, the building head matron. She welcomed me to the building. I said goodbye to Mother. We didn't shake hands, hug, or kiss. I think she was too conscience-stricken to look at me. Mrs. McCarthy led me on a tour of the building ending in the sleeping dorm where she led me to my cubicle. It was a small room about seven feet wide by ten feet long. It was enclosed by three walls, one of which had a window, and a drapery covered entranced. The cubicle had a neatly made up twin bed with a stuffed bear at the head, and there was a four-drawer dresser. Mrs. McCarthy told me this was to be solely for me. I was very pleased, I had never had a room of my own, and to have my own dresser was pure luxury.

She opened a dresser drawer. "Here's your clothes for the rest of the week." She pulled open another drawer. "Here's your pajamas."

I had never had pajamas. I was looking forward to wearing them. For a time I wondered how they knew my clothing sizes, then I remembered that Mother, when filling out the application for entrance into the home, had to give my height and weight, eye and hair color, and clothing sizes. After telling me all the rules and expectations, Mrs. McCarthy assigned Robert Wheeler to show me around the home grounds.

Robert was about my age. He had a round, chubby cherub-like, rosy, healthy-looking face and a good smile. There were acres and acres of green grass, shrubbery, trees, and flowerbeds. There was so much to see I literally could not take it all in. Robert introduced me to guys from our building as "the new guy, Jack." Some were friendly. Some were not. I was used to that. One of the guys was pointed out to me as being the toughest guy in the building, Bob Lanari. That kind of information was always good to have. My instincts told me to steer clear of him. My guide steered me back to our building for lunch. Mrs. McCarthy assigned me a seat at one of the five large round tables in the large dining room. She introduced me to the seven guys I would be seated with.

Three of the dining tables seated eight people. The other two tables where the two matrons sat with the youngest boys could seat nine or ten small people. The tables were set very formally with white linen table clothes and napkins with wooden napkin rings. The place settings included a dinner plate, a bread and butter plate with a butter knife across it, a large glass goblet, a dinner fork on the left of the plate, a knife, soup spoon, and teaspoon on the right of the plate. Each boy had his own wooden napkin ring identifiable by the decal picture on it. The food was served family style in large bowls and platters and a large pewter pitcher of milk. Each boy was expected to eat a full portion of the food served. We stood behind our chairs and said grace before the meal. We then sat down and awaited the first serving dish to be passed to us. (There was an older boy designated as the head of the table who served himself first and passed the serving dish to his right.) The head boy was responsible to see that we observed the proper table manners and cleaned our plates. We had to ask him to excuse us before we could leave the table. I subsequently had to learn all the table and other manners, many of which I was unaccustomed to. "Jack, keep your left hand in your lap unless you're passing a plate or using your knife."

After lunch we toured the rest of the very expansive property of the home. There were three other buildings for children: Lincoln Hall, the older boys' building; Washington Hall, for younger girls; and Logan Hall for the older girls. There was an infirmary with nurses on duty around the clock, a power house which contained the coal-fueled boilers which heated the buildings and provided hot water, a dairy to process the milk products from the home's dairy cattle, and a large greenhouse where all the home's many flowers and shrubs began. There was an apple orchard, a duck pond, the superintendent's home, and a statue of Mr. Stratton. The home also had farms where beef cattle and hogs were raised, and crops were planted too.

Life at the home was different, but not bad. I made friends right away. I just had to adjust to the daily routine which was more structured than anything I had heretofore been exposed to, with the exception of the Day Nursery of my kindergarten era. The typical summer day for boys[29] began with the matrons awakening us at 6:30 a.m. (5:30 for those who had to practice musical instruments). We got up and dressed, putting our folded pajamas in the dresser. Our afterschool clothes were bib overalls, chambray work shirt, and high-top work shoes. At a later date, the bib overalls gave way to the more stylish Lee jeans. For school we wore corduroys, sport shirt, and low-

---

[29]   I assume it was the same in the girl's buildings.

top oxfords. We made our beds, making sure to tuck the sheet corners correctly, washed our faces, brushed our teeth, combed our hair, and went to breakfast at 7:00 a.m. After breakfast we had preassigned house duties such as dish washing. Our tableware was 1847 Rogers Brothers silver, which had to be polished every Saturday morning. There was pot washing, setting the tables, hauling coal, dusting, vacuuming all the carpets, and mopping all the terrazzo floors. The mopping solution smelled like the creosote used on railroad ties. It smelled real sanitary.

After the building passed inspection, we reported to a room on the back side of the administration building for outside work assignments, which for the younger boys was digging dandelions. We were given diggers and would line up at a designated area and form a line of diggers on our hands and knees and move along an expanse of grass at a snail's pace, leaving behind us a lawn free of weeds. The girls at the home worked in the laundry. We were paid for this work at a rate of ten cents an hour. We were paid in cash once a month. Of our earnings, 50 percent was placed in a savings account which could only be withdrawn when you left the home for good. Twenty-five percent was placed in an account which was paid out to you once a month during the school year when you were not working and earning. The remaining 25 percent was paid to us in cash.

In the lobby of the administration building, there was, mounted on the wall, a glass-covered show case displaying race tracks with little racers on them. The tracks were different colors, and there were numbers all around each track. Each kid at the home had their name on a racer, and it was positioned on a track according to how much money that kid had saved. The tracks had marks at one hundred dollar intervals. Once you had saved enough to pass the finish line, your racer was placed at the starting line of the next track. The gold track in the center was occupied by those who had the greatest amount of savings. Most of us were on the outer tracks.

At about nine forty-five, we would turn in our diggers and go to our building, put on our swim trunks, and go to the swimming pool, which was opened at ten. The pool was guarded by two lifeguards, male and/or female who were high school–age kids who had

earned the Red Cross lifesaving badge. There was also an adult counselor who taught swimming if you were interested. (You couldn't go
to the deep end of the pool until you demonstrated your ability to
stay afloat and maneuver your body from one side of the pool to
the other.) Swimming was co-ed for both the younger and the older
kids. Going to the swimming pool was not mandatory. This was free
time until noon, at which time we were expected to be in the dining
room with clean hands for lunch. There would be hand inspections
at the dining room doorway from time to time. The pool was closed
at eleven. Lunch was served at noon.

After lunch we returned to dandelion digging till two thirty.
The swimming pool was opened again at three, closed at four. This
was also time for baseball practice. Dinner was served at five. After
dinner our time was free till seven thirty, at which time we prepared
to go to bed. The lights were turned out at eight even though it was
not dark yet. I had been used to playing outside till dark and came
in only when Grandma called me to come in. This was the first time
I had changed my address and didn't have to fight someone to establish the pecking order. I avoided any direct confrontation with Bob
Lanari, the designated toughest guy in the building, but I took no
guff from anyone else. This approach led to peace ever after.

It wasn't long before Bob and I shared the unspoken honor of
"toughest." Neither one of us wanted to test the other. We settled
differences by accommodation, along with quid pro quo so that there
was no loss of face. Example would be, "Dicky and I had dibs on the
pool table."

"You weren't here, so we took it."

"I went to the bathroom and came right back."

"You weren't here, so I took it, and we've already started the
game."

"Okay, but when you finish, save the table and come tell us.
We'll be in the living room."

"Okay."

Bob and I also negotiated by sending intermediaries to speak
for us. (If things got too hot, we blamed the intermediaries.) We
never did fight, and gradually, we became close friends.

Betty and Mother came to visit me on Sunday.

"Uncle Walt wanted you to have these." Mother handed me two gold rings, one with a ruby-colored stone inset and the other a black onyx. Walt had joined the navy and didn't think jewelry would be appropriate. I wish I knew what happened to those rings.

Corporal Punishment

Though rarely administered, the home was not averse to use of the willow switch to maintain discipline. These were the times of "You spare the rod, you spoil the child." Corporal punishment was common. It was felt as Samuel Johnson had put it more than a century earlier: "Punishment which left no lasting detriment was just and reasonable."

Before bedtime we all got into our pajamas, clothing items I had never worn, and went to the lavatory to brush our teeth. There was a can of Colgate tooth powder for each two sinks; toothpaste was considered a fad that really didn't get your teeth clean. A large room filled with pre-teen unsupervised boys in their pajamas, water faucets and cans of tooth powder was a sure fire stage for chaos. It was a time of horse-play like coming up behind a guy and pulling his pajama pants down, water fights at the faucets and pouring white tooth powder on each other's head. One night, I wasn't in the mood and some guy pulled my pants down. I turned around and smacked him. He grabbed me and we tumbled to the floor and began pummeling each other. I wound up on top and had him pinned down when Mrs. Terhune came in with her willow switch. She lashed me across the back. The switch wrapped around my back and the tip snapped the skin on my chest and opened a small laceration. I jumped up to fight, thinking one of the guys had done something. I saw the Matron standing there with the switch at the same time she saw my bleeding chest. She dropped the switch and came to me all apologies and took me by the hand to her room where she wiped the wound, which had stopped bleeding. She put a band aid on it and settled me down in her soft upholstered chair. "Sit down here Jack I'll get you some cake and milk." The chest was merely scratched, but I played the role of a deeply wounded waif. After the last crumb of cake was devoured I forgave her. She hugged me and sent me to bed.

> News Break
> August 7, 1942
> Marines Invade Guadalcanal
> US Marines braved Japanese snipers and bombing attacks to advance about a mile on Guadalcanal in the Solomon Islands.

The School Year The Sweet Science of Boxing

T he daily fall and winter routine began and ended like that of the
summer but was filled in between with school, homework, sports;
baseball, football and basketball, or however one wished to spend
the time after school. Maybe reading, listening to the radio or just
hanging out with or without someone else. My favorite sport was
boxing. I liked the sport because each time you landed a punch it was
a victory kind of, and it was much faster than baseball or football.
One Christmas I got two pair of boxing gloves and used them whenever I could get someone to spar with. Often I could only get one of
the older guys to box because they knew they could beat me. I didn't
care; I just liked the action and every so often I could get in a good
punch or two. On one occasion I actually got one of the older guys to
quit because his nose was bleeding; he had lunged at me with a well
telegraphed wide right haymaker. I instinctively parried it with my
left and countered with a right cross right into his oncoming nose.
He dropped to the mat holding his nose which was getting blood all
over my boxing gloves.

"Chuck, I'm sorry," I pleaded kneeling down over him. "Stay
here. I'll get something for your nose."

I took my gloves off and went to the restroom and brought back
a roll of toilet paper. As he held the paper over his nose with one
gloved hand, I unlaced the other glove then he switched hands. The
bleeding soon stopped and I apologized again.

"That's okay," he said.

I went to the rest room with some toilet paper to wipe off my
gloves glad he wasn't mad at me because I knew that if he wanted to,

he could beat me up. I don't know how he explained his red swollen nose to the other guys. Only Chuck and I knew and I was mute on the event even though I felt really good about it.

We were taken to school by buses owned by the home. The grade school kids were taken to the Ivywild School. Junior high (grades seven through nine), kids went to South Junior High School and the high school kids went to the Colorado Springs High School, the only public high school in town at the time. Previously the home kids had attended the Cheyenne Mountain School, a K–12 school in a one-school district, whose student body was mostly made up of kids from the posh Broadmoor area. (The school was world famous for its square dancers.) Miss Lloyd, the home superintendent, decided that it would be best for the home kids to attend schools which were more middle class. She felt this would better prepare them for adulthood in a middle class society. She also thought the Cheyenne Mountain School's physical education program put too much emphasis on square dancing.

Ivywild School
My All-Time Favorite Schoolteacher

F all arrived and we piled into the school bus and were off to the Ivywild grade school. I entered fifth grade along with five of the home brothers. I was the new kid at school again, but this time, I didn't come alone. There were no pecking-order fights.

> News Break
> November 11, 1942
> Allied forces land in North Africa.
>
> November 28, 1942
> The Cocoanut Grove night club burns, killing 492 people, including motion-picture star Buck Jones.

Almost everyone has a favorite teacher in their past. Mine was Mrs. Morrow, the fifth grade teacher at Ivywild. She was like Grandma in so many ways; I loved going to school that year. This saintly woman in charge of twenty-five to thirty fifth graders had everybody's devoted friendship. In Mrs. Morrow's classroom there were healthy portions of warmth, patience, understanding, mirth and learning given daily to every child in the room. Each of us was made to feel that we were special, and we were to her. She was maybe fifty years old, kinda chubby, gray hair in a bun, soft voice and a warm smile. Our days were filled with vocabulary, spelling, penmanship, arithmetic, geography, science, music, and physical education. She drilled us daily on the Palmer method penmanship, a method of standardized cursive writing using rhythmic arm motion rather than just moving the fingers and hand. Each one of us was supposed to be writing in such a way as to produce letters indistinguishable from all other students. In our red Big Chief tablets with widely spaced lines we practiced making coils of circles over and over. Next, we would switch to writing slanted straight lines as if scratching out something on the page. We filled page after page on both sides of the paper. With the exception of phys. ed. and music, Mrs. Morrow taught it all. My favorite class was recess.

News Break
March 10, 1943
Germans surrender
North Africa in final defeat in Tunisia

I entered the fifty-yard dash in the springtime school-track meet. At Ivywild, who could run the fastest was like winning the Decathlon in the Olympics. It overshadowed who could throw a softball the farthest, whose relay team could come in first, or who could jump the greatest distance. My class mates told me that Eddie Hayes was the fastest runner in school. "He won the fifty-yard dash last year when he was in the fourth grade." We broke from the starting line together. Right away, Eddie pulled out ahead of me. A couple yards later Barbara Freeman passed me. I wound up in third place. A short guy and a tall girl beat me by twenty feet. Eddie got a blue ribbon, Barbara got a red one and I have no remembrance of my ribbon. From that day on until the next spring meet, I went to the athletic field almost every day and ran in the heat of summer and in freezing temps of winter. My routine was I ran fifty yards as fast as I could four times, then I ran the full length of the football field two times and jogged once around the quarter-mile cinder track. This was an obsession with me. The picture in my mind of the backsides of Eddie Hayes and Barbara Freeman crossing the finish line really spurred me on. I asked some of the guys in the building to come race me. I beat all comers at the home.

"Walker, you're going to win that race," some of the guys told me, but I wasn't so sure.

To make the story short, the next spring I did win the blue ribbon.

Each school during the war took part in the war effort scrap drive. We kids were encouraged to collect scrap items of metal and paper to be recycled into guns and tanks and other things for our fighting troops. There was a mountainous pile of scrap in every schoolyard. Propaganda posters touting the war effort were everywhere you looked, such slogans as "Uncle Sam Wants You. Loose Lips Might Sink Ships," and "Food Is a Weapon. Don't Waste It." The people were encouraged to buy war bonds to help finance the war. At school kids could buy Minute Man War stamps for ten cents to be placed in a stamp book. When the book was filled it added up to $18.75 which could then be turned in to the bank for a $25.00 war bond with a ten-year maturity date.

> News Break
> July 23, 1943
> American and British troops land in Sicily;
> Germans had withdrawn, Italians surrender.

The Homefront

The unemployed who for one reason or another were not in the military, found work at home in factories producing many things for the military. Women were in the military also and many of those who weren't found jobs in the factories right beside the men. "Rosie the Riveter," a famous poster, was seen everywhere. It depicted a young woman with dark hair and eyes and rosebud lips wearing a red bandana on her head, a blue work shirt with a WPB (War Production Board) button on the collar. Her shirt sleave is rolled up to show a flexed bicept and a clinched fist. She is saying: "We Can Do It."

As the war raged on the folks at home felt it also. Almost everyone had loved ones fighting over seas, that maybe they would never see again. Casualties were checked daily in the newspapers. Although there was full employment, there were shortages at home. Many goods and services were either rationed or no longer available. The reasons given were that in some cases there was no longer the manpower to produce "nonessentials" and the draft had taken many farmers and sent them to war.

Women could not buy silk stockings because silk was used to make parachutes. Much of the food that was being produced was given to the armed forces. The government in Washington DC controlled about everything. There was rent and wage control, as well as censorship of mail. The OPA - Office of Price Administration was created to prevent spiraling prices, profiteering and inflation. Many civilian goods were no longer manufactured because they were not considered "essential." Almost everything manufactured was needed by the military. There was full employment as the nation geared up to produce the things needed by the military. Food rationing was enforced by the use of coupons issued by the government. The coupons had expiration dates that would allow you only so much of any given food item within a certain time. The number of coupons given a family depended on the size and make-up of the family. Especially scarce was meat and sugar. Kraft macaroni and cheese was hugely popular. Gasoline was rationed and required coupons to buy. If you used up your coupons before the expiration date, you were out of luck unless you knew someone with a surplus of coupons, who would share, but even if you had stamps, there may not have been any gas available.

Butter was almost nonexistent. Oleo-margarine came into widespread use as a butter substitute. It was a plastic bag of white vegetable fat with a small packet of a dark orange colored dye. You squeezed the dye pack until it broke and then kneaded and squeezed the whole package until the white fat turned butter-yellow thus giving it the appearance of dairy butter. It was then shaped by opening the bag and squeezing it out into a bowl or whatever you wanted to shape it with. Placed in the fridge it would stiffen up like butter. It was a time of deprivation for just about everyone. At the home we were not pinched that hard for food because we had our own farm and dairy. Soldiers in combat were fed "C-Rations," which they carried packaged in four-inch cans in their backpack. A typical can would hold meat and potato hash. A second can had bread and desert.

Lincoln Hall I Move in with the Older Guys

I resided in Independence Hall about one year. In the summer following my fifth grade school year Miss McCarthy told me to report to Mrs. Foster at Lincoln Hall, that I was being transferred to the older boys building. Lincoln Hall was normally for boys in the 7th grade and above, but as there was an opening for another boy at Lincoln and there was a waiting list to get into Independence, there was an exception made. Walking over to Lincoln, I was wondering with apprehension what it would be like living with all those older guys. Entering the building, I looked first to my left, where I peered through a door window and saw a pool table and a piano. This was really big guy stuff. I then turned to my right and saw a room with a desk and chairs, which I figured was an office, but no Mrs. Foster. One of the older guys was coming down the long polished terrazzo corridor. I waited for him and quickly practiced to myself what I was going to ask him. When he reached me, he said: "Are you lost?"

"I'm supposed to see Mrs. Foster."

"She's upstairs."

He then walked out the door.

I found Mrs. Foster upstairs in a small room sorting clean laundry and putting it in cabinets on shelves marked with boy's names. When she saw me in the doorway, she put her sewing down and struggled a little to push her heft up off the chair.

She said matter-of-factly, "Well, you must be Jack."

"Yes, ma'am."

Mrs. Foster was a full sized woman with enormous breasts. She was about five foot ten and had on two-inch heels. From my four foot six perspective she looked seven feet tall. She had authority written all over her like graffiti on a subway wall. It was the kind of aura that some assume and others don't question. I certainly didn't intend such folly. Her graying hair was worn in a tight bun on the back of her head. It looked like a big donut. I couldn't tell her age. All adults were the same age to my eleven-year-old observation.

She said, "Let's go meet Mrs. Irons."

We walked down a long corridor like the one downstairs and stopped at an open door. Mrs. Foster walked in first. She turned and motioned for me to follow. I stepped through the doorway and saw a small delicate looking gray haired lady in a delicate looking small rocking chair holding a sock in one hand and a threaded needle in the other. There was a framed photograph of a US Marine on the little pedestal table by her rocker.

While she was putting her sock project into a full basket of socks which was placed on the floor to the side of the rocker, Mrs. Foster said, "This is your new charge, Jack."

She then turned to me. "Jack, this is Mrs. Irons. She'll show you your cubicle."

Her exit was swift. Miss Foster was all business.

Mrs. Irons smiled warmly, stood up and offered her hand to me while her other hand held my forearm. Her gentle hand shake, was soft but not limp. It implied warmth and caring. She said: "Welcome Jack, I hope you enjoy your stay with us. Come, I'll show you to your cubicle." We walked to the other side of her room where a door led into a long large room with three-walled cubicles all along the opposite wall. They were as the cubicles in Independence Hall; three walls, a window, a dresser and a bed. The opening was closed with drapes hanging from a brass rod. After leading me to mine, the little matron showed me the bathroom and led me back to her room and said: "Please have a seat." In a general way she laid out the Lincoln Hall daily routine for me and asked:" Is there anything you would like to ask me?"

"No, ma'am." She then took me on a tour of the building. Stopping in the library, Mrs. Irons pulled down a book and handed it to me. It was titled either *Etiquette* or *Emily Post*; I couldn't tell which.

"This is required reading for all the boys. It tells us the measure of how we should treat one another. Make good use of it and you will be rewarded in many ways."[30] On our way back to the second floor, she opened a door under the stair case. "If you need shoes, I'm sure you can find in here a pair that will fit you." I peeked in the space to view what looked like a hundred pair of used shoes of all sizes piled high in no particular order; just loose shoes, not even matched up.

"These are shoes that have been outgrown."

I was now the youngest in the building, whereas I had been one of the oldest in Independence Hall. However, I already knew some of the younger guys here. Some I had met at the swimming pool and others through activities sports and games. Mrs. Irons' room was just off the younger boy's end of the floor. Mrs. Foster, who was the matron in charge, had a room at the other end of the upstairs corridor, just off the older boy's cubicle area. Both matrons were widows. The building also had two private rooms intended for boys who were away at college,[31] but since all males age eighteen and above were subject to being drafted for the war, the rooms were now empty.

At Lincoln the cubicles were larger and we were allowed to stay up an hour later at night and each cubicle had a closet with a door on it. Such freedom and privacy. We sometimes, after "lights out," would go into our closets and read with the light of a flashlight. We took the mandatory bath every Saturday afternoon in the large and deep marble step-up-into tub. After the bath we put our worn clothes in the laundry chute which dropped them to a gurney in the basement. Next, wrapped in a towel, we went to draw clean clothes at a room where all the clothes were neatly folded and placed on divided shelves and marked with each boy's name. A matron would issue us two shirts (one for school, and one for after school), two pair of pants, two pair of socks and two pair of underwear shorts. The only reasons I can think of for each boy having his own personal clothing bin is that we were different sizes or maybe because (in deference to

---

[30] Emily Post was an American writer and socialite who became the most famous authority on how to behave graciously in society and business.
[31] The home paid for college if a boy or girl wished, and if they had graduated in the top 10 percent of their high school class.

the more tidy boys) some of us were sloppier than some others and had stained some of our play clothes which no one else would want to wear. Otherwise there would be no reason to distinguish as we all pretty much dressed alike. Wednesday, after school, we could shower rather than bathe (A bath was considered a more thorough means to cleanliness in those days. Very few homes had showers.)

Even though I was living among the older guys (some were seniors in high school), I still had to go over to the younger boy's building and take the school bus with the elementary school kids because I was only in the sixth grade. I thought I was a big deal riding among such immature children who had to go to bed at 8 o'clock. Sometimes you just don't fit in with your peers: I experienced this in how I dressed for school one morning. Living with the older guys, I tried to emulate them in as many ways as I could. It was a style among the high school boys to pull a standard long sleeved shirt unbuttoned, shirt tail out, over a T-shirt. Thinking this to be very snazzy, I acquired a T-shirt from one of them (the home didn't provide T-shirts) and wore this groovy outfit to grade school. The peasants, my classmates, not being as urbane as I, made remarks like, "Hey, Jack, your shirt's unbuttoned," or "Did you know your underwear is showing?" or "Your shirt's hanging out." After a morning of these ignorant remarks, I gave up. I tucked my shirt tail in and buttoned it, and never again tried to be sartorially groovy in their presence. There were other times in my life when I ran afoul of the norm and received rejection, but none so hard to understand as this was to me.

Living now among older more erudite guys, my vocabulary increased profoundly. I never knew there were so many words describing the sex act, the male and female genitals, the anus, urinating, masturbating, and breasts. Most of these descriptions were words of four letters. The war made some seldom, if never, used words commonplace: "Axis Powers," "Fascism," "Gestapo," "Fuhrer," "Nazi." We read these words daily in newspapers, and they were just as common on the radio. The soldiers and sailors themselves gave us such patter as ninety-day wonder, "buck-private," "Krout," "gung ho," dog-face," "swab-jockey," "copacetic," and "head up his ass," to mention but a few. We also adopted some of the lingo of the weapons of war: from the army; grenade' "pineapple," rocket launcher,' "bazooka," 'flame thrower,' Sherman tank,' howitzer and 'Ml carbine; from the Navy; submarine, torpedo, hospital ship, PT boat, destroyer, mine sweeper.

The newspapers reported a lot of geography to us of North Africa, Europe, Asia and the South Pacific. Americans were being killed in places we had never heard of: in Asia, places like Bataan, Okinawa, Burma, Korea, Mindanao, and New Guinea; in North Africa, Morocco, Algiers, Casablanca; in Europe, Messina, Anzio, Normandy, Cherbourg, Ardennes, and Bastogne; in the South Pacific, Guadalcanal, Iwo Jima, Tarawa, and the Solomon Islands. The names of world leaders, generals and admirals were known even to schoolchildren—names like Churchill, DeGaul, Stalin, and Chiang Kai Shek, were the good leaders. Hitler, Mussolini, Tojo, and Hirohito were the bad guys. Our well-known generals were McArthur, Eisenhower, Patton, Bradley, and Marshall; our admirals' names in common use were Nimitz, "Bull" Halsey, and Spruance.

Two of the most skilled and highly respected enemy combatants of the war were: Field Marshal Erwin Rommel and Admiral Isoroku Yamamoto. Rommel, known as the Dessert Fox, was the commander of German and Italian forces in North Africa. The stories of his abilities in dessert warfare and his skill at eluding allied forces are legendary. Later in the war he was linked to the failed conspiracy to assassinate Hitler. He agreed to commit suicide with a cyanide pill in exchange for the promise that his family would not be mistreated. Admiral Yamamoto, although the planner and executioner of the Pearl Harbor attack, was against it from the beginning. He had studied at Harvard and had served as Naval attach^ in Washington, DC. He was an outspoken opponent of the pact with Nazi Germany that he felt was not in Japan's best interests. Yamamoto commanded the Japanese fleet at the battle of Midway. He later was made commander-in-chief of all Japanese forces in the Pacific. His strategies caused us to lose many lives and ships. The US Navy intercepted and decoded a Japanese message giving details of Yamamoto's inspection tour of the South Pacific.

President Roosevelt ordered navy secretary Knox, "Get him."

The admiral's plane was shot down and his body was found in the jungles of Bougainville. Legend has it that Yamamoto, after the battle of Midway, reflected, "I fear all we have done is to awaken a sleeping giant and fill him with a terrible resolve."

He couldn't have been more prescient.

Lifestyle at Lincoln

The typical Lincoln Hall day began with waking up at six thirty. (If you played a musical instrument you were awakened an hour earlier to practice.) We started the day by making up our beds. (We were given one clean sheet each week which replaced the top sheet we were using. The used top sheet then replaced the old bottom sheet, which was put in the laundry chute.) We then washed our faces, brushed our teeth, got dressed. Breakfast was at 7:00 a.m. After breakfast each boy had an assigned task such as dish washing (the silverware was polished every Saturday morning), floor sweeping and mopping, sorting laundry, clearing the dining room tables and setting them up for the next meal, and hauling coal for the cook stove.

On completion of our morning tasks, we changed into our school clothes and waited for the bus. In the summer we reported for various jobs on the home grounds. We were paid for our work at an hourly rate based on our age and/or skill required to do the job. (The high school boys could make as much as twenty-five cents an hour) Pay day was once a month. There also was a merit/demerit system of twenty-five cents. Merits were earned by such things as good grades at school, volunteering for extra duties like window cleaning and wall scrubbing. Demerits were given for infractions of rules such as being late for meals, not showing up for your assigned chores, a messy bed, or if you were studying a musical instrument, not practicing each day. Fighting was worth double demerits. I once got ten demerits for uttering two words to a matron: "You're crazy." I didn't really believe she was crazy, and I didn't mean it in any personally disparaging way. It was just an expression I used when I felt I was wrongly accused. To my mind it meant, "I beg to differ," nothing personal. Working off those ten demerits was lesson enough for me to never use that wording again. We could work off demerits by volunteering to do extra chores the matrons might want done. (Usually it was window washing with ammonia and newspaper.) Merit earnings were paid once a year on Founders' Day with the same distribution basis as our wages. Founders' Day fell on Memorial Day, a day when all the home kids were taken by bus to the cemetery to attend a memorial service at the grave of founder Winfield Scott Stratton. We didn't mind this service because we knew that when we got back to the home we would get our envelopes of merit money.

Miss Lloyd, the superintendent, rewarded good school grades by inviting the scholars to dinner at her house about eight scholars at a time. This was always a fun evening because we not only were given a delicious meal, but in addition, we played many of the games from her vast collection. I usually had grades that qualified me for these events.

Every other Sunday morning, after breakfast and before Sunday school, three barbers came to the building and set up shop in the library. Haircuts were mandatory, and style choices were not offered. At the completion of after-breakfast chores we went to the library and waited our turn. The barbers all joked and laughed with us and with each other. It didn't take long once you got in the chair. There was no witch hazel, no talcum powder, and no whisk broom, just scissors, comb, and clippers.

Friday night was movie night at the home. The home theatre held about 150 people, and movies were shown year around. We had to shine our Sunday dress shoes and iron our suit pants to be inspected by one of the matrons before we could leave the building to go to the movie. *Lassie Come Home* (1943) and *National Velvet* (1944) were movies starring child actress Elizabeth Taylor. In my eleven- and twelve-year-old viewpoint, she was kinda plain-looking, and I didn't like the sound of her English accent either. Elizabeth and I were the same age. I found her to be a far cry from the beauty of my love, Mary Jean Oliver. In later years I was to consider Elizabeth Taylor as probably the most beautiful woman in the world and her accent charming. I also believe she was one of the world's best actors. The movie that made the greatest impression on me was John Steinbeck's *The Grapes of Wrath*. This movie of migrating poor people seeking a way out of poverty shaped my social conscience and political philosophy for the rest of my life.

There was a community of older people at the home who were provided cottages or apartments and assisted living and medical services. The infirmary and a cafeteria were nearby. The elders qualified for residence by being a needy senior of El Paso County and by turning over all their assets (other than personal property) to the home. The couples who occupied the cottages ordered groceries from the home's store house at no cost. The single men and women ate at the cafeteria. There were times when we would go by the cottages when some of the elder ladies would give us cookies they had baked. Some would let us pick strawberries from their garden. Miss Lloyd's maid gave us lemonade and cookies when we were working near the superintendent's house. The kids and the elders at the home had a good relationship. We knew their names, and they knew ours. They were like surrogate grandmas and grandpas to us.

We could have visitors on Sunday afternoons only. Mother and Betty had moved to Texas to be with my aunt Edith who had recently lost her husband, so Grandma took the bus to come visit me every Sunday. The kids who had parents or family could go home one Sunday a month after Sunday school. Grandma would be waiting for me outside the church, and Grandpa would drive us home. There would be a big Sunday dinner feast, and sometimes my cousin Duane would visit. Duane and I could always sit and talk for hours about the people, places, and things we had experienced since the last time we were together, and especially now since we could share the activities of our entirely different lifestyles. We could always make each other laugh. On Thanksgiving and Christmas I always brought one of my orphan friends to Grandma's. These Sundays seemed so short. I had to be back at the home by 5:00 p.m. for the evening meal, which on Sunday was served in the kitchen and consisted of peanut butter and jelly sandwiches with milk and potato chips, served by the matron who was on duty. Our cook's day off began right after Sunday lunch was served.

A Different Kind of Christmas

Christmas at the home was much different than Christmas at Grandma's. In early November we kids were asked to submit a list of presents we wished to receive. We could get everything we asked for up to a certain dollar amount which was determined by your age. At age fifteen, I was allowed a gift amount of one hundred dollars. However, the mandatory new suit each year was to come out of that allowance. A boy's suit cost about forty dollars, so I had the rest for things I really wanted like boxing gloves, ice skates, a baseball glove, and wood burning set. None of us knew the price of anything. We just put everything we could think of on our want lists and hoped for the best. To be fitted for our new suits, we would be taken in groups of about fifteen to town on a series of Sunday mornings, prior to Christmas, to the Perkins and Shearer men's wear, which was closed to the public on Sunday. Our old suits were saved for any new kids to wear until their first Christmas. There was a large Christmas tree in our living room each year that was decorated by the matrons and by guys working off demerits. The gifts and all the boxed and Christmas wrapped suits were under and spread all around the tree. When the matrons weren't around, we would prowl through the pile of gifts to find the ones with our name, shake, rattle, and listen to them for clues as to the contents, without much success.

Etiquette of the Dance

First Love

On New Year's Eve, we held a dance at Lincoln Hall and invited the girls from Logan Hall and the sixth graders from the Washington building. We rolled up the carpets of our living room, polished the terrazzo floor, and decorated with crepe paper garlands and balloons. Punch and cookies were served. The music was provided by our record player. We had a good number of contemporary records of the big swing band era as well as waltz music. Our dances were the slow two-step, the fox trot, and fast-stepping jitterbug, which only the older guys and girls seemed to know. There also were the Latin dances, Rumba and Conga. The girls came dressed in their Sunday best each with a dance card[32] tied to their wrist with a ribbon. We wore our Sunday suits with the well-pressed creases in the pants, white shirts, and ties.

"Remember, gentlemen, the young ladies are guests in your home. Treat them as such. Try to sign as many dance cards as you can so that no girl will feel left out. And remember, when the dance is over, you say "thank you" to the lady and escort her back to her seat or to her next partner, and then find your own next partner. Never let one of the young ladies walk across the floor alone. You should ask any lady who has no refreshment if you may get her some. If each of you will do these things, I will be very proud of you." These words

---

[32] The dance card was a small booklet with a small pencil used by ladies to record the names of the gentlemen with whom she will be dancing.

were given us as we huddled around Mrs. Irons about an hour before the girls were to arrive. It was like a Notre Dame pep talk by Knute Rockne.

We broke out of the huddle all fired up to be gentlemen for Mrs. Irons. She surely understood boys.

While dancing with Mary Jean Oliver in my arms, on New Year's Eve, all my twelve-year-old fantasies about this happening were realized, and more. Although we were ostensibly "girlfriend-boyfriend" and had been so for several months, and I had carved JW+MO on a tree down by the Admin building, we had no more than held hands. I never had the opportunity or nerve to try to hold her in my arms, although I thought about it often. When the first record, which was a dreamy love ballad, began, I watched the older guys walk across the floor where all the girls had migrated. They each asked a girl (as we were taught), "May I have this dance?" The girls smiled and said yes, some with a nervous giggle. They then began to glide onto the dance floor. This was all according to Emily Post and our dance teacher and especially Mrs. Irons, who taught us much etiquette such as a gentleman's duty to open doors for ladies and when walking with a lady, to keep to the street side. She said that originally this was a gentleman's way of protecting his lady from mud splatters from carriages.

I looked across the room and saw Mary Jean Oliver looking more beautiful than I had ever seen her. I finally got up my nerve to get up and start across the floor. The anticipation made my knees wobble. I reached the other side of the room and asked Mary Jean if I could have this dance. She smiled and held out her hand for me to hold as she rose from the chair with grace and charm. Standing face-to-face, she placed her left arm over my right shoulder and took my left hand in her right. Tremors ran up my spine as I placed my right hand around her waist and placed it on her back. All at once I felt the soft, warm flesh of her back and caught the scent of her hair and felt her head resting on my shoulder. I had always felt awkward in dance class, but on this night, I felt like I was floating as we moved about the floor. We danced two more slow dances together that night, but none more thrilling to me than the first one. Before the party ended we all formed a circle around the dance floor and sang Auld Lang

Syne. As we sang we held our arms around the person on each side of us. On my right side was Mary Jean Oliver. When the song ended, I kissed her on the cheek. She smiled and softly said "Good night." We held other dances after that, but that magical evening was the last time I held Mary Jean Oliver. "The love affairs of youth are oft short-lived" (*La Donna e Mobile*).[33]

---

[33] Giuseppe Verde's opera, *Rigoletto: Woman Is Fickle*.

The Ravines

The home was surrounded by acres and acres of ravines and prairie. The front gate arch faced west on Highway 115, which led to Cannon City, home of the Colorado State Penitentiary. Looking west across the highway was the prairie making a gradual slope to the foot hills of the front range of the Pike National Forest and Cheyenne Mountain. To the south, north, and east lay the ravines, for how many square miles, I don't know. Camp Carson was about two miles to the south. We hiked over to the camp from time to time to view the German prisoners of war. The prisoner area was fenced off with a twelve-foot chain-link fence topped with coiled barbed wire. The guards up in the tower would motion us away. Prisoner viewing wasn't all that exciting; once in a while we would see a figure walk from one barracks to another. I think we expected to see some ugly, mean-looking, monstrous, Nazis who raped, pillaged, and killed innocent women and children that we were always reading about in comics and hearing about on the radio when casualties were being reported. We had a hate/fear of these creatures and wanted to watch them in their cages. The ravine's hills, valleys, dry streams, and gullies offered up much healthier activities than prison gaping; watching Magpies adorn their nests with shiny objects always brought to mind how some people adorn themselves with shiny jewelry, watches, earrings and such. In the ravines there was a sizeable outcropping of iron pyrite, often called "fool's gold," this rock formation looked like a shiny metal with a gold-like color. It formed into hundreds of perfectly smooth sharp cornered crystals. When we chipped off some crystals with a hammer, it would let off big sparks like flint.

An old hay storing barn out in the ravines was a pigeon hunting and loft jumping paradise. The pigeons flew in and out of the loft, openings high up near the vaulted roof. The openings had long past lost their doors to the elements as had other parts of the barn. But there was still enough roof and walls to store hay. The open timbers in the loft were caked in years of pigeon droppings. From a distance they appeared to have been painted white.

"I got one!" yelled Reggie.

He had dropped a pigeon with a thrown rock. We all went to see where in the hay the bird had fallen. None of us had actually ever before hit a bird, we didn't know what to do with it when we did find it.

"Let's cook it," one of the guys said.

"They have disease," another guy responded.

We decided to bury it. After the "disease" remark, nobody wanted to touch it, so we just kicked it along on the barn floor planks till we got it out the door to a clearing in the brush. With sticks, we dug a grave just barely deep enough to accommodate the corpse. Covering it left a mound which one of the guys placed a stick cross. We all went back in and spent the next hour or so jumping from the loft onto the hay pile twenty feet below. On one such leap, I hit my head on a cross timber and hit the hay with blood streaming down the side of my head.

"Oh god, Walker, that's a bad cut."

He took his shirt off and put it on my wound.

"Hold that on there, we'll go to the highway and get a ride back."

We walked about quarter mile to the highway. I held the arm of a guy on each side of me while one of them held the shirt on the bleeding wound. I didn't feel any pain. I was in shock I guess. I felt dizzy and kind of sick to my stomach. Luckily we caught a ride right away from a middle-aged man who looked at the opening in my head.

He whistled and said, "Oh boy," then said, "It's not too bad, it's just bleeding a lot."

He drove us the three miles to the home. The guys directed him to the infirmary. The good Samaritan delivered me to the arms of good nurse Ms. Jacobson, who cut the hair around the wound, washed it, and bandaged it, then put me in a bed. Later in the day Dr. Houf showed up, and for whatever reason, he used metal staples to close the incision rather than stitches. I was released soon after.

The ravines were acres of hills, valleys covered with sagebrush, yucca, scrub oak, prickly-pear cactus, and tumbleweed. I often went alone to my fort of brush and tree limbs. I saw myself as living off the land like the mountain men I had heard of. At these times I would eat the pear of the prickly-pear cactus and wild onions just to prove I could survive in the wild. The prickly pear was sweet eating, but hard to peel. The onions were strong and barely edible, but I convinced my pallet that these were sustaining life. The yucca plant with its long sharp blades had beautiful white blossoms whose stamens could be made to look like little people. Down one of the ravines, there was an old, unused rutted roadway leading to a large age-weathered open shed near a retention pond. We skated on the pond in the winter and skipped rocks, gathered pollywogs, and salamanders in the summer. The old shed housed some old horse drawn ore wagons with deep bottoms that cranked open to dump the ore. The large wooden spoked wheels were rimmed with an iron band and there was a foot-pedal brake which forced a large wooden wedge against the iron rim. We guessed that they had belonged to Mr. Stratton when he was operating the gold mine. We could just picture these old relics loaded with gold. The wagon shed was a favorite place to go smoke whenever one of us got hold of a pack of cigarettes by hook or crook.

I had developed a large cyst on my thigh. It was turning red and beginning to hurt. I showed it to Mrs. Irons.

"Jack, you go over to the infirmary and show that to Ms. Jacobson."

It was a painful walk over to the infirmary. Ms. Jacobson had me sit in a chair while she called Dr. Houf.

She said, "Doctor will see you when he comes tomorrow. We'll keep you here and put some cold packs on your leg."

The ice packs on the leg reduced most of the pain. I listened to the radio and looked at a stack of *Life* magazines and *Saturday Evening Posts*. A good dinner was brought to my room, and there was ice cream for dessert. After lights out, I listened to the radio till I fell asleep.

Next morning when Dr. Houf showed, he told Ms. Jacobson, "I'll need to open this up and remove it."

She prepped the area well, then the doctor, with a can or bottle of something, sat down at the bedside and told me, "Jack, I'm going to freeze the cyst. You won't feel a thing."

He sprayed my leg with stuff from the can.

"I'm going to prick you with a pin. Tell me if you feel something."

He pricked, and I jumped.

"We'll spray some more."

I felt that pin pricking me two more times I wished he would quit doing that. The sore area was more painful now than it had ever been. "Jack, I want you to bite down on this towel and hold on to these bed rails. I'm going to open the sore and remove the cyst. It will hurt, but it won't take long. I know you are brave enough to do this."

I did as he instructed and closed my eyes.

"Are you ready?" he asked.

"Uh-huh," I replied.

He cut open the skin. I bit that towel with every muscle in my jaws and squeezed those bed rails till the pain in my fingers was almost unbearable. I felt the tears well up and run down the side of my face.

"It's all over, Jack. You are a very brave young man"

Ms. Jacobson bandaged the wound and wheeled me back to my room.

"We're going to keep you here for another day. I want you to stay off that leg. You can stay in the wheelchair, but no walking around."

The next day Dr. Houf released me and gave me a ride back to Lincoln Hall. "No running now till I see you next week, okay?"

I assured him I would obey.

Cowpokes, Trappers, and Farmers

The work horses grazed in the ravines when off duty and were surreptitiously used by four us as cowponies. We helped each other get up on the horse. The last guy would have no help, so would wait his turn. We rode bareback and without bridles. This was my first time at riding a full-size horse. Once I got lifted and mounted, I leaned forward, grabbed a handful of mane, and back-slapped the horse on the haunch. The startled horse lunged forward, and I slipped off the rear on to a pile of road apples. Once the horse got rid of me, he returned to grazing. Next time I stayed on and tried to get her to gallop by smacking her haunches and nudging her with my heels. She continued grazing for a few minutes then decided to take a walk, so I had to imagine we were at full gallop chasing stage coach bandits. The other guys weren't having any better luck. Draft horses just don't make good bandit-chasing steeds. Even after we lifted two bridles from the stables and lashed them with the reins, they would not chase bandits. Our disappointment didn't last long. We continued to mount our trusty mares and ride off into fantasy land. We four each had a favorite horse, and we named them. My mount went by the name of Blaze because I just knew that if she wanted to, she could race over the prairie like a blue blaze. After falling in that pile of horse manure, the seat of my pants was soaked and smelly. The guys all stayed their distance from me walking back to the building where I took a garden hose to the pants out on the lawn.

Bob Wheeler and I had a short career as trappers. We had acquired two rusted, spring-jawed traps and set them in the ravines near two burrows in the sagebrush where we had seen jack rabbits in the ravines. We pulled a couple of carrots from the victory gardens and placed them carefully where the powerful steel jaws of the trap would capture if not kill our prey. Bob and I could hardly wait the next morning to finish our chores and go retrieve our game.

Trap number one was absent; the carrot and the trap had not sprung. I lightly touched the bait area with a stick. Bamb went the steel jaw and snapped the stick in to. We were baffled. At the next trap the jaws had sprung, but no rabbit and no carrot. We tried this one more time with the same results and gave up our trapping ambitions. I imagined that the rabbits were nearby rolling in the dirt laughing at these two dimwits, and for the longest time, I wondered if they told the story to other rabbits and maybe even pointed us out to others saying: "There's one of the dummies now." A day or two later I saw a rabbit rapidly thumping the ground as I approached. The thumping sounded like "dumb-dumb-dumb-dumb." I stooped to pick up a rock, but he disappeared into the brush.

The best summer of all at the home was the time I worked as helper to Mr. Reilly in the greenhouse. It was junglelike in the glass-covered building. The aroma of rich earth and growing plants was intoxicating. It was hot and humid, but there were fans blowing like ocean breezes. Mr. Reilly was a small grizzled elf-like little man with sun-browned hands and face. His fingernails were full up with rich black earth. The snow-white hair fringing his head like a Trappist monk's tonsure was thick, as were his profoundly wide, unruly eyebrows. He looked like Friar Tuck in overalls.

In June when I arrived at the greenhouse, there were hundreds of seedlings in little papier-mâché cups in trays on tables throughout the building. Mr. Reilly planted them in the early spring. Some were budding already. Leading me throughout the greenhouse, he named each of the many plants. I was curious and energetic, but even though I was of that age when a child can learn anything, I committed but a few of the plants to memory. I do remember names like bleeding heart, daffodil, crocus, tulip, and nasturtium. "The nasturtium leaves are good to eat. Here, taste one." The leaf was tasty, but kind of sharp like black pepper. "This beauty here is the Colorado State flower," he said with a certain reverence in his squeaky voice. "The columbine grows in every mountain meadow in the Rocky Mountains." Out in back of the greenhouse was a forest of small and large shrubs which he led me through naming them for me. I only retained lilac. He spoke of how plants create oxygen for us as well as providing beauty.

To this day most all the names of plants Mr. Reilly introduced to me are beyond my ability to recall. But I do recall how much pleasure I had each morning taking a wheelbarrow full of plants from the greenhouse out to the many flowerbeds on the home grounds and on hands and knees placing them in the ground in patterns as Mr. Reilly directed. The little old man spent so much time on his hands and knees that his bib overalls were permanently dirt stained at the knees.

Back at the greenhouse my job was to water all the plants using a fine mist hose nozzle. By the end of June everything was in full bloom, and I was spending a great deal of time hoeing weeds from the flowerbeds. I also walked the grounds setting water sprinklers. Frequently I would stop by the lily pond and watch the water skippers scoot across the water's surface and the iridescent, colorful dragonflies fluttering their transparent wings. They were shaped like little helicopters. Sometimes I'd see a frog or two. The greenhouse work was fun, but the most fun of all was listening to the stories Mr. Reilly told of growing up in the 1880s in a small Kentucky town on the Ohio River, where as a boy he worked on a river barge. The stories sounded like they were right out of a Mark Twain anthology. He also laid some Irish philosophy on me: "It's a long road that has no turnin'." I hated for that summer to end. I so enjoyed that summer I wish the lessons had stayed with me. Mr. Reilly told me he would like to have me back the next summer, which I gladly agreed to do, but by the time summer came around again, I had left the home.

The home farm raised crops and livestock and operated its own dairy. One of our jobs in the spring was to plant corn. Mr. Hawkins, the farm manager—a big, tired-looking, ruddy-faced man in bib overalls, flannel shirt, big high-top work shoes, and a well-worn straw hat—gave us each a bag of corn kernels and lined us up in a freshly plowed field about three feet apart.

"Take a long step forward, and dig out a small hole in the earth and place about three corn kernels in the hole, cover the hole back up, and take another long step and repeat the process until you reach the other end of the field." (It looked like a far distant destination.)

When we reached the end of the field about an hour later, we were given a drink of water out of a canvas water bag and allowed to sit in the shade under a big old cottonwood tree for about twenty minutes. Mr. Hawkins then had us move over and start back the way we had come repeating our now experienced corn-planting activities. At the end of this row, we were taken back to Lincoln Hall in back of the stake-bed truck we came in. We were back in time for the morning swimming session.

After lunch we were taken back to the cornfield for an encore of the morning's performance. We didn't go back to the cornfield after that day until July when we were given hoes to hoe the weeds out from around the cornstalks, which by this time were waist high and beginning to show small ears on them. While working, we sometimes would sing song verses of various poems and songs which I'm sure boys still do—deathless prose like this:

> One bright day in the middle of the night,
> two dead boys got up to fight.
> Back to back they faced each other,
> drew their swords and shot each other.
> A deaf policeman heard the noise,
> came and arrested the two dead boys.

And there was this:

> Ching ching chinaman hanging on a fence,
> trying to make a dollar out of fifteen cents.

Another favorite chant was this:

> Had a little monkey,
> fed him ginger bread
> Along came a copper,
> hit him on the knocker

175

Now my monkey's dead.

There was one lengthy song about a hearse going by. We also sang pop tunes like this:

> I'm an old cow hand from the Rio Grand
> and my legs ain't bowed, and my cheeks ain't tanned.
> I know every trail in the Lone Star State,
> 'cause I ride the range in a Ford V8.

A song we especially giggled about was an Arabic sounding-tune:

> There's a place in France
> Where the women wear no pants,
> and the dance they do
> Would be enough to kill a Jew.

Another pastime was creating and telling little moron jokes: "Why did the little moron throw butter out the window? He wanted to see butterfly." There were hundreds of them. When I first heard these jokes, I thought *moron* was a nationality.

Swimming and Tending the Victory Gardens

Ill-Gotten Fish

Our large swimming pool was nine feet deep on one end and one foot deep on the other with an attached wading pool on the shallow end. We had three diving boards: a one-foot-high board, a six-foot, and a nine-foot. At the shallow end, at about three feet deep, was a water slide. There was an elevated lifeguard's chair. I couldn't swim when I first came to the home, so I was restricted from going to the deep end. Within two weeks, I had learned to dog-paddle across the pool and was then given a pass to enter the deep water. By the end of the season, I was able to do elementary dives off all three diving boards and entered swimming competitions in the Swimming Carnival held in late August. The following season I received my Junior Red Cross Lifeguarding certification.

After leaving the pool, we lay on the smooth hot tennis court to dry off. Before getting dressed, we showered in the basement to remove the chlorine smell from our bodies. There were three showerheads and a floor drain. We spent a lot of time standing two to a shower. We told jokes and laughed until wrinkles appeared on our hands. With the other guys in the shower watching, it always got a laugh to stand behind an unsuspecting lad and pee on his leg as the shower water rushed down his leg. He would see the other guys laughing and turn around to see what was funny. "Walker, you shithead, I'll get even with you." We all laughed it off. Each one of us was at one time or another the peed-on guy.

Summertime at the home had us tending the victory gardens as part of the home-front war effort. Labor and transportation shortages made it hard to harvest and move fruit and vegetables to market, so the government encouraged everyone to plant gardens and provide their own produce. These gardens were also considered a "morale booster" in that gardeners could feel they were involved in the effort to win the war. Some of us carried a salt shaker in our pockets for flavoring celery, radishes, and cucumbers we sampled when picking. The salt was also used to neutralize the sourness of the green apples we picked from the orchard.

On one of our hikes in the mountains, we came upon a small stream filled with trout. The fish were so crowded we literally pulled them out of the stream with our hands and put them in a makeshift bag made of one guy's shirt. We walked upstream and came upon a building on the shore of a pond which was identified by a sign which read, Colorado Parks and Wildlife. "Oh my god, this was a fish hatchery." We made a fast retreat and took our ill-gotten catch home where our cook prepared them for us after making us gut and clean them. On another hike up along the stream in Cheyenne Canyon, we came up on a cache of pop and beer some picnickers had put in the stream to keep cool. A couple of our guys took bottles of ginger ale, and two of us took a bottle of beer each. When we got back home, we mixed cups of beer and ginger ale. As best I remember, it wasn't a bad drink.

Recreation, Circumcision, and Poison Chicken

T he older boys and girls automatically belonged to the Recreation Club, which held parties, picnics, carnivals, hay rides, and treasure hunts. At the parties held in Lincoln Hall we played parlor games like charades and I spy as well as card games and Ping-Pong. The picnics were held at the pavilion in the ravine behind Lincoln Hall, where we cooked hamburgers and hot dogs on a stone grill. The carnivals were held in the gym. Individuals or groups set up homemade booths with games of chance or skill with prize play money going to the winners. The winnings could be used to purchase cookies, cakes, and other goodies which the girls had made. The treasure hunt clues led us all over the many acres of the home site. The moonlight hay rides were especially fun if you could be in the hay with a girl you particularly liked.

My first summer at the home, I was sent to the infirmary where I was given a physical exam by Dr. Houf. He told me I was healthy; he then told the nurse to schedule me for tonsillectomy and circumcision surgery. He said he was going to remove my tonsils and circumcise me. I knew about tonsils being removed. I knew kids who had that done to them. I had no idea what circumcision was. When I got back to the building, I told the guys what had transpired.

One of the guys said, "After you get your tonsils out, you'll get all the ice cream you want."

That information lightened my fear load some.

"What is circumcise?"

"That's where they cut off the skin in the front of your peter. We all had it done."

That scared me. I started giving closer looks at "peters" after that. It was true. They had all had it done.

The surgeries took place simultaneously at a local hospital within the month. I was returned to the infirmary to recover. I did get a lot of ice cream offered to me, but everything tasted like the ether anesthetic which was still in my lungs. I didn't feel like eating anything for a day or so. My throat and my "peter" hurt too much. Miss Jacobson, the head nurse told me that these surgeries were to prevent infections. While convalescing, I listened to soap operas on the radio all day long and learned all the advertising jingles by heart. There was a hair oil called Wild Root Cream Oil which constantly ran ads with this jingle:

> You better get Wild Root Cream Oil Charlie.
> Start using it today.
> You see you will have a tough time, Charlie,
> keeping all the girls away.

Another ad for hot cereal aimed at kids was sung by movie star cowboy Tom Mix. It ended like this:

> So take a tip from Tom,
> and go tell your mom.
> Hot Ralston can't be beat.

I was in the infirmary one more time; it was with food poisoning. One of the guy's parents shipped him some fried chicken in a box through the post office. As I remember, it was sent from Oklahoma. He shared it with three of us. I woke up in the middle of the night and vomited on the floor of my cubicle. I woke up Mrs. Irons and told her what had happened. I don't know what took place then, but I wound up in a hospital bed in the infirmary. When I woke up the next morning, the other three guys were bedded in the room also. For about three days, we lived on Jell-O and pillow fights.

The Trumpet and I

I t was while I was in the sixth grade I became interested in music. We had a radio in Lincoln Hall, and I began listening to popular music programs. I especially liked the trumpet sounds of Harry James ("Ciribiribin"), Louis Armstrong ("When the Saints Come Marching In"), Bunny Berigan ("When the Angels Sing"), and others. Also there was a high school-age boy in the building named Bert Clibon, who was an exceptional trumpet player who played the first chair in the Colorado Springs High School Orchestra. He was also exceptional in that he treated us younger guys as if we were human, and although he was an exceptional and natural athlete, he preferred his trumpet to all else. The guys on the various competitive athletic teams were always begging him to play. He would only consent if there was a dire need for him to play, such as an injury to another player. Bert Clibon was my hero. I wanted to be like him, so I told Miss Foster I wanted to play the trumpet.

She said, "After your chores on Saturday morning, you go to the administration building and see Mr. Fink, the music teacher. He will arrange for you to take lessons. Just remember this, you will get up each and every morning, without fail, at five thirty and practice one hour before breakfast. If you can't do that, you will not be allowed to continue with lessons, and your instrument will be taken away."

"Okay," I said.

When Saturday came, I went to see Mr. Fink. His door was closed. I heard the "do, re, mi, fa so, la, ti, do" of a trombone struggling through scales coming through the transom. I sat on one of the three chairs outside the door and waited. A high school girl from Logan Hall came in carrying a violin case.

She said, "Are you next?"

Before I could answer, the scales started up again. After about four full scales, there was silence.

I said, "No, I'm here to see Mr. Fink about taking lessons."

"Then you go ahead. I can wait."

I thanked her. The door opened, and out came Reggie Burch, one of the guys from my building, carrying a long case which I guessed housed a trombone.

He said, "Hi, Walker."

I nodded, and he went on down the hall.

I hesitantly walked to the open doorway of the room Reggie had just exited. The room was small, bare, and uninviting. There was a window without curtains. The blank walls were a dull off-white smooth plaster with Victorian crown molding. The floor was scrubbed clean hardwood. It had been varnished at one time, but now it showed patterns of foot traffic and was warped in places. There was a tall cabinet of shelves where a man with his back to me appeared to be rearranging papers on one of the shelves. I stayed in the doorway waiting. He slowly and carefully turned around. He was old, like Grandpa old. His face was creased like the Grand Canyon and his eyes were so deep set I couldn't even tell if they were open. His nose was large as was his mouth. His large hands were disfigured with knobby swollen joints. His gray head of hair was thick and wavy. The crevassed face broke into a toothy smile as wide as the Grand Canyon.

He said in a soft baritone voice, "And who do we have here?"

"I'm Jack Walker."

"Well, come in, Mr. Walker."

I stepped into the room. He offered me his twisted right hand, which I gingerly shook, holding three of his fingers. He sat down and asked: "What can I do for you?"

"I want to learn how to play the trumpet."

"Well, I think that can be arranged," he said warmly. He then inquired why I especially wanted the trumpet.

I told him, "On the radio I've heard Harry James play the trumpet, and I wish I could play like that. And I like to listen to Bert Clibon play his trumpet. I think he is really good."

"Bert is one of my best students, and I also like Harry James," he said.

He got up and walked across the room and opened a door to a closet full of shelves of black cases of all sizes. Some were obviously violin cases; the others were unidentifiable. He bent over and pulled a black well-worn case from the bottom shelf and returned with it to his chair. He opened it to reveal a tarnished brass trumpet. He fingered the keys, then put the mouthpiece in and ran an eight-note scale up and back down.

He said, "The keys are a little stiff, but you can wash them off and they should be okay."

After showing me how to remove and replace the keys, Mr. Fink showed me the finger positions for the scales and gave me a well used beginner's lesson book. He opened to the first lesson, which showed the finger positions for the notes.

He said, "Take this and practice the first lesson, and I will see you next Saturday at"—he stopped and consulted his lesson calendar—"let's say ten fifteen?" He didn't wait for my response. "I'll see you next Saturday then. If anyone else is waiting, send them in."

Mr. Fink and I met each Saturday morning as I struggled through the first of several lesson books to come. Each lesson got harder and harder, but my confidence grew with each one completed. After about six months, Mr. Fink thought I was ready for a recital that was being presented by the Ivywild School. For my debut into the world of Bach, Beethoven, Brahms, Mozart, and Spike Jones, he selected country gardens, an old hackneyed English folk tune that I'm sure every music teacher of beginners has heard countless times. I practiced that tune so many times that by the time of the recital, I was sick of it. After being introduced by Mrs. Sonderson, the school music teacher, in my white shirt and tie, I stood on the stage and gave my best rendition of country gardens. The audience of parents met its obligation and applauded. I never played that song again.

I studied the trumpet for five years with Mr. Fink, and I played third trumpet with the Stratton Home Symphony Orchestra before the first year was out. Bert graduated from high school and left to join the army. I then moved up to second chair behind George Vaughn. Later, at age fourteen, I was given the first chair. Now I was the principal trumpeter in the section and got all the good solos and other parts. I no longer had to sit and count off endless bars of music until I could play a few notes. Mr. Fink said I was the youngest ever to sit in this position. In the South Junior High School, I also had the first chair position. (There was only one other trumpeter at the school, maybe two if you count the girl who had only had one lesson so far.) I also played the bugle in the school color guard. My trumpet and I were constant companions. I practiced, as required, each morning in the Cloak room among all the coats and galoshes, and again each evening, running scales struggling for the high C note, playing popular tunes, trying different mutes, and experimenting with improvisation.

I was truly touched by a gospel/blues song being played on the radio by a trumpeter called Bunk Johnson. The tune was "Just a Closer Walk with Thee."

At my next Saturday lesson, I told Mr. Fink about my feelings toward this song. He knew the song well. "I'll see if I can get you a copy of the sheet music."

The next Saturday he brought it to me and guided me through it. I practiced that song over and over until, to me, it sounded like the wailing soulful trumpet of Bunk Johnson. I've since learned that the tune is often used in New Orleans funeral marches. I was in the advanced lesson book at the time, so Mr. Fink let me experience and play things outside the lessons. He even let me improvise some once in a while.

"Musical improvisation should be creative, but still stay within the meter and rhythm of the score. Just as in life, it's okay to be creative and different, but not so different that you become alienated from society entirely."

I continued with my Saturday lessons and daily practice until I left the home at age fifteen.

In the ravines one day Richard Allen and I heard a trumpet delivering "When the Angels Sing." It was beautiful and like mice drawn to the Pied Piper, we were pulled by the sound to the source. We hiked about a quarter mile over hills and gullies and came upon a young man playing his horn standing by a car that had been driven off the Pueblo highway and onto a two-rut road used by the home's tractors. He stopped playing when we approached.

"Gee, you're really good," I told him.

"Thank you. I'm just practicing. The horn sounds much better out here than it does in my apartment." I told him I played the trumpet and wished that someday I could play as good as him.

He said he had been out of practice while he was overseas in the army and that he hoped he could catch on with a band once he got his lip back. We left him to his practice, and even though Richard and I returned to that spot several times after, we never saw him again. I hope he was successful in finding a band 'cause he was really good. Richard and I were composing a swing tune we called "Lincoln Hall Stomp." It was never finished. Richard kept the written score when I left the home. He died fighting in Korea and big band swing music was on its way out and was being replaced by the jazz sounds of Charlie "Bird" Parker, Dizzy Gillespie, Miles Davis and Thelonious Monk.

Amazing Grace

Before each meal, we stood behind our chairs, and one of us, depending whose turn it was, said grace. Many of us could get about halfway through it and mumble the rest of it sort of phonetically to get the lyrical meter. We would start with, "Our Heavenly Father, we give our thanks for this blessed food. Guide us . . . [mumble, mumble, mumble]," and end with, "In Jesus name. Amen." Then we would all quickly pull our chairs out and sit down and begin the meal. In private, we joked about that prayer by treating it like we had tired of the prayer-giver's rambling, "For Christ's sake, Bob, say amen. Let's eat."

Religion was never mentioned in my family. This was all new to me. I was taught right from wrong. I was also taught the concept of fairness and to always say "thank you" and "please." These things, along with periodical admonishments about calling people names, was about the extent of my moral training up to this point.

We put on our suits and dress shoes on Sunday, after household chores, in preparation for Sunday school. We were each given a nickel for the collection plate, which we often gambled away by flipping coins "heads or tails." There were times when one guy would wind up with about all the nickels. The word got back to Miss Lloyd that "the boys are not bringing their donations to church." After that all the nickels were given to the oldest boy at each church. The home required that we all go to Sunday school. If a child had not been raised with a strong religious preference, they were, for reasons unknown to me, sent to the United Brethren Church.

The church was held in an old Victorian house on South Nevada Avenue. It had a wide railed front porch and front door with ornately beveled glass. In the entryway there was an old hall tree with a lift top storage bench. It only had five double hangers for coats, scarves, and such, so it couldn't be used for any sizeable congregation. It was a carryover from the glory days of the house as a residence. The living room and the adjoining parlor were used as the church nave. A lectern stood at the far end of the living room in front of a table with a cross on it serving as an altar. On the wall behind the table was a large white banner lettered in black and gold: "Whosoever Believeth in Me Shall Have Everlasting Life." The rest of the room and spilling into what had been the Parlor, were about fifty metal folding chairs in rows facing the lectern. On each chair was placed a hymnal book.

Sunday school was held in a back room which may have been the Victorian maid's quarters, since it was right off the kitchen which was still being used by the church. There was a wall hanging poster painting of Jesus in his long white gown and sandals surrounded by children. He was a good-looking guy with a tanned face, long hair, and a well-trimmed beard. Lettering beneath the painting read: "Suffer the Little Children to Come unto Me." I took that to mean that if kids are suffering, they should go see him.

Sunday school at the United Brethren was not co-ed. The girls went to a room upstairs. The school curriculum was basically the telling and reading stories from the Bible. Each and every Sunday we began the class singing "Jesus Loves Me." We heard about a talking snake in the Garden of Eden and a story about the man Moses who made the sea dry up so he could get through to escape some Egyptians. And there was the story about Moses going up on a mountain and having a conversation with a burning bush. My favorite story of all was the one about the guy Jonah who was swallowed by a big fish and lived in its belly for three days until the fish after being spoken to by God, vomited out Jonah onto dry land. We were told that these stories were from the Old Testament (whatever that meant) and that next we would be hearing stories from the New Testament (coming attractions). I hoped the new stories would get us away from the funny words like *thee, thou, begat, maketh, verily, smite*, and so on, which, to me, detracted from the stories.

The New Testament seemed, to me, to be about the adventures of one man, Jesus, a carpenter-turned-preacher who ran with a bunch of apparently single unemployed guys, one of which was a former fisherman. They were called apostles. There were a few women along who would "provide for them from out of their means."[34] They walked around by the Sea of Galilee and helped Jesus spread the Word to people about loving one another. Jesus could walk on water, cure sick people, and bring dead people back to life, even himself after dying on a cross. Our teacher told us that if we believed in Jesus, we would live forever and go to a wonderful place called heaven and that if we didn't believe, we would burn to death in a place called hell. Bible stories got confusing sometimes; on one hand we were told that God was merciful. On the other hand, we were told he would smite you if you didn't obey him. Reading the barely intelligible seventeenth-century King James–approved version of the Bible—which seemed like a foreign language (words like "begat," "didst," "verily," and "holdest")—wasn't conducive to young boys' comprehension, let alone retention.

On those occasions when our teacher didn't show up, we attended the regular church service. I never knew what that preacher was talking about, but it was entertaining watching him walk back and forth, his voice rising and falling with the message. He was not monotonous at all. We did learn and sing some lyrics from the hymnals, such songs as "The Old Rugged Cross," "Rock of Ages," "Nearer My God to Thee," "Tell Me the Old Old Story," and my favorite, "Little Brown Church in the Vale." These were sung by the entire congregation. We could sing as loud as we wanted to the inharmonious tones of the accompanying tinny piano played exuberantly by a little gray-haired lady who sang her heart out as she deftly fingered the old worn keys.

I was not too long recovered from the trauma of realizing that Santa Clause and the flying reindeer were not true, that Jack's magic

---

[34] Luke 8:2.

beanstalk didn't really grow beyond the clouds, that shoe-making elves don't really come out at night to help cobblers, that the tooth fairy wasn't really a fairy, and that fairy godmothers can't turn pumpkins into coaches. Now I was expected to believe a new set of tales called the Old and New Testaments. I was beyond skeptical at this point in my eleventh year of life. I just plain did not take them for the truth. Nevertheless, they were good stories, and I enjoyed hearing them. I never did grasp this idea of life after death, or the concepts of heaven and hell. Although I didn't buy into these ideas, life after death did tweak my imagination as to what it would be like: If I reached a greater age than Grandpa did, would he be younger than me in the afterlife? Do they play baseball in heaven with their wings on? Do rats and spiders and snakes go to heaven? Visualizing these ideas made me laugh. "He's a God-fearin' man," I often heard grown-ups exclaim. They spoke as if it was good to live in fear. I always wondered what the man was afraid of.

The church wanted all the children to sign a pledge which read, "I will never smoke cigarettes or use tobacco in any form as long as I live." I didn't understand this at all. I fully intended to smoke cigarettes, pipes, and possibly cigars. Every adult male I respected did these things. The radio and the magazines were full of cigarette ads: Camels ("More doctors smoke Camels than any other cigarette"), American Tobacco Company ("Lucky Strike Means Fine Tobacco"), Liggett and Meyers Company ("ABC, Always Buy Chesterfields"), and The Phillip Morris Company used a midget bellhop yelling, "Call for Philip Morris." Almost every famous Hollywood actor and athlete did magazine ads for cigarettes. I would have smoked at that tender age, if I was allowed, even though Grandma told me, "Smoking will stunt your growth." I didn't sign the pledge. I would have been giving up one of the major symbols of being a grown-up. Mr. Fielding scanned the pledges he had distributed and saw that one was returned blank.

He asked, "Who didn't sign their pledge?"

Mine was the only hand in the air.

"Why didn't you sign this Jack?"

"Because it wouldn't be true."

"Don't you want to go to heaven?"

"I don't know."

He exhaled in exasperation and said, "Okay, if that's the way you want it, but just remember, Judgment Day is coming."

He was one of those who believed that every word in the Bible was true just as God had spoken. The subject of smoking was never broached again.

Mr. Fielding, a slight middle-aged, pasty-faced, pious man with shiny black well-oiled hair, slicked straight back from his high pale forehead, was a night watchman for several downtown stores. He walked a beat and checked doors and windows for break-ins. The stories he told us about his experiences in the dark alleyways were always attention-getters. He was a good storyteller.

"I'm not afraid to walk down the dark alleys checking back doors because I know Jesus is with me," was something repeated every Sunday. It was later discovered that he had been robbing the stores. It was a big newspaper story. He didn't deny the charge. He said he did it because he needed medicine for his sick wife that he couldn't afford. He lost his job as a watchman, was ordered to repay all his victims, and was put on probation. Later I learned he was working in one of the banks as a guard. They gave us a substitute Sunday schoolteacher.

I changed churches. Some of the older guys and a couple of my closer friends went to the Baptist Church, on Kiowa Street, so I followed. This was a regular church, not a converted house. It even had a bell tower and tall colorful stained-glass windows depicting seraphim and cherubim, and regular padded pews. The Baptist Sunday school class was much larger than at the United Brethren, and best of all, they didn't take attendance. Opportunity to skip class was glaringly obvious, and a few of us took advantage of this serendipitous windfall. The bus would drop us off at the entrance to the church. We would hang around at the bottom of the church stairs giving little Lord Fauntleroy Sunday morning smiles and greetings to people going in, then when the bus was out of sight and before the crowd got too small to blend into, we would sort of saunter off down the street and around the corner to the Stratton Coffee Shop in the

Continental Bus Depot for Cokes and jokes and sometimes cigarettes if one of the guys had some. Behind the cash register counter was a display of Trojans (condoms). We wondered if they would sell them to us, but none of us had the nerve to ask. I don't know what we thought we would do with them. We weren't getting any. Hanging out in the café making jokes to each other about all the people we saw going in and out of the depot was our Sunday School until it was time to go back and mingle with the Baptist congregation coming out of church and catch the bus back home.

Escapes, We Do the Palace, Root Beer Floats Thievery and JoJo the Dog-Faced Boy

T he matrons habitually attempted to enlighten us by preaching such platitudes for children as (at bedtime), "Early to bed, early to rise, make a man healthy, wealthy and wise." And there was, "Children are to be seen, not heard," and, "If at first you don't succeed, try, try again." For us musical early morning risers, there was, "Rise and shine," and, "The early bird gets the worm." (Not if the worm sleeps in.) They went on and on. This was Grandma all over again. Grown-ups didn't seem to catch on that these pearls (of wisdom) were being cast on swine.

> News Break
> September 12, 1943
> Allies go ashore in Italy. American and German
> forces locked in furious combat near Naples.

These news bulletins never told us in any detail how the fighting men were getting along. John Steinbeck had written in *Time Magazine* that there were really two wars, one of maps and logistics, campaigns, ballistics, divisions, and regiments, and the other a war of the homesick, weary, funny, violent, common men who wash their socks in their helmets, complain about their food, whistle at girls, and bring themselves through as dirty a business as the world has ever seen and do it with humor and dignity and courage. Front-line journalist Ernie Pyle and cartoonist Bill Maudlin were our life-lines to the common soldier. Pyle told us that many of our GIs felt no hatred of the Germans they were killing in order to stay alive. He listed some of the silly gifts soldiers received from home: cans of Spam, house slippers and silk socks, to mention a few. He ridiculed politicians who were worried about whether the soldiers would be able to vote, when soldiers were concerned with staying alive. Bill Mauldin told us of the common soldier by use of sardonic cartoons of two combat-weary infantry dog faces, Willy and Joe, who stoically undergo the daily tribulations and dangers of war.

AWOL Adventures

"**D**o not leave the home property without permission" was a cardinal rule. Of course permission was granted only if there was to be certain adults to take responsibility for you, such as a matron, the home superintendent, or under some circumstances, a relative. With this in mind, we sometimes slipped out the gates unseen by these certain adults. One of our favorite places to slip off to if we had enough money for admission was the Broadmoor Ice Palace (formerly the Broadmoor Riding Academy). On our way walking to Broadmoor, we always stopped by the reservoir to watch the prairie dogs nearby scurry here and there, in and out of their holes. They were so used to us they weren't alarmed at all. Continuing our walk, as we entered Broadmoor proper, we passed great multiacre estates with high walls and iron gates. These people were more than millionaires. JP Morgan would have classed them as having real money. This community was without stores, sidewalks, or any other displays of crass commercialism or plebian activity. The epicenter of all this affluence was Spencer Penrose's posh Broadmoor Resort Hotel, known as the Queen of the Rockies.

The polo ponies and riders were fun to watch as we passed the Broadmoor Polo team field. We sometimes stopped at the nearby army remount station stables to pet the horses. Contrary to general belief, the army still uses horses and mules. There is no substitute for animal pack transportation in unforgiving mountainous terrain. The Ice Palace was luxurious, smooth, slick, Zamboni-treated ice (unlike the ponds, lakes, and reservoirs we were used to). We skated until the place was emptied for the Pikes Peak Skating Club.[35] We would hang around and watch the champions train. On one of these excursions, I fell on the ice, and someone ran a skate blade into the side of my mouth. One of the guys got me some toilet paper to blot the blood. We decided to go home, which was a walk of about two miles. My mouth was cut open, and I couldn't tell anyone because I was engaged in a forbidden act when it happened. I kept a piece of toilet paper on it and avoided the matrons the rest of the day. Next morning my mouth was sore, but it had stopped bleeding. I could take only small bites of food because I was afraid if I opened my mouth wide, it would break open again. It finally healed, and my secret remained undiscovered. We usually stayed on the home grounds and skated on the duck pond where a muskrat lived, but the duck pond didn't compare to the large smooth ice and surroundings of the Ice Palace.

One time Richard Allen and I snuck off to go to town to buy some sheet music. The bus was filled with young soldiers from Camp Carson. As we stepped onto the bus, we were greeted with a resounding chorus of soldiers singing "Ninety-Nine Bottles of Beer on the Wall." Once we caught on to the less than complicated storyline, we joined in, "If one of those bottles should happen to fall, there'd be ninety-six bottles of beer on the wall."

Some of us snuck out once in a while to walk a mile down the highway to the Ivywild drugstore for a ten-cent root beer float in a big frosted glass mug. Sometimes these wonderful soda fountain creations were paid for by deposits we got for returning Coke bottles. And sometimes these bottles were ill gotten from the shed at the back of the drugstore. On one such criminal quest for bottles, Richard and I got surprised by a man from the store. Richard was near the door. I was in the back of the shed crouched behind a lot of boxes. The shed door opened.

"WHAT ARE YOU DOING IN THERE?" a loud male voice blurted.

My heart was beating like an African drum. I was safe, until, "Jack we're caught," I heard Richard's voice ring out. I sunk to the floor, then I heard, "Come on out of there, you."

---

[35]   Later renamed the Broadmoor Skating Club, home of many Olympians.

I gave up and showed myself and meekly walked out. (James Cagney would have said, "You'll never take me alive, copper," and come out with guns blazing.) The man had grabbed Richard by the arm, and when I appeared, he roughly grabbed and painfully squeezed my arm with his other hand.

"What were you doing in there?"

"We were just looking around," I whined.

He warned us, "You stay away from here. If I catch you here again, I'll call the police and have you arrested." He let go of our arms with, "Now get outta here." No root beer floats that day.

On another clandestine adventure, I snuck away alone with a free pass to the circus in my pocket which I had found outside the church. I rode the bus to town and walked nine blocks out to the circus grounds. Having never been to a circus, I was filled with exciting anticipation. I showed my ticket to the man at the entrance to the Big Top tent. He read it to me: FREE ADMISSION in large bold print, and in very small print beneath it, "Admit one to side show of choice" He then explained to me in so many words that I was allowed only in one of the side shows, like the snake charmer or the seven-hundred-pound fat lady or the three-headed calf. "And JoJo the dog-faced boy." My heart sunk down to my stomach. I didn't care about any old side show of freaks. I wanted to see clowns, the man on the flying trapeze, the flying Wallendas, and elephants and lion tamers. I choked back the tears and walked away. I felt cheated by the circus, and I have hated them ever since.

The Vigorous Varied Life

We had a lot of picks of things to do at the home; we played cards a lot, games like rummy, old maid, and war. One deck of cards we had was illustrated with the actual silhouettes of war planes of the US, Great Britain, Germany, and Japan. We learned to identify these planes by heart: Corsair; Mustang, B25, and Flying Fortress B17 (American); Spitfire and Hell Cat (British); Mitsubishi and Zero (Japanese); Messerschmitt and Junkers (German). The Ping-Pong table was well used. One of the guys had a Jews Harp, or Juice Harp, which I never could get any music from. There was always a community crossword puzzle in progress on a living room table. The library enjoyed optimum popularity as did the well-appointed, carpeted Billiards Room. We shot eight-ball and straight pool on a vintage Brunswick pool table of ornately tooled and polished cherrywood. The four large table legs were art pieces that would more than rival the Corinthian pillars of ancient Greece. The table surface was a large thick slab of marble covered tightly with dark green wool felt. The six pockets were woven leather. The table was reputed to have belonged to Mr. Stratton. Just as old and as ornate was the cherrywood cue stick rack mounted on the wall holding nine cue sticks of different lengths and weights. The rack also shelved the ivory pool balls. Across the top was a thin metal rod holding scoring beads. Even the ball rack was vintage cherrywood with brass inlaid brackets at each of the three corners. The room, for lack of space elsewhere, housed one of the two upright pianos of the building. You had the feeling that this room was to accommodate gentlemen engaged in a gentlemen's pastime. "No more than 4 persons allowed in the billiards room at one time," read the sign on the door. This was strictly enforced. If violated Mrs. Foster would lock the room up for two weeks, and the guys who caused that penalty were in deep trouble with their peers. I spent a lot of time at the pool table, playing mostly just slop pool or when alone I would practice various shots learning at what spots to hit on the target ball from various cue ball positions in order to make the target ball go where I wanted it to go. My pool game was ranked as one of the top five players in the building, of which there were probably no more than about fifteen of us who used the table.

There was a variety of sports activities. Our athletic field had a regular one-hundred-yard grass covered football field, goal posts and all. Surrounding the field was a quarter mile cinder track. Down at one end of the field was a backstop for baseball and a sawdust pit for high jumping and pole vaulting. Football was played without helmets or any other protective equipment. We would invite some guys from town to come out for a pickup game on Saturday after-noons. Our football was mostly a running game and we never place kicked. The extra point was by drop kick and kickoff was by punting. We fielded two different age group baseball teams in the Colorado Springs Little Leagues. Miss Lloyd saw that we had all the equip-ment we needed and she saw to it that we suited up in the best of uniforms of grey pants and shirts, with blue caps and socks. MSH was emblazoned across the front of our shirts in large blue letters. We had a gym with a regulation sized basketball court. In season, these three athletic activities, and trumpet practice, were my after school destinations right after "Nutrition," of graham crackers and milk, or sometimes cinnamon toast left over from breakfast.

None of our recreational activities were mandatory. Some guys listened to the after-school children's radio programs, on our big console Zenith in the living room. Some practiced their musical instruments. Others might play ping pong, or cards. After school till dinner time at five, was free time for us. After dinner was study and homework time. If we had no homework we might listen to the radio and hear Edward R. Murrow of CBS, broadcasting the European war news from London which had been bombed nightly and unmercifully by the German Lutwaffe. Murrow sometimes gave live broadcasts as he flew on bombing missions. I remember one of his famous quotes about fighting the war was, "Difficulty is the excuse history never accepts." He always signed off with, "Good night and good luck." And then there was Westbrook Pegler, a famous newspaper columnist who ranted daily about the White House dictator Franklin D Roosevelt, the Commie Unions who he compared to Hitler's "goose-steppers." Gabriel Heatter would come on the radio with: "Good evening, everyone, there is good news tonight." And then tell us of all the carnage taking place around the globe. One such report I will never forget was the announcement that all five Sullivan brothers serving on the same ship had died when their ship was sunk by a torpedo from a Japanese submarine.

Radio programs during the war were commonly interrupted with war news bulletins. In the early years we heard that the Nazis discriminated against Jews, but we heard nothing of the killing of millions of Jews, nor did we hear of the starved slaves of the concentration camps and the ovens where bodies were burned by the thousands. Only little by little did this unbelievable news gain credence. After the war the whole story of the holocaust was revealed. I hated Germans for many years afterward for allowing such insane terror to exist. Years later while a college student, I wrote a Political Science term paper wherein I stated: "The German people will do it again when they hear the drums of war." My professor, a German Jew, noted my paper with, "Although your position is defensible, it disturbs me."

In the summer mumblety-peg was a popular game we played with our pocket knives or our dandelion diggers. In the winter when the ponds were too deep in snow to skate on, we sledded on the drive which curved down the ravine behind Lincoln Hall which led to a picnic pavilion. We made huge snow men and built snow forts for snowball fights. Ice balls were "no fair." Violators would be branded "cheaters" forever after, or until dinner; whichever came first. Our sleds would fly through the air off the ramps we built and sometimes crash land. The only injury I ever remember was when Robert Russell couldn't get his sled to turn on the curve and he hit a big boulder head on. His nose was split open and bleeding. He was crying. We put him on a sled and took him to the infirmary. He looked funny later on with stitches down his nose. We teased him about using his nose as a hood ornament.

Another past time was to sit on the hillside overlooking the highway to Pueblo and see who could identify the make of the most cars. Each auto in those days had distinct styling. "Body by Fisher" was the coveted statement sought by the auto makers. Many of the auto styles of the past were originated and custom-built by the Fisher Body Corporation. There was the sleek 1940 Dodge with its split windshields, its distinctly designed radiator grille topped off by a lion hood ornament. The 1938 Buick Road Master had horizontal bar grilles on each side of the hood and at the rear a trunk built into the body. The wood paneled station wagons were easy IDs, as was the Model A Ford Coupe with rumble seat and hooded windshield. Because cars of that time had higher ground clearances, they all had running boards under the doors to step up on to enter. Hood ornaments were artistic metal sculptures like mastheads on a ship; Ford had a racing greyhound, Dodge, a charging ram, Plymouth, a sailing ship, Packard, a winged woman, Pontiac, an Indian head. These cars were built of steel by people, not robotically turned out cookie cutter models of today. If, while watching cars go by, we saw a load of hay, we immediately in unison broke poetically into:

> Load of hay, load of hay,
> Make a wish and look away.

Providing we looked away and never saw that load again, we had every confidence that this might be the time that the wish would be granted.

One of our most common contests out in the ravines was to see whose stream of pee would go the farthest. Whenever we had enough guys together, we played Red Rover or go to the dairy and use one of the barns to play Ante Over, using some rolled-up rags as a ball. Another fun game was Follow the Leader, where every guy had to follow and do exactly like the leader; if the leader jumped over a fence and you couldn't, then you were out of the game. We chose the leader by playing rock, scissors, and paper. When tired of following, we might play "leap frog" by pushing up and over the guy in front of you who is bent down like a pummel horse; then you bend down and become the horse. Or we might just play dog-pile by throwing one of the guys down to the ground and all pile on top of him. Pom-pom- pull-away was played on the athletic field. When we could find a rope and get enough guys to play, tug-of-war was played across a muddy pool. More sedate games we played were croquet and blind man's buff. The yo-yo was big for some of us. After endless hours of practice, I learned some basic yo-yo tricks like the throw-down, the sleeper, walking the dog, around the world, and rock the cradle. Some of the more difficult tricks were beyond my skill level. Wrestling in the grass took up a good portion of our spare time. This sport often led to somebody getting so intent on winning, that a real fight would erupt and two friends would become enemies. I learned to jump-rope from the girls, a skill I later used in my boxing practice. We used the entire football field for playing tag and crack-the-whip. You had to be able to run fast over a great distance. Many hours were spent climbing the numerous trees on the home grounds. To show off my strength, I used to go over to Washington Hall, and with four to six girls riding, I would walk in circles, pushing their merry-go-round like an old horse-drawn thrasher. "Oh, Jack, you're so strong," was the whip motivating me to push faster. Many times since, I've served as some woman's mule. Nevertheless, I love them.

It was rare for any of us to get mail, but on occasion, after school, I would find that a V-mail had been put on my bed. V-mail was a secure method to correspond with soldiers and sailors during the war.

A V-mail letter would be censored by the government to insure that no sensitive information was disclosed. It was then photographed and put on microfilm and then forwarded. The person receiving the mail would get a photo copy of the letter. The censors would blackout any words they felt were sensitive. It was felt that the V-mail method cut down on valuable shipping space also. You could get the very thin paper V-mail forms at the post office. Because of the censoring you could never know where your soldier or sailor was writing from. Also the letters were pretty outdated by the time you got them. Kenny also sent me a sailor suit he had tailored from one of his uniforms. He included a white hat. I wore this uniform in a school play wherein we acted the parts of ourselves as grownups. I was a navy doctor.

It was a crisp fall day. With brown bag lunches, we all climbed up into the back of the stake-bed tuck. About thirty of us were going to go climb Pikes Peak. We drove through Manitou Springs and headed up Ute Pass on Highway 24. Turning off the highway we continued to climb on a twisting turning road so steep it had to switch back and forth on itself until we reached Glen Cove, a way station which had originally been a settler's cabin on the old carriage road. From here we continued by foot six miles of gravel road, steep climbing, cold wind and thin air to the summit. To coin a cliché; the view was spectacular. There was a 360-degree panorama of mountain after mountain and the endless Great Plains to the east. We took it all in quickly. However, we were hungry and cold and found a place behind the summit house out of the wind and ate lunches that were just as cold as we were. We hurried back down the road and froze to near death on the way home in the back of the truck.

Passed around till they were dog eared, were the Big Little Books. These were comics in a bound book format about four inches square and two inches thick. They were passed around until they fell apart from use.

Flip Books got a lot of play. They were small books with a series of pictures and when you flipped the pages rapidly, the pictures appear to move or animate like you were watching a cartoon movie. Our literary tastes also ran to the surreptitiously acquired *Esquire* magazine which had the "pin-up" drawings of Alberto Vargas and George Petty depicting beautiful scantily attired ladies in provocative poses. This literature and the bare breast pictures from Africa, Asia, and Polynesia viewed in our library of National Geographies, was our first experience with the female physique.

"Ball four. Take a walker. Walker the talker, Jones moans for ice-cream cones." Punning and rhyming each other's names was a creative laughter producing boredom killer, along with parody creations on popular songs like the song "It's Magic" was versed "It's Tragic," or the Harry James's theme song "Ciribiribin," we called "Cherry-Flavored Beans." And to the lyrics "you laugh and i hear violins" was reversed to "you laugh and spit runs down your chin." There were many more. We made kites of sticks, newspaper, flour-water paste, string, and rags tied together for a tail. We flew them (some of them) out on the open athletic field in the winds of March. The field was also the site of our risky bomb making. We had discovered that by putting a small amount of calcium carbide[36] in a glass jar, add water, and quickly close and toss it, it produced a gas causing a combustible explosion which sent glass shrapnel flying everywhere. This comes under the category of stupid youth as was our skating on the deep reservoir without really knowing the thickness of the ice. At that age we felt that courage, though often misplaced, was more manly than was safety.

Bob Wheeler and I cut a golf ball open to see what they were made of. We had heard that in the very center was a little ball filled with acid. With Bob's pocketknife, I cut the tough white outside cover of the ball and found what looked like a lot of rubber bands wound around and around to form a ball. I Continued cutting on the rubber strands and they began to unwind little by little. I reached the core ball about the size of a large marble. This we guessed held the acid. We wanted to see the acid, but were afraid it might get on our hands and eat them away. We hid it under a rock down by the pavilion until we could figure out how to safely open it and use it. We then went to the duck pond and skipped rocks on the water. The golf ball core might still be under that rock.

"MSH succumbs to Demons 35–0," read the sports-page article in the *Gazette* on the day after our first excursion into Little League. We got better with time and practice. Miss Lloyd loaded all of us in her station wagon to go to games. Our games were all played at Monument Valley Park. The infield was dirt and the outfield was weeds. There was an all-colored team called the Clouds of Joy. Every one of them could run, hit and catch better than any other team

---

[36] Calcium carbide was sold at the hardware store for lighting miners' lamps and for use in toy cannons.

in the league. After each game Miss Lloyd took us to the Johnson, English drugstore soda fountain and let us order whatever fountain concoction we wanted. My favorite was Chocolate Soda. We crammed into booths, talked baseball, and ate ice cream. The Soda Fountain made us forget the score of the game, unless, of course we had won. The marble top counter, high stools and mirror behind the counter were pretty common to all Soda Fountains. The man behind the counter in the little white cap and apron was called a "Soda Jerk," short for soda jerker, so called because of the jerking motion used on the carbonated water (soda) fountain handles. Even a "coke" was made with Coca Cola syrup and a couple jerks of soda. The Soda Fountain menu offered all kinds of ice cream and soda concoctions: banana splits, hot fudge sundaes, root beer floats, cherry phosphates, malted milk shakes, and even ice-cream cones.

Next day in the *Gazette* we would check out the sports page to see box scores if only to see our names in print; walker ss hits 0, runs 0, errors 0. We didn't have big league baseball team in the west. The westernmost teams were in St. Louis, which we considered as "back east." St. Louis had the Cardinals and the Browns. Stan Musial of the Cards was my favorite player (1943 batting average 357). I wrote him a letter asking for an autographed picture. He sent the autographed picture along with an Eversharp pencil shaped like a baseball bat with his signature on it. It was probably the most thrilling thing to have happened to me up to that time. Right away I had to show the picture and bat pencil to all the guys on the team. Those treasures were displayed on my dresser along with a picture of trumpeter Harry James for the remaining three years of my stay at the home. There were only sixteen major league baseball teams, eight in each league and they didn't move from one city to another. The Dodgers were in Brooklyn at Ebbets Field. The New York Giants played in the Polo Grounds, at Coogan's Bluff, Upper Manhattan. The White Sox were in Comiskey Park, and the Cubs were and still are in Wrigley Field, Chicago.

News Break
November 23, 1943
The Battle of Tarawa
US Marines make amphibious landing at Tarawa
Atoll in the Gilbert Islands.

Burn-out was one of our favorite games: two guys wearing ball gloves playing catch with a baseball throwing as hard as they can in order to see whose hand burns out first. We also played a pitching game; one guy is the pitcher, the other the catcher. The catcher called balls and strikes on invisible batters until there were three strike-outs, then the two guys switched roles. This went on until nine innings were played. Runs could only be achieved by being walked around the bases. There were times when two or three of us, after lunch on Saturday, would just lie on the grass and watch clouds drift by. In the clouds our imaginations saw the shapes of animals, trains, people, cars, buildings, bridges and mountains.

When we tired of that, we would go over to the dairy where the big breeding bull was corralled. He looked to be twice the size of the milking cows. If a heifer was corralled with him, we might get a chance to watch him screw her. If he were alone, we would amuse ourselves trying to anger him to charge us. This was done by trying to hit one of his huge soft ball sized testicles with a pebble. We were rarely successful.

The remainder of the afternoon we might go down to the Power House boiler room, peek in a window, looking down into the basement to locate the boiler tender, old Mr. Jack Fink (the music teacher's brother). He usually was sitting near his radio smoking his pipe. He wasn't crippled, but he moved slowly and bent over like he was carrying something heavy and his knees hurt. He had a false left hand which was gloved in brown leather. I don't know what it was made of, but we always talked about his "iron fist." Once we had him spotted, we went down to the door which opened into the basement, opened it unseen by him, and threw a piece of coal to the other side of the room, banging one of the big boiler water tanks. When he went to investigate, we slipped in to the boiler room and over to the opening to the underground tunnel system which led to the basements of all the buildings.

Beautiful Girls And the Curve

The tunnels were tall enough and wide enough to walk in and there were light switches every so often. These were concrete utility tunnels for the electric wires and the plumbing pipes. There was only one way in, but we could exit at any of the buildings. We heard girls laughing up ahead and turned the tunnel lights out.

"Look at the knockers on her," whispered Johnnie.

I could have smacked him. We were at the tunnel exit at Logan Hall, the older girl's basement where they showered after coming in from the swimming pool. We looked through a wrought-iron grill. These were grown-up high school girls. I was awestruck. I gasped. I couldn't speak and could hardly breathe. I had never seen girls naked before. They were all laughing and having fun in and around the showers. Some were standing under the showers while others were drying off, and some were sitting on or straddling the nearby benches. One girl was combing another girl's long black, curly hair that tumbled all the way down her back to almost touch her bottom. Two other girls were chasing each other around the room snapping each other with towels.

Once over my initial shock, I began to take in this forbidden, stunning visual feast. This experience has remained vivid in my memory as a tipping point and passage from childhood to adolescence. My eyes went first to breasts; they were all sizes beautifully sloping down and out from the chest to be peaked by nipples of various sizes and colors; some pale pink and some darker almost brown. Each nipple was circled by a ring of color matching the nipple itself. From the nipples the breasts gently curved down and back toward the chest forming alluring globes and when they raised their arms the breasts were lifted. Whether their breasts were ample or modestly small, they all curved beautifully. Next I noticed their bellies and the exotic pubic mounds. Their bellies sort of pushed softly out presenting the small cavities encompassing the belly buttons and then rounded on down to the small pubic hair mounds where the thighs begin. Everywhere I looked there were soft flowing curves. The plump girls had plump curves. The slender girl's curves were more subtle. Even the homely girls had curves. The sun-tanned arms and legs were contrasted to the silky smooth white skin of their torsos. Their backs beginning from the shoulders started with a long subtle curving sweep down then a more pronounced curve into the lower backs, only to curve back out to begin to form the round firm cheeks of their bottoms which reminded me of upside-down hearts. The bottoms, framed by the softly rounded hips, curved down to meet the thighs which smoothly tapered down to the knees. Their dimpled knees were soft and round, not knobby and bony like guys knees. The muscles of their arms and legs were smooth and soft. The calves of their legs curved attractively down to trim ankles connected to small feet. I noticed also that their waists were distinctly smaller than their hips (except for the chubbier girls). Guy's bodies have curves also, but the curves of their muscles are not as subtle and graceful as are girls'. It seems to me that the male body is designed as an instrument for physical strength. The female body is a work of art. Necks and shoulders of these girls were attractive in how their necks curved softly down and out to blend in to the soft silky shoulders which then curved out and down smoothly rounding in to the upper arm, and softly tapering on down to the elbow. The delicate forearms gracefully curved and tapered down to small wrists and hands. Even their faces took on a new look to me that day. The oval seemed to generally define the face shapes. The ears and noses were small. The eyes were large and smiling. The cheeks were rosy and the lips were naturally red and beautifully shaped and when laughing revealed pure white teeth. I guess the beauty of it all was in the way the curves were arranged. The thoughts running through my head were not prurient in any way. I just felt I was experiencing something new and beautiful. The vision of these girls was entrancing and unforgettable.[37] I couldn't believe these were the same girls I saw every day. I knew these girls all, but never did I suspect there was such beauty covered up by their clothing. It was like viewing a gallery of Roberto Ferri paintings. I'm sure they were unaware of the simple perfection of their naturally beautiful bodies. I don't think girls of my twelve years of age had all these curves.

That day I fell in love with the female form as a natural art form not matched by any artists of any artistic genre past or present. I looked at these girls and have looked at all females, whether saints or sinners, in this light ever since. Though enraptured with what I had seen, I felt guilty of having invaded the privacy of these beautiful girls. I didn't speak with the other guys of how this affected me. Listening to their banter, it was something to joke about. This experience and later occasions in my life with the female mind, personality, sensuality and other characteristics, has made me glad to be a man. The French say it best, "Viva la difference." Some of the guys went shower peeking one more time and were detected. The tunnel entrance was thereafter locked. That shower room picture remains banked in my memory. This was an epiphany for me. My attitude toward girls changed from that day on. It no longer meant anything that they looked awkward running and throwing. Girls were no longer just sissies.

As I grew and matured some, I learned they also could possess intelligence and strength beyond that of males'. Growing up, I never used degrading terms to describe females, nor did I ever find humor in so-called dirty jokes. As an adult, I have always considered the sex act as a natural sensual engagement of two individuals delighting all the senses. I've found sex delightful, but never funny. Over the years I've always taken pleasure in viewing the curve wherever I encounter it; the sleek sloping curves of a Ferrarari, a spiral staircase, ripples in a pool when you drop a pebble, wind shaped curving sand dunes, violins, vases, the round pillars, and curving domes of ancient cathe-

---

[37] My twelve-year-old vocabulary could not have adequately given full measure to what my eyes revealed. These descriptions are my adult attempts to give insight to my senses at the time. I only knew I was in the presence of beauty.

drals, rainbows. Would the moon be as beautiful if it were square? Isn't wavy or curly hair more pleasing visually than straight hair? Even the rugged peaks of the Rocky Mountains eventually slope gracefully down to meet rounding foothills before washing on to the alluvial rolling plains. Appreciation of the beauty of the female form is not confined to men. I've read that the nude female form in art has been purchased by more women than men. It is a universal taste just as sugar is.

Bedtime Radio

The Sheriff Comes for Us

Before lights out, and after brushing our teeth and getting into our pajamas, Mrs. Irons let us come into her room and sit on the carpet to listen to her radio. One of my favorite programs was *First Nighter*. The show created the image of being in a Broadway theatre. The narrator whispered from his third row center seat. When the show was about to begin, he whispered, "The house lights have dimmed, and the curtain is about to go up on tonight's production." I was magically transported to a seat in the Little Theatre off Times Square. At the intermission, you would hear the announcement: "Smoking in the outer lobby only." After a commercial, there would be a curtain call. This was radio theatre at its best. While keeping our eyes on the radio as if we could see the characters, we even listened to such sight-necessary performances as Charlie McCarthy and Edgar Bergan, a ventriloquist act, and to tap dancers competing in talent contests. Almost every broadcast signed off with a patriotic song, of which there was no shortage at that time. There were the songs of the individual armed services: "The Marine's Hymn," "Anchors Away," "The Caissons Go Rolling Along," and "The Army Air Corps Song." Other popular patriot tunes are, "Praise the Lord and Pass the Ammunition," "Star-Spangled Banner Waving Somewhere," "A Wing and a Prayer," and I'll never forget the Andrews Sisters singing "The Boogie-Woogie Bugle Boy of Company B" or Kate Smith's "God Bless America." Much of the popular music lyrics, though not of the patriotic genre, were ballads lamenting the separation of lovers. The titles tell it all: "Give Me Something to Remember You By," "I'll Be Home for Christmas," "It's Been a Long, Long Time," "I'll Be Seeing You," and "I'll Never Smile Again."

> News Break
> February 18, 1944
> US carrier aircraft destroy 270 Japanese fighter
> planes at Truk Island in the Carolines.

On one of our chaperoned hikes into the nearby mountains, up Cheyenne canyon and up and around Cheyenne Mountain, we were returning downstream following South Cheyenne Creek to the 180-foot drop of Seven Falls. To the side of the falls was a wooden staircase of 224 steps (we had counted them on earlier hikes) that led steeply down to the bottom where there was a trout pond and a souvenir shop. We walked down the steps having fun in the spray of the falls. At the bottom we milled around watching the rainbow trout in the pond and looking at all the curios in the shop. About an hour after we got back to Lincoln Hall, Mrs. Foster rounded up all the hikers and sent us to the living room. Walking into the big room I saw Miss Lloyd and a tall man in the brown uniform of the El Paso County Sheriff's Office. He had a leather holster on his belt with a gun and held a Stetson hat in his hand. My heart beat so hard I could hardly breathe. I knew we had been caught.

Ms. Lloyd softly said, "Have a seat, boys."

We sat, some on chairs and others on the floor.

She then turned to Mrs. Foster. "Is this all of them?"

Mrs. Foster nodded.

"Boys, this is Deputy Sheriff Wilson [pseudonym]. He has something to say to you." She turned and nodded to the deputy, who stepped forward and in a deep commanding voice, "How many of you boys were at the Seven Falls store this afternoon?"

We all raised our hands.

"Well, after you left the store, several items were missing. We have good reason to believe that these items were taken by some of you. If they are not returned, there will be serious consequences."

At this point, Ms. Lloyd stepped forward and said, "I want each one of you to go up to your cubicles, and if you have any of these items, bring them down and put them on the table in the Ping-Pong room. And then return here."

We all trudged upstairs. I got my little brown alabaster bear out of hiding in my closet and took him down to the Ping-Pong table. The table had about a dozen such items on it. We all met back in the living room.

"Is this everything?" Ms. Lloyd asked.

In unison, we said, "Yes, ma'am."

"If this is all of it, there will be nothing more said about this. If things are still missing, there will be a search conducted by the sheriff's office, and if something more is found, the boy or boys responsible will be punished severely, so I ask again, Is this everything?"

In unison, we said, "Yes, ma'am."

She then dismissed us.

Skeet Shooting
At the Cabin We Escape the Fire

"How do you fire this thing?"
Returning home from one of our mountain hikes, four of us left the main group to make a cross-country shortcut and had come upon a skeet shooting range. We figured out how to work the spring-loaded skeet throwers which were mounted in two little wood shacks about thirty yards apart. Having seen skeet shooting in the movies, we knew the small opening in the shack wall was for firing the "clay pigeons" through. There were boxes of the clay discs stacked up in each shack. After using the throwers to send a few discs flying out into nowhere, from each shack, we discovered we could aim the throwers. This knowledge gave us the idea to launch the discs and hit the other shack. The artillery battle was on; two guys in each shack firing clay pigeons at each other; one guy loading, the other firing. The delicate clay birds crashed and shattered against the shacks, making a lot of noise.

None ever came through the opening at either shack. We tired of this after about twenty rounds apiece and hiked on home.

News Break
March 4, 1944
US planes bomb Berlin for first time.

"FIRE! FIRE! WAKE UP!" I awoke to hear Ms. McCarthy yelling.

The cabin was on fire. Some of us had our sleeping cots out on the porch. Others were up in the loft. The kitchen was engulfed in flames. All twenty boys and matron scrambled away to safety. Looking back, I saw the entire cabin was aflame and nearby tall pine trees were burning. This was now a forest fire. The noise of the crackling pine trees burning and the wind blowing was frightening. I had never seen such a sight. The flames reached far up into the night sky, and sparks flew everywhere. The earsplitting, cracking sound of the fire was terrifying. We made our way down the drive to the main road along the creek. We were lucky that William Fritz had gotten up to go to the bathroom and saw the fire in the kitchen. This was my first trip to the big log cabin. It had been built for the home kids to spend a week in each summer. The cabin had a large main room with a stone fireplace. There was a small kitchen and a staircase leading up to a loft for sleeping. We slept on canvas army cots with wool blankets folded in such a way as to affect a sleeping bag. Some of us chose to put our cots on the porch and sleep under the stars which shine bright in the clear mountain air away from the garish lights of civilization, but this, my first night, was a nightmare to remember.

A couple of the older guys took off running down the road to find a telephone. The rest of us stayed with Mrs. McCarthy by the side of the road and waited. We saw the gradual early predawn come, and eventually the clouds were bathed in sunlight. We were all shivering in the early morning mountain air while picking and eating blackberries by the creek. The two runners returned and reported that they had called Miss Lloyd and that a truck would be on the way to pick us up. I don't know how the fire was ever subdued.

The following summers we spent a week at the cabin site, chaperoned by Mr. Tatum, our activities guy. A large tent was raised within the cabin's, still standing, stone foundation. There was a portable generator for electric lighting. The well water pump was still useable and the stone built outhouses were still standing even though the roofs had been burned off. We cooked on the remaining stone grill. Most of the guys slept in the big tent, but a few of us went down in a nearby draw and put up lean-tos, put our blankets down on pine boughs and counted falling stars. Sighting the first star of the evening always elicited this:

> Starlight, star bright,
> First star I see tonight,
> I wish I may,
> I wish I might
> Have the wish I wish tonight.

Down in the draw we were free to do anything we wanted. Someone always had cigarettes. We were a pretty good distance from the main tent and thereby also the outhouses, but we took along toilet paper so that was no inconvenience.

The older guys in the draw took me on a snipe hunt. "Hey, Jack, let's go on a snipe hunt."

"What's that?"

They explained that a snipe was a special kind of bird that lived in the mountains and that the only way to catch them was for one of us to get located up on the mountain side and beat two rocks together while the other guys went down the mountain to drive the snipes up. "The snipes are attracted to the sound of the beating rocks, and will walk right up to you. You pick them up and put them in this gunny sack." I sat in the dark on that mountain side beating two rocks together for about an hour and not a snipe was stirring. I decided to go down and see what the matter was. I could find no one, so I made my way back to the lean-tos. Those guys were all sitting around a campfire roasting marshmallows.

When I walked in to camp, they all laughed.

"Jack did you catch any snipes?"

I realized I was the butt of a prank.

"You dirty rats," I laughed. I felt real dumb. One of the guys handed me a marshmallow right off the coals to pacify me. The following year I was one of the pranksters.

Mr. Tatum told us stories around the campfire. They were of his own creation made up during the telling. "Tootsie the Green-Eyed Mosquito with Silver Spurs" and "Awful Face the Awful" are titles I remember. The plots were long ago robbed from my memory bank. I do remember though that Awful Face married Horrible Face. We were in stitches from the very beginning to the end of these absurd creations.

News Breaks
June 6, 1944
Allied Forces Invade Normandy, France

July 21, 1944
Americans Capture Japanese Held Island of Guam

August **25**, 1944
Paris Liberated

September 15, 1944
American Forces on German Soil

South Junior High School

"Take off your shoes, and run through the sticker field," was the first-day greeting we new seventh graders received at South Junior High School. A bunch of older guys were gathered around initiating the new arrivals. If a neophyte refused to take his shoes off and run through the school ground field of dead weeds containing stickers, they would gang up on him and take his shoes off and shove him onto the field. I refused and was ready to fight the three guys approaching me, but Cousin Duane stepped between them and me.

"He's my cousin," he said no more.

The three guys backed off and sought other prey.

In three happy years at South Junior, I enjoyed intramural sports in softball, basketball, speedball (soccer), and volleyball; we played homeroom against homeroom during the noontime break. My homeroom name was Rustlers. Mr. Wattenburger was our homeroom teacher. He was a tall, well-built man with a balding head and a pockmarked face. He had been the coach at the Boys Club but got tired of spending every night at the club. He controlled the homeroom whenever he needed to, but usually the half hour each morning after he took attendance and made announcements, we spent casually socializing; the guys talking sports, the girls talking guys. My two best friends at school were Harold Potts, a tall, slim colored guy and Don Snell, a short redhead. The three of us made up the nucleus of any and all Rustler sports teams. All others were support staff. We were always in the playoffs, if not champions. One of the stalwarts on the team was a stocky Chicano kid about three years older than the rest of us. Paul Alverez, or Pauly, had flunked a year or two and had dropped out of school on his own one other year. Paul always came to school in a suit with high-waisted, wide-legged, pegged cuff pants, known as drapes. The suit jacket had wide padded shoulders. It was a modified Zoot Suit. He had long gleaming hair combed into a style to become popular, the California DA (duck's ass), or ducktails. His image was every bit the "Pachuco."[38] He carried a switchblade and was always talking in detail about the "chicks" he had screwed. I think he said either "pussy, ass" or "tits" in English or "panocha, "culo," or "tetas" in every other sentence. His antics on the ball court were not any help, what with his shoving, punching. And his swearing at the referees: "Besa mi culo,"[39] or some English utterance just as obscene. He often was kicked off the floor for some offence or other. But Mr. Wattenburger said we had to let everyone play who wanted to. Paul dropped out again toward the end of ninth grade, after teaching me more Spanish than I learned in my general language course.

On game days we "homeys" didn't take the bus back to the home for lunch; instead, we brown-bagged with a lunch meat sandwich, an apple, and a dessert of some kind. I also took part in boxing and track, high jump, pole vault, and fifty- and one-hundred-yard dashes. Track events, rope climbing, calisthenics were coached in the boy's gym class where we changed into khaki-colored gym shorts and white T-shirts. In the locker room some of the guys were really timid about changing clothes in front so many other people. Up to this time, only their parents had seen the skin between their ankles and their neck. Some went to the toilet stalls and others went to stand in the corner to change. After that first day some started to wear their gym clothes under their street clothes on gym days. We from the home were well used to seeing each other run around naked. That's when we snapped each other with towels on bath and shower days. We "homeys" also took long showers together after getting out of the chlorinated swimming pool.

I didn't distinguish myself in track, but in ninth grade going into the boxing semifinals, I was matched with Emilio Garcia, who

---

[38] A young Zoot Suit–wearing Chicano or Mexican gang member.
[39] Kiss my ass.

outweighed me by many pounds. He was a big, fat kid. His biceps were bigger than my waist. I probably weighed no more than his legs. Butterflies were dancing in my stomach before the match. We fought three one-minute rounds. He chased me all over the ring in the first round. He caught up with me a couple of times and each time he telegraphed a big roundhouse punch which I was able to slip away. I went into a clinch with him after the second punch went by. The clinch was a mistake; Emilio walked me all over the ring then threw me against the ropes like he was getting rid of a candy wrapper. The bell rang ending the first round. I hastily sought the safety of my corner bench. That one-minute round seemed like an hour. The sixteen-ounce gloves, the size of small pillows, felt like lead bricks. After a drink and a few minutes' rest, it was announced that he had won the round. I wasn't surprised. I knew I was going to lose this match. Accepting the fact that I was going to lose and realizing that he had not hurt me, I relaxed, and then it came to me that although he was big and strong, he was slow. Maybe I could dance in jab him and back out before he could respond. My plan worked. He was just too slow to catch me. I hit him all over and he never caught me. Many of my punches bounced off his forearms, but scored as punches landed. He was too big for me to hurt and I was too nimble for him to catch. I won the second and third rounds. I now was to fight for the Heavy weight title. The title match was scheduled for the next week. There's not much to tell of the title match. Lee Ornales. A small muscular athlete was strong and fast. I couldn't hit him or catch him. Lee was punching me at will. He won the first two rounds so the third never took place, which saved me from total humiliation. Next to sports and band, I liked singing in the choir. Singing three-part rounds like "Frere Jacques" were the most fun, and easy to get lost in. I remember the hymn: "The Lost Chord" sounded like a lament for the dead. The Negro spiritual "Dry Bones" I found funny. "Down in the Valley" was the easiest to sing. Periodically we would put on our white shirts and black bow ties and give a concert either for the junior high students, the PTA or across the street to entertain the "little kids" at the Lowell grade school. Each morning the three of us in the Color Guard draped in blue and gold capes raised the Stars and Stripes. Actually the other two guys did the raising and I accompanied them with my renditions of "To the Colors." On occasions when the flag was lowered to half-mast, I played the mournful Taps.

It was sad that some kids didn't even get one valentine on Valentine's Day. The valentine cards were put into a box in each homeroom and distributed before class on February 14. The popular kids got lots of cards and the rest got fewer. It was an unfair and insensitive activity. I hope it has been abolished in our schools. I wish I could say that I either sent cards to these kids or that I had shared my cards with them, or had at least complained to the teacher about this injustice, but I was just as insensitive as my peers.

"What is your opinion of our stopping the program?"

This was Miss Snyder, my math teacher, a small bird like skinny little hook-nosed woman, about fiftyish, who wore her coal black hair in a bun pulled so tight that we kids thought it prevented her from ever smiling. Her question to me had to do with a near riot in the auditorium. I don't know what caused it, but we were being shown a movie with the house lights turned off. Someone in the darkness yelled out something teenage-funny, and someone else responded, then a third voice and then another, including my own, till many voices were creating such a cacophony that the teachers monitoring the event, turned the lights on. Silence. "I'm ashamed of all of you." (I never understood why teachers thought their feelings about us had any meaning to us. We all felt that we were non-persons in the eyes of grownups.) These degrading words came out of Miss Snyder.

She went on, "The program will not be resumed. Everyone, return to your classes."

Everyone moaned.

On my way back to class, I encountered Ms. Snyder in the hallway. That's where she sought my opinion, for some reason beyond my limited bank of wisdom.

"You did the right thing. I think the kids now know you will not let them get away with that kind of thing." (If I had learned anything in my thirteen years, it was how to feed grown-ups what they wanted to hear.)

She was so impressed with my response that she stopped another teacher walking by and said, "I want you to hear what this boy has to say. [I don't think she ever knew my name.] Tell her what you just told me." I repeated my for-teachers-only opinion as best I could. (It's hard to repeat a lie verbatim.) "Well, I hope so. That was disgraceful."

She walked on. Ms. Snyder and I walked together to the math class. My math grade didn't improve, and Ms. Snyder never learned my name, nor ever smiled at me. At least when the Lone Ranger rode off, someone asked, "Who was that masked man?" Not Ms. Snyder.

Next to band and gym, my favorite class was woodshop and mechanical drawing. After we built the obligatory book ends, we could choose our own project with the provision that upon completion we pay for the materials we used. I chose to build a desk with a pull-out drawer and shelves at one end. It was sort of art deco in that the shelf end was rounded off. Mr. Archer the teacher thought my choice was pretty ambitious and suggested I should reconsider. I didn't waiver. I wanted to build that desk. He gave in and said: "Well, okay, go to the stock shelves and check out your materials." I worked pretty much independent of his help. "Where did you learn so much carpentry?" He asked. I told him my Grandpa had taught me the most, but the Boy's Club had taught me also. The project turned out well and I got an A grade on it. All along I thought the home would surely pay for the materials. However, when it came time to pay I had left the home and had spent all my savings on a new trumpet and new clothes. I didn't want to ask Mother for money. I knew she had little to spare. I had to leave the desk with the school.

My first real prurient experience came in the eighth grade in a classroom taught by Gertrude Glick, a tall long-legged woman. Her figure was more than beautiful with curves in and out from her ample breasts down to her waist and around her hips and down her long legs. From behind when she walked up the aisle, we pubescent boys watched her marvelous bottom sway back and forth with each step. Those times when she would sit on the front of her desk and cross her legs a little carelessly would cause all her words to be lost to every testosterone-loaded boy in the room. There's no telling how many erections she caused in one day. In addition to the foregoing qualities, she also was very nice. My memory will let me remember no more about that class. I don't remember what she taught and I don't know how I ever passed.

Violet French stabbed me with a pencil in the palm of my hand. It was headed for my heart, but my hand intercepted it. This violent act was committed when she was seated in front of me in general studies class. Her braided pig tails hung down to the front of my desk I lightly pulled on one. I wasn't ready for what happened next: She spun around with the speed of lightning with a pencil in her right hand making a back-hand motion towards my body. Without thinking, I instinctively put up my hands. The sharp pencil lead sunk deep in my palm and broke off. It didn't bleed much before I held a piece of notebook paper over it. The teacher, facing the blackboard, didn't see us. I held the paper over the wound. The pain wouldn't let me concentrate on class. I was glad I wasn't called on for anything.

After class was over, I got to the restroom and put a paper towel on it. The notebook paper was soaked red. I put two extra paper towels in my pocket. All I was thinking was, *How do I stop the bleeding? And how do I prevent teachers and matrons from knowing what happened?* A funny thing was, through all this—the stabbing, the bleeding, which stopped by mid-afternoon, and the pain, which diminished at about the same rate as the bleeding—I felt no animosity toward Violet French. From that point on I felt only that she was a violent person who could hurt me and I better stay away from her. This was pure self-preservation instinct. I kept the paper towel on my hand and went to science class.

"The seat of his pants is so shiny you can see things in the room reflecting off the shine like a mirror." That was the common story we told each other about the pants to the suit science teacher Mr. Sims wore every day for three years. He was slight, of medium height with dark, shiny, neatly combed and oiled, wavy hair. He had dark heavy eyebrows to match his head-hair. His black shoes were as well shined as the seat of his pants. His face and his nose were both thin and sharp and there were well defined natural creases running from each side of his nose, down around his mouth; not from age; he wasn't that old; forty at the most. (I was beginning to see that all grown-ups were not the same age.) Science class offered a modicum of geology, astronomy, biology, chemistry and weather-climate earth science. All of us liked Mr. Sims; he made science fun with all of the experiments. We demonstrated that gasoline fumes are heavier than air and they flow like water, that helium is lighter than air and makes balloons rise We did a biofeedback project showing how the mind can communicate with the hands by using a piece of string and a button. We proved at what temperature water boils and at what temp it freezes. Mr. Sims also had a collection of fossil trilobites in rocks that were imbedded more than a thousand years ago. Out in the school yard we learned the three necessary element of fire; fuel, heat and oxygen. "If we take away any one of these elements, the fire will go out." He made three different fires in metal buckets and extinguished each one by eliminating one of the three elements. He eliminated heat by using water. He removed oxygen from the second fire by smothering it with the bucket lid. The third fire which had been made with some small pieces of kindling wood was put out by removing the wood pieces which had not caught fire yet thus leaving only the one stick to burn out.

> News Break
> March 8, 1945
> Allies cross the Rhine River
>
> March 25, 1945
> Americans capture Okinawa
>
> March 26, 1945
> Iwo Jima Captured
>
> The five-week battle of some of the fiercest and bloodiest fighting of the war has ended.

I think I got my reading habit from wanting a reading certificate with my name on it. These were awarded if you read and wrote an acceptable report on at least five books during the school year. Up to this time, my literary tastes ran to Superman. Popeye, Batman and other like scholarly works. I checked out a book, skimmed through it as fast as I could, wrote a report and checked out another book. With each book I began to run into more and more passages which got my attention. While reading the 5th and final book I was reading and concentrating on most of the sentences and was actually enjoying the reading of it. I've rarely been without a book nearby ever since. All during my navy years I had a paperback in my back pocket. Today I always take a book to read while waiting in Doctor's Offices or when waiting for my wife in the hair salon.

"I was a ninety-seven-pound weakling," read the ad for Charles Atlas's "Dynamic Tension" method of body building. The ad showed a drawing of a skinny wretch in swim trunks having sand kicked in his face by big bullies. Below that was a photo of Charles Atlas in swim trunks posing his very muscular body. This ad ran in every comic book preying on the fantasies of young boys.

In 1945 the news kept breaking fast:

April 12, 1945
President Roosevelt Dies. Vice President Truman sworn in.

April 30, 1945
Adolph Hitler commits suicide.
Russians thrust into Berlin.

May 7, 1945
Germans surrender unconditionally.

July 25, 1945
Italian partisans execute Mussolini and hang him upside down for public display.

August 6, 1945
Atomic bomb dropped on Hiroshima, Japan.

August 9, 1945
Atomic bomb dropped on Nagasaki, Japan.

September 2, 1945
Formal surrender of Japanese Government takes
place on USS *Missouri*.

Shortly after Germany fell and became occupied by the Allied Forces, we began to hear and read of our troops engaging in flourishing black-market operations. Soldiers would buy cigarettes, watches, and cameras at the PX and resell them to Germans and Russians for two hundred times what they paid. A fifty-cent carton of cigarettes would bring one hundred dollars on the black market. War brings out the best in people.

On August 6, 1945, the city of Hiroshima was totally destroyed by the first atom bomb ever used in a war. The death and destruction caused by the bomb in this city, the world had never experienced before. A hundred thousand people were killed, almost all buildings were leveled. The Japanese didn't surrender until after a second atomic bomb was dropped on Nagasaki three days later with the same devastating effect.

The Killing Ends

T he news of President Roosevelt's death was devastating to me as well as others. He was the only president I had known in my thirteen years. I didn't know what we were going to do without a president. I knew nothing about the law of succession, even if I had known I still wouldn't have accepted that people would just automatically name someone else to take his place and think that was alright. My mind finally came around to know it was true, but my heart wouldn't let it go for a long time.

At war's end men and women in uniform began coming back into civilian life. "Taffy" Thompson, a twenty-year-old homey who had served three years in the Marines, drove up to Lincoln Hall where John West, Reggie Burch and I were hanging out in front of the building. Taffy was in civvies and working for a company delivering pastries. He was on his way to Camp Carson. "How would you guys like to take a ride with me out to the PX?" It was our midmorning break. We had about two hours till lunch so we piled into the back seat of his car. "Be careful, those boxes are filled with pastries. You guys can have some, but don't eat them all. They are for the PX." We dug into those boxes and glommed onto those pastries like flies on dung. There were glazed donuts, cream filled Twinkie-like cakes, assorted cookies and brownies. We sampled at least one of each. My favorite by far was the Twinkie. Skimming down the highway to Camp Carson, we were in hog heaven stuffing our mouths and throwing wrappers out the window. Taffy said he made this trip once a week and that if we wanted to he would meet us at the home gate and take us along. Johnnie, Reggie, and I met him a few times after that. We kept it a secret from the other guys.

On one trip back from the PX, Taffy nonchalantly asked, "You guys been getting any lately?"

We knew what he meant, and we three who still had our cherries, in unison, answered nonchalantly, "Naw," like it was a temporary condition or hiatus for us. Taffy knew we didn't get any. Our ages ran from my fourteen years to Johnnie's sixteen. In those days, we thought there were good girls you didn't even try anything with and there were bad girls who would put out. We didn't know any bad girls. The ex-Marine then began telling us stories of his sexual exploits while in the service. We sat up on the edge of the back seat, wiped cake and stuff off our faces with our sleeves and became all ears. Taffy pulled over and parked by the home entrance to continue his tales of conquest. He told of babes with big asses and big tits, officer's wives he fucked, and a hot California dame that put out to all the marines in San Diego. He gave us some of the intimate details we were panting to hear: 'The first pussy I ever felt, it was all wet. I thought she had peed her pants, but that's just the way they are, so don't be surprised when you feel down there." We silently filed that information away for what we hoped would be future use.

"What if you had to pee while you were doing it?" I wanted to know.

"You can't pee when you have a hard on." That's how our sex education took place; older guys passing down what they had heard, not always what they had actually experienced.

Many Splendors

In ninth grade I fell in love with Sally Green, a pretty, vivacious, blond eighth grader. We spent every possible moment together each school day. We laughed together. We held hands, hugged and even kissed while being half hidden by an open locker door. It was an exciting romance. To me, she was the epitome of perfect in every way. She came to all my school sports events. My athletic performances were for Sally; no one else. We ate lunch together on game days. We were only separated during classes. Our affair was the love of innocent children. After school I had to catch the bus back to the home, and Sally walked home with her girlfriends.

Some of the other guys at the home had townie girlfriends also. To carry on our wooing, after Mr. Drumiller, the Dairyman locked up and went home, we climbed through an unlocked window in the dairy to use the phone to call the girls. "Tell her good-by Walker; you've been on the phone for fifteen minutes." While we waited our turn, we sampled cheeses and ice cream. We four Lotharios— Bob Wheeler, Bob Lanari, Maurice Armentrout, and me—snuck off the home on Saturdays now and then to meet with our beloveds to hang out in one of the girl's living rooms. There was lots of hugging and kissing. Nothing heavy. These were "good girls," not "bad girls." We all went for walks together, gabbing, laughing and holding hands. I often imagined being grown up and being married to Sally. In Art class when we were designing homes, my rendering was of a home with a nursery for lots of children belonging to Sally and me. I always wanted a large family. It's funny how you can sometimes remember little things like the time on one of these gatherings when Sally gave me a pair of red ski mittens for my birthday. These clandestine Saturday trysts were truly wonderful fun fairy tale times until the sweet sorrow of parting when we had to take our carriage (City Transit Company) back to the home before it turned into a pumpkin.

There was a burglary at the general store one night. A case of chocolate-cream cookies was missing.

Mrs. Foster called us all into the living room and announced the dastardly deed and asked if any of us knew who had done it. We were all dumb about the event. Some were truly unknowing. "If one of you did this now is the time to confess. If we find out later it was one of you, it will go much harder on you." There was not a peep out of anyone. We just all looked around at each other like we were looking for the culprit. "I will give the guilty one till lights out to come tell me. After that, if no one shows up, there will be a full investigation and the punishment will be severe." She then dismissed us. Johnnie, Reggie, and I would meet periodically down in the basement near a cubby hole in the wall leading to a crawl space to indulge in chocolate cream cookies.

It was a cold but sunny Sunday when Kenny and Uncle Walt, who I thought were at sea with the Navy, came to visit me. My uncle was accompanied by a beautiful young woman. "Jack, this is your Aunt Eileen." I had heard that he got married. I liked her right away. She laughed easily and asked me questions all about my likes and dislikes and she wanted to know all about the home. She seemed so genuine and nice. Although Sally was my true love, I also fell for my new Aunt. In my late teens, in my wallet, I carried a photo of her taken when she was eighteen. I would show it off as my girlfriend.

While peeing and gazing into the large urinal in front of me, the question came to me: "Why is it we can talk about tears, a fluid draining from our eyes, but it's not acceptable in polite company to talk about pee or poop coming out of our bodies?" and "Why is this called a rest room? Nobody rests here." I also wondered if it was really true that shiny patent leather shoes would act as a mirror which would reflect up under a girl's dress. I never found out.

Grandma Dies

I Leave the Home

Grandma had suffered with abdominal cancer for about a year of radium therapy before she died in 1946. Mother, Betty, and Aunt Edith had returned from Texas to take care of her. It was late afternoon. I was in the basement practicing my music lesson.

"Your mother is here to see you, Jack," Mrs. Foster announced.

It wasn't Sunday. I was confused. I went upstairs and there was Mother and Aunt Edith. Mother, deeply somber, said, "Let's go to the car." I thought I was in trouble of some kind, but I couldn't think of what of the many rules of conduct I had violated that would call for Mother to have to come see me. We got into the car, three of us in the front seat of Aunt Edith's DeSoto. I was sandwiched in the middle. I had developed butterflies in my stomach. We drove down by the duck pond and parked. Mother held my hand and softly said: "Grandma died last night." I was stunned. I felt numb and disconnected. All my senses went numb. Mother's voice became far off: I had no idea what she was saying. She hugged me for a long time. I don't know how much time had elapsed before her voice returned to normal. My butterflies turned into tears cascading down my cheeks. I couldn't actually cry. I couldn't speak. "The funeral will be held Friday. Ms. Lloyd has given permission for you to attend if you want."

I still couldn't speak, and I didn't want to hear anyone else speak. I wished she would just shut up about it.

"Do you want to attend?"

"No!" I barked. I just wanted her to leave me alone. The three of us sat in silence for how long, I have no recollection. The sun had long since settled behind Cheyenne Mountain. We were now on the shady side. The sun's rays were only showing on the highest clouds. The air grew cool. "I have to go to dinner."

I wanted them to leave and take this situation with them so I could get back to my life. I was dropped off at the building. Mother kissed me and said: "Call me if you want to talk. I'll be out to see you Sunday."

She drove away, and I drove all that ugly conversation out of my head, but I still couldn't shake off the strong sadness and loneliness I felt. I didn't relate it to the message Mother had delivered. It seemed like a bad dream. Sleep didn't come easy. It was a chore to eat. Slowly I went through day upon day of "poor me" to "Why wasn't I nicer to her" to "How could the family let this happen? Did anyone even try to help her? Who was the quack doctor that let her die?" to "I hate cancer. What is it? Why hasn't someone found a cure?" Mother had told me sometime previous that Grandma had cancer and was being given radium treatments. I thought that was a cure, not just a put-off of the inevitable. During that time, I preferred to be alone whenever the choice was mine. I went out into the ravines alone and cried.

I pounded my fists into the earth. My knuckles were red and swollen. At school I just sat through each class until the bell rang, not knowing what was taking place. I think if I had let myself cry a little more, it wouldn't have eaten on me so long. However, in time I came to accept that no one was at fault but at times I forgot that Grandma had died and then the reality would hit me again. Total acceptance took months. I guess losing someone dear to you is part of coming of age.

It was a cold Sunday afternoon in early November 1946 when Mother came to visit. First she told me that I had a new cousin, that Uncle Walt and Eileen had a baby boy. "They named him Michael." Later on in her visit she, out of nowhere, said "What would you think if I went to see Miss Lloyd about taking you out of the home?" I couldn't believe what I heard. Was this an idea that just crossed her mind?

"Do you mean it?" Her record of keeping promises wasn't good.

"Yes, I mean it. If you want to leave, I'll call Ms. Lloyd tomorrow."

"Yes, I really want to leave." I didn't ask where or with whom I would live, where I would go to school or any practical questions. I just thought of the freedoms this presented: I could wear stylish clothes, I could smoke cigarettes, I could walk home after school with Sally Green. I could stay up late at night.

"I want you to promise me one thing."

I interrupted her. "I promise I'll get a job and I'll work around the house and stuff." I wanted to assure her I wouldn't be a burden in case she had second thoughts.

"That's not what I'm talking about. What I want you to promise is that you won't talk to anyone about this until I get it all settled."

I promised her I would not talk even though every part of me wanted to scream it from the mountain tops. She called me Monday evening and informed me that Ms. Lloyd was going to take care of all the paper work and that I should be able to leave by Saturday. She asked if I had told anyone yet. I lied. I had told my best friend Richard Allen and swore him to secrecy. Somehow every guy in the building knew about it. Richard said he had only told his sister but had sworn her to secrecy so we figured Miss Lloyd must have said something to Mrs. Foster. The waiting until Saturday was almost unbearable. Each hour of the day dragged. I told Sally and my two "Townie" homeroom friends.

The most popular book of 1946 was Dr. Benjamin Spock's "Common Sense Book of Child and Baby Care." Rather than teaching children to respect authority, Spock taught parents to instead be more considerate of the child's feelings and preferences. Many parents were influenced by Spock. I often heard young mothers start a sentence with "Dr. Spock says." There are those today that feel that the post war children of the "baby boom" grew to become the coddled, self-indulgent, self-gratifying, Spock-raised "me" generation. If it feels good, do it to excess.

In retrospect, I look back at the home with fondness and a great sense of gratitude. It was an unbelievable place for orphans and other needy children to grow up. It was a far cry from the Oliver Twist work house of half-starved urchins. And we didn't have to earn our board and keep like Little Orphan Annie. We had all the advantages, and more, that money could buy, we just didn't have the traditional family. The home provided security, stability, and freedom from want. I didn't appreciate it at the time, but I now think that Mother's decision to take me out was a mistake, as will be revealed in the following trials and results of my high school dilemma. To place me there she had to show a need. To get the home to release me to her care, she had to show that the need no longer existed. I don't know what changed. I suppose there was a means test of some sort.

Even though I didn't appreciate it at the time, the home was unquestionably a great place to be for a poor kid of a struggling single mother during the war years.

Postwar Teens Freedom's Charms

Freedom has a thousand charms to show, that
slaves, howe'er contented, never know.
—William Cowper, 1731–1800

If freedom is the absence of unwarranted rules and an opening to
do a lot as you wish, then in my fifteen-year-old mind, I was free
on the day I left the home for good. Mother came as promised to
take me to my new home. It was a cold but sunny Saturday morning
in December as I anxiously stood near the front door of the building
looking down the road for her to come. By the door all my clothes
and personal things were neatly packed in two large cardboard boxes.
I was leaving much richer (in more ways than I knew) than when I
arrived. Earlier I had turned in my trumpet to Mr. Fink. We skipped
my music lesson and just talked a little.

"Jack, I hope you continue with your music. You've come too
far to stop now." With that, he gave me the name of a teacher in town
he wanted me to see. "I'll call him and tell him you will be getting in
touch with him. Will you do that?"

"Yes, sir."

He handed me a slip of paper with the teacher's name and phone
number. Mr. Fink patted me on the back and wished me good luck.

Life on the Outside

A s we drove out under the entrance arch of the home, I was thinking of what my new life would be like, staying up late, smoking
cigarettes, and walking Sally home every afternoon in the new, stylish
clothes I would buy. I had saved up five hundred and some dollars in
my five and a half years at the home. It was given to me in a savings
pass book in my name. I knew the first thing I would buy would be
a pair of Penny Loafers, some almost white corduroy pants. White
sweat socks, T-shirts, and some neat shirts. At the home we wore
the more sensible but less stylish darker colors. Next, I would buy
a new untarnished trumpet like the ones I saw in Downbeat and
Metronome played by Harry James, Louis Armstrong, and Bunny
Berigan. I could hear my new shiny trumpet sounding "I Can't Get
Started" just like Bunny Berigan. He had died about the same time I
went to the home, but his music continued to be played on the radio
and if I had any style it was influenced by him.

My new home was at 1705 North Nevada Avenue; a nice house
in an upper class neighborhood. The North side generally was known
to be the domain of those with incomes well beyond the subsistence
level. Aunt Edith owned the house and lived there with Mother, Betty
and Florence "Johnnie" Johnson, a roomer/friend/nurse. Aunt Edith
and Mother shared a bedroom upstairs. Johnnie had the downstairs
room and Betty had the other upstairs room. Mother explained to
me that it had been agreed that Johnnie would be leaving as soon as
she could find another place. "Until then you can share a room with
Betty. She will sleep on the cot and you can have the bed. Betty will
move downstairs when Johnnie leaves."

Though in junior high, we were allowed to try out for the high school football B squad. I made the team, but didn't stay for the season. This wasn't my game. Macho peer pressure pushed me in to it. The first day of practice I was standing on the sidelines watching the guys run plays. "Are you running?" the coach yelled at me. I didn't hear him clearly. I thought he wanted to know who I was. What I heard was something like, "Are you Runyon?"

"I'm Walker!" I yelled back.

"Get your smart ass over here."

I walked over to him. He was a big, gorilla-size guy with a beat-up face. His voice sounded like his throat was filled with ground glass; very intimidating. He was as loud, rough-looking, and acting as the head coach George Porter was smooth and soft-spoken. Porter was brains; this guy was muscle. "Drop down and give me one hundred pushups." While I was on the ground pumping up and down, the action on the field moved away, and the coach was no longer standing above me. I quit somewhere in the forties. I stayed on the team long enough to play in the first preseason game against the Deaf and Blind School. All the guys on their team were deaf. I don't, to this day, know how they called signals silently. Just all of a sudden out of the silence, their center would hike the ball and at the same time their entire team was in motion. They were tough too; when you attempted to tackle one of their running backs, he would just grunt and run right through you. My football career ended in the second quarter of that first game: I was attempting a low tackle on a running back. His heel kicked into my forehead right between the eyes. I was helped off the field by two team mates. By the time we reached the sideline and I got seated on the bench, my nose and forehead had swollen to the point that my eyes were almost covered up. I was looking through small slits. The coach asked: "Who's your family doctor?"

"Dr. Brian." (Mother's employer.)

"Where's his office?"

"Down town on Tejon Street."

"Any you guys got a bike?"

A couple guys stepped up, and the coach told one of them to give me a ride to the doctor's office. I rode on the handlebars of the bike barely able to see as we wound in and out of the five or six blocks of down town traffic. "Well what happened to you?" Mother asked. I told her the story. She put an ice pack on my eyes and the swelling went down some. "You sit here for a while then I want you to take the bus home." At home I got a look at my face in the bathroom mirror. I looked like a panda with my two black eyes. That's the whole story of my short unimpressive football career.

Betty introduced me to hillbilly music on the radio. To be polite while we were reacquainting from our five-year separation, I listened with her to the strains of Ernest Tubb, Red Foley, Bob Wills and his Texas Playboys, Eddy Arnold, "The Tennessee Plowboy," and Tex Ritter. All this stuff came to us from some radio station in Del Rio Texas. I actually considered this music as being for hay seed, backward hicks. One of their commercials I remember well—"Get your statue of Jesus Christ, it glows in the dark."

"Jack, don't expect a lot of Christmas gifts like you had at the home," Mother cautioned.

"That's okay. I don't expect anything. I'm just glad to be home." Christmas morning there were gifts under the tree. A large gift box had my name on it, and when I opened it, I recognized the new suit I had been fitted for at the home. All the other gifts from the home were under the tree also. Aunt Edith told me they had been delivered one day while I was at school.

I was allowed to stay at South Junior for the rest of the school year, even though I now lived in the North Junior district. Each morning Mother packed me a lunch and gave me a dime for bus fair to school. The student fare was five cents one way. Nonstudents could buy the little dime-size bronze tokens with the CS stencil cut issued by the bus company, which were sold in amounts as few as three, or packs of fifty or so and were cheaper to use than currency. I didn't always ride the bus. Weather permitting, I would walk the twenty-three blocks straight down Nevada Avenue and pocket the dime. Ten cents would buy a two-scoop ice cream cone. If I bought a one-scoop, I'd have a nickel to spare. After school I walked home with Sally and then walked up the railroad tracks to go home. Some mornings I would get up early and walk the tracks down to Sally's so I could walk to school with her. I spent a lot of time with Sally after school and on weekends. Her mother often asked if I wished to have dinner with them. I once in a while accepted.

Sally's father, a fireman, once asked, "Does he live here?"

John Green barked, but he was nice to me. The Greens would include me when they went to the race track out east of town on Highway 24.

"I hope the wind's blowing north tonight," Mr. Green would say in reference to the fact that the race track was south of the Babcock Hog Farm. It was a small race track used for midget race cars and stock cars. This was our Indianapolis 500 and locally the drivers were just as famous as the Indy drivers. The most famous race in Colorado Springs was on the mountain: the Pikes' Peak Hill Climb. And the most famous mountain race car driver was Louis Unser, known endearingly by locals as "The Old Man of the Mountain." The race was twelve miles up the mountain to the 14,110-foot summit. The road was gravel with over a hundred turns some of which were hairpin curves with deadly drop offs. From the start to the summit the track rises 4720 feet. Louie Unser had a total winning record of nine titles, three second and two third place finishes. Some of these races were against Indy 500 drivers. Two more generations of Unsers went on to win as much or more than Louie. But for my generation, he was the legendary native son and "King of the Mountain."

Mother to Mom

Music Career

It was not easy for Mother to have a fifteen-year-old boy in the house who she hardly knew. For the past 5 years I had been raised by strangers. She had not been privy to my development from a 10-year old to this youth who now stood taller than her. I think especially appealing but yet uncomforting was my formal manners: "Yes, ma'am," "No, ma'am," "May I be excused?" (when leaving the dinner table), and "May I go to?" (when wanting to go somewhere). The longer I lived with her, the more I began to feel of her as a friend rather than an adult and gradually dropped all the formalities and we became the closest of friends for the rest of her life. From this time on I called her Mom.

I had bought a lot of new stylish clothes, including penny loafers, white cords, some shirts, and a reversible wind breaker. Now I needed a good trumpet. In the music store on North Tejon Street, I picked out a beautiful golden Reynolds trumpet. The salesman said I could try it out in the back room. Back among the shelves and boxes, I ran my fingers over the trumpet valves. I hardly had to press them at all. They moved to the slightest touch. Not like my old horn. The mouth piece was the newer larger size which was easier on the lips. The bell was beautifully engraved and the valve finger buttons were inlaid pearl. I blew hot breath into it before inserting the mouthpiece and again softly breathed into it after it was inserted. This warms the metal for a more mellow tone. I ran some scales first just to warm up. The valves responded to my touch with such ease and the tones emitting from the bell were like nothing I had ever known. I ran a few riffs to get acquainted then broke into "Ciribiribin" followed by "When the Angels Sing." About this time a young woman of twenty-some years, I guessed, came back in the store room.

I stopped playing. "You're very good where did you learn to play like that?"

"I studied with Mr. Fred Fink at the Stratton Home."

"Well, you're certainly good, are you with a band?"

"No. I played with the Stratton Home Symphony, and I'm in the South Junior band."

"I sing with a small swing dance band and our trumpeter can't make it to our next dance for Peterson Field Saturday night. Would you be interested in sitting in? You'll get five dollars for the evening." (This is about sixty dollars in 2016.)

"Sure, I would," I said, trying to hold my elation in check. "Where do I go?"

She gave me directions and a phone number. "I'm sure the guys will be glad. We've been worried about what to do with half our brass section gone."

The other half was a trombone. After we shook hands and exchanged names (her name was Vera), she went back up to the sales room. After blowing the spit out, I wiped the trumpet with the soft cloth I found in the red velvet-lined case and carefully placed the horn inside, snapped it shut, and carried it up front with the intention of buying it. It struck me, while walking up to the front of the store, *I wonder how much it costs.* I had spent a lot of money on clothes. I only had a little over three hundred dollars left in my savings account and this was a real professional instrument like the horns played by Harry James, Louis Armstrong and Bunny Berrigan. Vera was at the cash register. I placed the case up on the counter. "I'd like to buy this. How much is it?"

"Just a minute, let me check" She got some information from inside the case and looked through some papers in a file drawer. "Here it is. That trumpet lists at $289, but since you are now a professional musician, there is a ten per cent discount." She did some figuring with pencil and paper. "Jack you can have that trumpet for $265.30 including tax."

"Okay, hold it for me. I have to go to the bank to get some money." My savings account showed a balance of nearly three hundred dollars. I took it all and closed the account. Back at the music store I bought a Harmon mute, a straight mute and an advanced trumpet method book. From this point on I was going to have to be self-taught. The mutes and the book cut deeply into my forty or so left over dollars and I still had to go to the dime store to buy a toilet plunger to mute with. "See you Saturday Jack." In brief, I took the bus out near Peterson field and began my professional music career. The music was all standard swing ballads and not difficult at all. I even treated myself to a few improvisations on the solos. At the end of the gig the band leader paid me and my professional career was over.

News Break
April 15, 1947
Robinson Breaks Color Barrier

Jackie Robinson breaks major league color barrier as first Negro player. He will start today at first base for the Brooklyn Dodgers.

Summer in the City

Sally and I decided to break up toward the end of the school year, since I was going on to high school and she still had a year to finish in junior high. I was saddened about the breakup, and at the same time, I was looking forward to my first summer away from the home. I envisioned getting a job and having some money. Don Snell, from my homeroom, was the only friend I had outside of the home, and he moved away right after school closed. I walked the downtown streets asking businessmen if they needed anyone. I also checked the want ads in the gazette *Telegraph*.

I forget how I made the connection, but I wound up as the infield coach for the younger Little League baseball clinic held at Monument Valley Park three mornings a week. My picture was in the newspaper with a caption something like: Jack Walker goes through his paces as infield coach, etc. I was made to pose for the picture as if I were fielding a grounder. I treasured this picture for years. I don't know where it is now. Maybe my daughter Valerie has it. One of the coaches at the clinic was also coaching the American Legion baseball team sponsored by Blick's Sporting Goods.

"You used to play for the Stratton Home, didn't you?" he asked.

I told him I had. He asked if I would like to play for Blicks. I went to a couple of practice sessions and was made the shortstop.

While continuing my search for a real job, I ran into a classmate, Bob Matheson, who was also trying to find a job. We both had knocked about all the doors downtown to no avail.

"Let's go over to Manitou and look," I suggested.

"How do we get there? I don't have any money."

"We can hitchhike," which we did.

Manitou, though in full swing with the tourist season, was to disappoint us just as Colorado Springs had.

"Let's go catch a ride up to the Cave of the Winds."

We walked up past the "Manitou water" pump to the road leading up to the Cave. We watched the old Pierce Arrow touring cars go up the road filled with tourists who all waved at us. Being a tour driver seemed to me to be the best job in the world. We caught a ride to the entrance and asked the guy at the entrance if they needed any help. He told us that all the summer Guides had been hired and there just wasn't any help wanted. We walked back down the mountain road and caught a ride back home. Bob and I agreed to meet at Busy Corner the next morning. After we exchanged phone numbers we parted. I walked the seventeen blocks home and up in my room listening to the radio. It was about 5:00 p.m., when the phone rang. Aunt Edith answered it. "Jack it's for you. It's your sister." I wondered what she wanted.

"There's a Busboy Wanted sign in the window of the Blue Spruce restaurant. If you get down here right away maybe you can get a job."

I got off the phone, borrowed a nickel from Aunt Edith, caught a bus downtown, talked to the head waitress, and went to work on the spot.

The Blue Spruce

Sex, Almost

The Blue Spruce Restaurant was the largest and most popular restaurant in town. It was located right downtown on Pikes Peak Avenue near Tejon Street. It was busy day and night. I was introduced to Doug, a guy in a white jacket who wasn't much older than me. "Get Jack a jacket and show him what to do. He'll work the back four booths and two tables." I followed Doug back through some swinging doors. He went through the right door. I started to push open the left, when it flew back at me. I almost collided with a waitress hurrying from the kitchen to the dining room with a tray held high on her shoulder. I stumbled back awkwardly and managed an "excuse me."

"Watch where you're going," she said without missing a step, nor even giving me a look.

I could have been a dog in her way. It would have been given the same cutting retort. The kitchen was a large hot busy and noisy place with waitresses coming and going and cooks yelling out orders. The smells were wonderful. There was a salad Chef working behind a counter with large clear glass door refrigerators behind him. A long steam table filled with soups, sauces, and vegetables of all kinds. Behind the steam tables four cooks/chefs in tall puffy white hats, and white jackets that had two rows of five buttons that looked like tied knots. All had Mandarin collars. Their pants were sort of black and white finely checkered looking. There were ovens and grills with meats frying and baking. One chef was carving slices off the largest piece of beef I had ever seen. Back behind the kitchen was a room with a long table with benches on both sides. This is where the employees eat." Next to that room was the dish washing machines which were manned by two men scraping, washing and drying just like at the home.

After being fitted with a starched white jacket, Doug took me to my assigned station. A booth had just emptied.

Doug pulled a large aluminum tray from a stack nearby and said, "When someone leaves, we clear the table as soon as possible and reset it for the next people. If the table cloth is soiled we change it. There are table clothes in that cabinet where I got the tray. When new people are seated you pour them water from the pitchers over there. The silverware is in the drawers."

He taught that when pouring water, you don't just pour into the glass on the table. You pick up the glass and pour it three quarters full and place it back on the table and that at the tables always serve from the left side. "We also pour the coffee and the tea and watch to see if someone wants a refill. The more service you give will get you more tip money." Doug explained that the waitresses were required to chip in ten percent of their tips for the bus boys and if you did an extra good job for some waitress, they sometimes would give you something extra. 'There's only three of us so we're kept really busy trying to keep up with fourteen booths and twelve tables.

I had been hired to work straight nights from three to eleven. This meant I couldn't play baseball for Blick's Sporting Goods. The job went well. I was kind of slow and awkward at first, but I became much better and eventually earned extra tips on a regular basis, as Doug had said would happen. It was a hectic job with very few moments of rest. The large restaurant was busy always. The hard working, fast moving waitresses were all nice to me. I was even the favorite busboy to a few of them. Off the dining room was a bar room and upstairs was another bar which I remember had a dance floor. I reported for work one afternoon and was told I would be going to the city jail to serve dinner to the prisoners. This sounded scary. I'd be locked up with killers, thieves and other criminal types. One of the cooks got me all lined up with eight covered metal canisters.

Each had been filled with a large hot dinner. The cans were snapped together in two carrying racks, four to a rack. I carried the racks up to the police department and told the cop at the desk what I had. He said, "Wait a minute, I'll get an officer to take you back there. *Oh my God I'm going to need an armed cop to take me "back there," wherever "back there" was.* I pictured a dark dungeon filled with blood thirsty murderers and such. A smiling policeman came through the doorway and said: follow me." I followed him a few yards down a well-lit corridor to a large lighted room with bars. Inside the cell guys were milling around two guys sat at a table playing cards. As soon as they saw me, the card game stopped and those just milling around went and sat at the table. They were all in civilian clothes, no striped prison garb like I expected killers to be wearing. The officer unlocked the gate.

"Put the cans on the table and bring the racks back out here."

As I lay down each canister, a prisoner took it. I took the racks back outside the gate. The officer locked it and showed me where to leave my racks.

"Yesterday's cans are over here. Take them back with you."

This became my daily job for the rest of my Blue Spruce career. I learned that my murderers were actually being held for such things as drunk driving, petty theft, driving without a license, etc. About two weeks after I came here, the head waitress quit, and the restaurant hired a head waiter named Sam. He was an impressive looking tall dark haired guy who wore a uniform of white tuxedo shirt with black buttons, black bow tie, white Eton jacket, black tuxedo pants and highly polished black shoes. He looked like a regular big city maître d'. Sam took a liking to me and made me busboy-at-large, meaning I was to scan the whole dining room and pitch in wherever I might be needed. He also let me wait on tables when the waitresses were busy. This allowed me to make some pretty good tips. He taught me many things about the servers craft: He emphasized that if I were a waiter I should get to the table within two minutes after everyone in the party is seated, smile and greet them with, "Good evening, I'm Jack. I will be your waiter this evening. Would you care for anything to drink before you order?" As I was only fifteen, Sam told me to take the liquor orders and bring them to him to serve. "Never eat or chew gum while waiting tables and never initiate conversation with the people you're serving. If your jacket gets soiled, even a little bit, change it as soon as possible. Nobody wants to be served by a sloppy looking waiter." There was more. I don't know for sure. But I think all this advice paid off in tips.

Out in the kitchen the banter between waitresses and cooks was often bawdy if not downright dirty for my tender ears: "Hey, Louise, I bet you'd like to have this." The cook had stuffed something down in his crotch creating a large bulge. As he spoke, he held his hand on the bulge and shook it. Louise looked at him while she was taking plates off the steam table. She laughed at him and responded, "If you mean would I like a head of rotten cabbage in my pants, the answer is no." I knew every dirty word and expression like any teenage boy, but I had never witnessed this kind of conversation between men and women. At first I was embarrassed and pretended I didn't hear it, but this one cook kept it up all night every night. He was put down every time regardless of which waitress he accosted, "Hey, Carol, wanna play hide the weenie with me?"

"Your weenie is so small it's always hidden."

After I got over being embarrassed by this palaver, I then began to overhear waitresses use words and phrases I thought only "bad" girls used. More than often I heard waitresses exclaim, "Shit, fuck you, shove it up your ass, bitch." They also conversed about "giving it" to some guy last night. There were expressions like, "I fell head over heels in bed with him." They didn't seem to care weather I heard them or not. I guess they thought I was just a dumb kid. They were right.

It was mid-July when I was asked if I wanted to go on a midnight picnic which was being put together by the waitresses. "We'll go out to Austin Bluffs after work Friday night." Doug the busboy said he was going to bring a gallon jug of wine and would give me a ride. It was a moonlit night in the Bluffs. We ate sandwiches, pickles, olives, and potato salad, all brought by the cooks. It was a fun time listening to all the banter and laughter. Ava May, a pretty waitress who was a nineteen-year-old college student from Texas asked me If

I would like to go for a walk with her. As we walked along a moonlit trail, she held my hand. I was thrilled that this beautiful red-haired nineteen-year-old young woman would want to hold my hand. We walked for a while then turned around and went back to the picnic. Ava got a blanket out of her car. "Here we can spread this out over there behind those rocks and lie down and watch the stars in the sky." As we lay there holding hands, she rolled over facing me and put our hands between her legs. I turned and faced her, and we kissed. She brushed her tongue over my lower lip. It felt good so I opened my mouth a little, and she slipped her tongue into my mouth, touching my tongue. It was my first French kiss. We held each other tighter and continued to exchange tongues as she squeezed her thighs tighter over our hands. I was so excited I was trembling. Ava unbuttoned her jeans and placed my hand inside her panties. This was ecstatic. I was stiff with excitement. "Hey, where did Jack and Ava go?" came a loud voice from the group. I withdrew my hand, and Ava buttoned her jeans.

"Here they are."

We got up and joined the group. The rest of the night I hung out with the group and drank lots of wine. Doug took me home drunk. I slept on the couch for what remained of the night. That was my first being drunk, and when I awoke, I experienced my first hangover. My head truly felt like it was split by an axe. Mom knew the symptoms. "What you need is a hair of the dog that bit you." What in the hell was she talking about?

She returned with a shot glass. "Here, drink this." It was whiskey. The smell almost made me throw up. "Drink it."

Is she crazy?

"Go ahead, drink it, you'll feel better."

It went down and stayed down.

"What were you drinking?"

"Wine."

"Never drink wine. Stay with beer and good whiskey. Wine is poison."

I slept the day away and went back to work that evening still feeling a little woozy and vowing never to drink wine again.

Next day back at the Blue Spruce everyone was in good spirits. Ava treated me like we had never met. I was dumbfounded. Did I do something wrong?

"La donna e mobile."

She quit about two weeks later to return to Texas.

Odone's

The week following the party Sam announced that he was quitting to go to work at the newly opened Odone's restaurant. A week later, he came by the Blue Spruce and told me they were looking for a busboy and that he had told them about me. He said they paid the busboys thirty-five cents an hour plus tips. The next day I went to Odone's and spoke to Gino Odone, one of the two brothers who owned the restaurant. He was very soft-spoken. I could hardly hear him. His hair was coal black and slicked down like the 1920s pictures I had seen of Rudolph Valentino. He said he needed a busboy who could also wait tables. And work shifts eleven to seven, or three to eleven. "Sam tells me you are the person I should hire." His face tried to smile. "When can you start?"

The following Monday at 10:30 a.m., I showed up at Odone's in my white shirt, bow tie and black pants. I met Jimmy George, the head waiter, a stocky middle aged guy with a big smile. "Sam tells me you can do it all" He got me one of the short white Eton jackets just like the waiters. There were no women working here. The place was all new with wall-to-wall thick plush carpeting. Sam was in the group around the bussing station when Jimmy introduced me to the waiters. The four young waiters were all college boys. They were fun to work with. That summer they taught me the lyrics to "Abdul Abulbul Amir" and the poem "The Shooting of Dan Magrew." Odone's was small; there were only four waiters in the dining room and Sam worked the tables in the lounge. I was the only busboy.

Baseball or Base Pay

There was a Colorado Springs all-star baseball team being formed. I tried out for an infield position and was chosen as the shortstop. I had an old worn out pair of baseball shoes that I held together with friction tape. The guys used to rib me about patching the hole in the soles with the funny papers. "Hey Jack, What's Popeye doing today?" Our games were to be played at Memorial Park which was acres and acres of prairie with a stingy baseball diamond on it. The first game we played was on a Saturday afternoon, against a Denver team. I don't remember who won I only remember we drew the biggest crowd I had ever seen at a ball game. Even Mom and Grandpa came. There was even an announcer on a loudspeaker: "WALKER GOES DOWN SWINGING." The game was scheduled early enough for me to still get to work on the late shift at Odone's. The next game we had was scheduled during a time when I was expected to be at work. I told the coach I couldn't play. He came to Odone's and talked with my boss who then let me off for the game. I later had to just quit baseball all together. The team was going to be travelling to other cities. I needed my job. I had promised Mom I would work and pay for my clothes and spending money. Even during the school year.

Kenny had gotten married in Australia and had sent word that his bride would be coming to America to await his soon to be discharge. Nancy, the new Mrs. Lankard arrived at 1705 North Nevada Avenue on what date I have no inkling, but I do know I fell for her right away. She was beautiful, warm and full of humor, and her accent was really cool. She and I hit it off right away. One time when I had just come from the bathroom Nancy remarked, "Jack, your pants are unzipped," so I zipped them up. "You zip your pants in front of a lady?"

"You want me to unzip them. I can do that." I reached for my fly.

"Oh, Jack, you're such a clown."

We would carry on like that all the time. When Kenny came home, they moved to a place of their own and he went to work for Douglas Jardine, a former Admiral in the "Sea Bees"(CBs Construction Battalion). Jardine's construction company hired a lot of ex-navy men.

Uncle Walt came home from the war with the beautiful Eileen. He went right back to work for Lorigs "peddling rags" as he used to call selling clothes. Also he and Vern Pollart, his long-time friend at Lorig's, bought and sold income properties on the side. They even leased the second floor above Lorig's and rented out rooms. At one point Grandpa had a room up there and served as the manager. My uncle tried many things on the side; he bought and sold used cars after cleaning the engine with kerosene.

"If you clean the engines this way it doesn't look so obvious that it was just done to sell the car. It looks like an engine that has been taken care of."

He tried carpentry also; with help from his neighbor, he was building a garage one Sunday when Grandpa and I drove up. The two builders were up on ladders with a long board to be used as a rafter. One was holding it up at the ridge beam while the other was holding the lower end down at the top wall plate. The each had a pencil and were marking the board where they would have to cut it.

"What are you doing?" Grandpa asked.

"We're measuring the angle for the rafters," Uncle Walt replied.

"Here, take your ruler and measure from the top plate to the top of your ridge beam. Now measure from the wall to the center here." He pointed. "Now we know the run and the rise." He did some math with his pencil on a rafter board laying across two saw horses. He then took the framing square and drew an angled line at each end of the board. He picked out a cross-cut saw from his son's tool box and was about to start sawing when Uncle Walt almost jumped off the ladder and said: Dad-What are you doing?"

"I'm cutting you a rafter." He started sawing along the line he had made on the board.

"Dad, we only have just enough boards for this job. We can't afford to experiment with a board."

"Don't worry. This board will fit."

After he made the second cut, he said, "Here, try this." They hoisted it up and it fit perfectly. Grandpa measured and marked the rest of the rafters and left the sawing to the two would-be carpenters.

Aunt Edith and the Jug

"It's so hard to believe that such a competent nurse could be like this."

Aunt Edith was a sure enough problem drinker. She only knew how to drink till she passed out, like that was the sole purpose of drinking. Many a time I watched Mom try to wake her and get her sober enough to get to work. (She was an RN at the Saint Francis Hospital, where Mom worked.) Mom would force black coffee down her and put cold wet towels on her head. Edith would give a goofy smile and drift off. Mom would slap her.

"EDITH, WAKE UP."

Sometimes Mom's efforts paid off, and sometimes she would have to call the hospital and make excuses for her absence. Mom tried hiding the liquor bottles, but Edith was clever. She somehow knew to look under the bed, in the dirty clothes hamper, in the oven and in the washing machine. She also knew all the nooks and crannies in the basement and the garage.

Every time Edith got drunk and passed out, Mom would say to me, "It's so hard to believe that such a competent nurse could be like this."

One night when I came home, Edith was passed out on the couch.

Her hair was a mess. One shoe was off, and her skirt was pushed up way above her knees. She had vomited all over her blouse. I got her awake and got her upstairs and in to the bed. I took her soiled blouse off her and put it in the bath tub. At breakfast next morning she was her cheerful self and said nothing of the night before. On another occasion I came home to the same scene only this time the living room was filled with smoke and flames were leaping from the couch. I dragged Edith off the couch and on to the floor. I then doused the flames with several pots of water. The front door was still open and smoke was pouring out. I hoped no neighbors would see this and call the fire department. Edith was still on the floor, and I couldn't wake her, so I put a chair cushion under her head. Mom was working the late shift and didn't get off till eleven. Betty was out with some friends.

Mom got home and saw the mess, including her sister on the floor. "This is the last straw. I'm putting her in Brady's."[40]

"Should we get her upstairs to bed?"

"No. Let her stay on the floor. She can see what she caused when she wakes up. We'll throw a blanket over her, and she'll be okay."

Next morning Edith asked what had happened. She had found her way upstairs and into bed sometime during the night.

Mom told her what had happened and in an extremely pissed-off tone, "Edith, someday you'll burn the house down with all of us in it. This has got to stop."

Mom went on to berate her sister. Edith just gave one of those Scarlet O'Hara "I'll think about it tomorrow" shrugs and poured herself another cup of coffee. I was eating as fast as I could so I could get out of there. A couple of nights later when I got home, Mom was home. She said she had found Edith passed out drunk in the dry bathtub fully clothed and that she had called an ambulance to take her to Brady's.

"She fought the ambulance drivers, and they had to put her in a straitjacket. In the morning I have to go sign some papers to admit her for detoxification."

---

[40] Brady's is a small psychopathic hospital in Colorado Springs. It is often attended by the rich and famous incognito. Alcoholics Anonymous was in its infancy at the time.

255

The Joy Ride

Edith was held at Brady's three days against her will. While she was gone, her car keys were in a bowl on the kitchen table. I had the less-than-bright idea of using her car even though I didn't have a driver's license. The summer previous, using Edith's De Soto, Mom had taught me to drive with my learner's permit. Automatic transmissions were not standard equipment at the time, so we struggled with my jerky releasing of the clutch. The gear shift was on the floor with three forward speeds and a reverse. In time I reached a minimal skill level in coordinating the clutch with my left foot, the gear shift with my right hand, the brake with my right foot and the steering wheel with my left hand. It was a Saturday afternoon, a beautiful sunny autumn day. I had been in high school about three weeks and already knew a lot of kids that hung out at the Davis Sweet Shop. I didn't have to work that day. The High School had a football game that afternoon. Mom was at work. The De Soto was in the garage. It would make a big impression on the kids at Davis's if I drove up in that De Soto. I backed slowly out of the driveway onto Del Norte Street and headed for the Davis Sweet Shop.

"Hey, Doak, where'd ya get the wheels?" (My nickname was "Doak" only because I shared my last name with a famous football player at SMU whose first name was Doak.)

Some of the guys in the sweet shop had seen me pull up and park across the street. I don't know what story I told them about the car. I do, however remember that for that afternoon my social status among my peers was elevated a notch or two. Even a couple of girls came by the booth where I was sitting with Bob Lacey and Edgar Howard. "Are you going to the game Doak?"

"Yeah. You want a ride?"

"Oh, could we? That would be great." In the place at that time there was a former CS High School football great, Andy Pavich, an ex-GI. He and a beautiful girl were sitting in the next booth. He came to our booth. He came over and introduced himself to us (like we didn't know him.) You couldn't talk CS High School football without using his name. Pavich football stories were legendary. His photos were posted in the school football trophy case.

"Jack, I overheard you say you were driving to the game. Could you take two more passengers?"

"Sure."

Now I didn't only have wheels, but celebrities asked me for rides. He called me Jack, like he knew me. The high I was feeling I had never felt before. Doak was walking out the door with Andy Pavich, his beautiful companion and two popular school girls. In my imagination the conversation in the Sweet Shop was going something like, "Man, that Doak is something, isn't he?" or, "Some guys have it all." And the girls would say, "I've heard he's a real fun date."

"Sally Green, a friend of mine at North Junior, went steady with him at South Junior last year. She said he was a really neat guy." Such is the way my Mittyesque[41] mind worked. After I dropped my passengers off at Washburn Field, I thought I'd just take a drive around town and revel in my newly won social status. At a stop sign, a car pulled up next to me. The driver was Kenneth, a friend of Mom's. He motioned me to pull over, which I did. He parked behind me and got out of his car.

"Your mother is worried sick. Give me the car keys, and get in my car. I'm taking you home."

My newly won social status had been reduced to "child caught playing with adult toy without permission." On the ride home,

---

[41]   Walter Mitty, a fictional character given to grand and elaborate fantasies, daydreamer.

my driver chastised, "I don't know how you could do this to your mother." There were other berating comments all the way home.

When we pulled up in front of the house, I saw Mom standing on the front porch. The thirty-foot walk with Kenneth from the car to the porch seemed like a mile. I knew I was really in for it. Mother and Kenneth had a few words. As he was leaving, I heard him say, "When Paul returns, have him call me, and we'll go pick up the car."

Mom's friend Paul had been out looking for me also.

"Well, Jack, did you enjoy your ride?"

"I guess so," I muttered.

"You're going to promise not to do that again, aren't you?"

"Yes, ma'am."

"Well, the important thing is you are safe."

She hugged me, ruffled my hair, and walked into the house.

Evicted

A unt Edith was not happy about her sister committing her to "an insane asylum." Mom told Betty and me that Edith was kicking her out of the house because of the Brady thing, "You two can stay here until I find a place for us." She moved in with her nurse friend Johnnie. Edith brought a Truck driver boyfriend home from somewhere. They just sat around and got drunk every day. I later heard she bought him a new tractor/trailer costing $30,000. Betty told me Mom had called and that she had found a place for us. We were to bring only those things we needed. My memory refuses to conjure up just how we moved our stuff, but I remember with lucidity the third story attic apartment we moved into at 801 East Boulder Street. Our living quarters were up in the gables and dormers of the old Victorian mansion. The east and west exterior walls slanted along the lines of the roofs rafters. There were three furnished rooms surrounding a kitchen. Each room was a separate rental unit with all sharing the kitchen stove, refrigerator, and cupboards. Mom rented two of the rooms. The third was occupied by a single man who moved out shortly thereafter. His room became ours also. Now we had a kitchen of our own and Betty could have a room of her own. The bathroom was right at the top of the stairs which we shared with a couple across the landing. The owner lived on the first floor. He was a colorful guy who went by the name of Speedy Allen. Mom knew him from way back. She told of his getting his nickname back in the prohibition era as a bootlegger. He now was a bail bondsman who hung out in the courts with a pocket full of cash ready to put up bail for any defendant who might appear to be able to pay for it. Speedy was like bail-bond ambulance chaser.

"Jack, I had to do some real fast talking to get this place because Speedy didn't want some loud rowdy high school boy running up and down the stairs. I assured him you were not that type. I'm asking you not to make a liar out of me. Okay?" What could I say—"Oh no, you're not getting me to agree to that." One end of my room had an old table and four chairs, no two were alike. This area served as our dining room. One end of Mom's room had a couch, two end tables with lamps and a visibly worn overstuffed arm chair. This area served well as a living room where we sat and listened to the radio. The new address would be a short eight block walk to school or take the city bus which stopped right in front of the house.

It had been in early August I was being fitted for new shoes by my Uncle Walt at Lorig's.

He asked, "Are you planning on working nights at Odone's while you're going to school?"

As he spoke, he reached into my shirt pocket and took my cigarettes and put them in his shirt pocket. Nothing was said. He did this often. I had learned not to complain, because I didn't want to hear his lecture on my being too young to be smoking.

In answer to his question, I replied, "Yeah, I was planning on it."

"That's some pretty long and late hours when you have to get up in the morning to go to school."

"I can do it." He seemed not to have heard me.

"There's a job here for a stock-boy after school. This would make you a good job and you'd get off work at six. You'd have time to do your homework, play your horn or cat around. You come over here we'll get you some new threads and a good leather jacket for school and you'll be set. How would you like that?"

"That sounds neat. I'll have to give notice at Odone's."

"You give them two weeks' notice, and I'll tell Junior [Mr. Marx Lorig] you'll be starting right after Labor Day."

Stock Boy in High School

"New students, report to the auditorium," read the sign over the desk where a man and a woman were handing out sheets of paper with those "You are here" floor plans of the school, two buildings each with two floors. There were also directions for the returnees. I saw kids I knew from South Junior, and I saw guys I knew from Junior High inter-school sports and American Legion baseball. My two best townie friends from junior high, Don Snell and Harold Potts were not in the crowd. I knew Don had moved out of town, but the reason for Harold's absence was unknown to me. I had not stayed in touch with him over the summer. We were divided into alphabetical groups and assigned areas of the auditorium. I was with the U, V, W, X, Y, Z group. We were sent to the upper level.

We all milled around trying to decide where in the upper level we should sit. Some of us guys from South Junior sat down in the back row. Some others followed. A teacher finally showed up and got everybody seated down on two rows.

As she handed out sheets of paper, she loudly explained, "These are your class assignment sheets. Your faculty counselor is in the lobby he will call your name and one at a time you will go to the lobby and he will help you pick out the five classes you will be attending this semester. You will then hand in your assignment sheets at the front desk."

I had heard from the older guys at the home that in high school you could pick your own classes. They were called "electives." This sounded neat even though I couldn't figure out why we needed counselors if we had "electives."

The counselor called off the names one at a time. While I waited I looked over the assortment of classes on the sheet. There was some good stuff here: band, orchestra, choir, and gym. There was even Swim with an explanation that swim classes would be held at the YMCA. There were other classes, but they didn't interest me. I was the last person remaining in our group. I guess there were no X, Y, or Zs in this group. I waited impatiently to be called and when it seemed I wouldn't be called, I left my seat and went to the lobby to see what was going on. There was no one there. I pondered my situation a bit and then sat down at the counselor's desk and filled out my assignment sheet: band, orchestra, choir, gym, and swim. I handed the sheet in at the front desk. The lady at the desk, with only a cursory glance at my registration sheet, gave me a locker number and told me the orchestra people were meeting on the auditorium stage.

While walking to the orchestra class I was thinking, "Man, this is going to be a fun school, nothing but music and sports."

The first day orchestra class was spent getting acquainted with the teacher, Mr. Jackson, who was my teacher at South Junior. He was now the band/orchestra director at the high school. He took attendance and told us: "Bring your instruments tomorrow and we will begin tryouts for any chair positions not filled by returnees. For today will all of you who were in orchestra last year take the positions you held. There were but a few of us new people left standing. The first and second chairs of the trumpet section were occupied.

"You new people, take the remaining seats."

I went to the trumpet section not too happy that there were two trumpeters ahead of me. When we were all seated Mr. Jackson passed out a sheet of paper to each section.

"I want each of you to write your name at the number on the page corresponding to where you now sit. This will not necessarily be a permanent arrangement. Starting tomorrow we will have tryouts for positions." The bell rang about that time and we filed out heading for our next class. I had to walk a block away to the YMCA. I knew when the orchestra tryouts were complete, that I would be sitting in that first chair. I was eager to hear that guy who occupied it presently."

I wonder if he can flutter tongue or lip trill. Can he hit a high C? The rest of the day went well. At the YMCA pool, the teacher/coach said we would play water polo, and racing and diving contests and sometimes just free time. The band class went about like the orchestra practice with the exception that we were to be fitted for band uniforms and taught marching band formations. I didn't like the idea of uniforms, and when he announced that we would be playing at all home football games and marching at half-time, I knew band was not for me. I wondered if I could maybe drop band and take something more to my liking.

At noon I ran into Johnnie West, a buddy of mine from the Stratton Home. Johnnie, a senior, had left the home a year before me. He took me down to the Davis Sweet Shop, where all the kids hung out. We got a booth and we were joined by two other guys, one I knew from baseball. The place was crowded and loud. We ordered hamburgers, and fountain cokes. All the jocks were there in their letter jackets and there were more beautiful girls than I had ever seen in one place. Guys were draped over the pinball machine watching the player bump the machine to make the ball obey. When it didn't, the most mournful choir of "Oh" could be heard a block down Nevada Avenue. A guy and a girl (she wore the letter jacket) were making selections on the jukebox while the box loudly gave forth with "Peg o' My Heart' by the Harmonicats. There were two guys on the pay phone in the vestibule leading to the back entrance. A couple of girls dropped by our booth and joked with the guys. I would have stood up if I hadn't been sitting on the inside. It's lucky I was on the inside. I'm sure such an act of gentlemanly behavior would have been ridiculed by my peers probably thought of as cute but discomforting by the girls. This was really the life I wanted to live.

After we finished eating one of the guys said, "Anyone got any smokes?"

To which I responded, "Yeah' and whipped out a half pack of Camels."

All of us lit up and knew we were suave. The guys told me I should pledge the Chiselers club. They said the Chiselers were all regular guys, not goodie-two-shoes like the Bachelors. The Chiselers was Johnnie's club, so I said okay.

One of the guys was reading the newspaper. He put it down and said, "Willy Sutton broke out of prison."

Sutton was a famous bank robber, who also became famous as a prison escapee. He was asked once, "Why do you rob banks?"

His reply was, "That's where the money is."

From that reply was born "Sutton's Law," which states that when diagnosing, one should consider the obvious.

My first class after lunch was gym. The gym coach said we would be taking tests of strength and athletic abilities as well as playing basketball and dodgeball. In choir we actually got to perform a few pieces. The choir teacher had to move a couple guys, who thought they were tenors, over to the baritone section. Their voices had changed over the summer. After school I ran into some guys I knew and walked with them down by Davis's where I had to part and walk on down to Lorig's to begin my new job as stock boy. I reported in with Uncle Walt who then took me to Mister Lorig, who I had known for as far back as I could remember. All my clothes came from Lorig's.

"We're glad to have you Jack. Are you ready to go to work?"

"Yes, sir."

"Well, the first thing I need you to do is run some packages over to the post office. Your Uncle will show you where they are. You'll need some money."

He opened the cash register and handed me some bills. "Get a receipt, and bring back the change and give it to whoever is at the cash register."

Uncle Walt took me to the back room and got me all lined out with the packages. There were two middle aged ladies working back there at sewing machines.

"This is my little nephew Jack." (I was six feet tall.)

When I returned from the post office, Walt took me down stairs where all the back stock was kept on deep shelves. The passage ways between shelves were barely wide enough to slink through and the lighting was sparse with two or three small bare bulbs hanging from the ceiling. There's no other smell like the rich aroma of a stock room full of brand-new garments. "Vern, Jack's ready to go to work, Do you have anything for him to do?" This was Vern Pollart, the store manager. He was the only person who had worked at Lorig's longer than Walt. "Welcome Jack." I had known Vern all my life also. He brought up the time I had come in with my money from caddying and bought a new suit. "That suit wouldn't fit your six-foot frame today. How old were you?"

"I think I was about ten."

"I've been telling it that you were seven."

Vern had been taking inventory when we interrupted him. He had me moving stacks of Levis and Oshkosh overalls from one location to the next as he tallied them.

We did this for about an hour.

It was nearing closing time when he said, "Let's go upstairs. We can finish this tomorrow."

Upstairs he showed me a drum of something that looked like sawdust saturated with oil and the oil smelled like furniture polish. He handed me a bucket with a scoop that was nearby. "This is a sweeping compound, Scoop out a bucket full and spread it thinly all over the floor then take that broom over there and sweep it all up and dump it in the trash can there." He explained that when sweeping up debris the sweeping compound picks up dust and prevents it from kicking up and settling on the merchandise. It was nearly six pm when I finished sweeping.

At the stroke of six Walt said, "Let's get out of here."

We went out the back door which had a large and loud cow bell hung over the door knob this was the security system. You could not go in or out of that door without loudly broadcasting the event.

"I'll give you a ride home."

On the way home Walt asked how I liked the job. I told him I liked it and that the time went really fast.

He said, "That's good. Vern said you were a good worker. He's going to show you how to make up price tickets tomorrow."

Orchestra tryouts were underway when Mister Jackson called me to come down stage. "You're wanted in the office."

He gave me a hall pass so I wouldn't be set upon by hall monitors. Walking down the corridor I wondered who wanted to see me in the office, and what for. Being called to the office had always been something to dread. That's where punishment is dispensed. At the office I waited until the stern looking bird like little lady at the desk looked up from her paper shuffling and said: "Well?" I presumed this was a short cut way to say: "How may I help you, son?"

"I was told to come to the office."

"What's your name?"

After I told her, she shuffled some more papers and came up with the one she wanted. She perused the paper a moment then gave me a look like she had just read that I was a criminal. "Have a seat." She picked up the phone and dialed a few numbers. "He's here." She put the phone down. "Mister K. will be here in a few minutes," she said without looking up from her stacks of paper.

"Walker?" he asked. I stood up. "I'm Mister K." He didn't offer to shake my hand. There was not even an attempt to smile. I will never forget Mister K.; He wasn't short, but his legs were. His long torso rose from the stump-like legs upward to reach nearly six feet to the top of his head. His belly was rounded out and over his belt. The face was jowly, pale and uninteresting. A large nose supported a large pair of horn rimmed glasses. The large head showed signs of early male pattern baldness. "Let's go over across the hall." He led. I followed. It was an odd sight, this six-foot man walking with such small prissy steps due to his little legs. We walked into an empty class room.

"Take a seat."

I slid into one of the desk-chairs as he took a seat behind the desk. I think some teachers feel that sitting behind the desk gives the impression of authority.

"Who counseled you on your class schedule?"

"No one." I was still at a loss to know what this was all about.

"Were you with the other sophomores at registration?" As I was beginning to answer, he cut me short, "Never mind. I'm your counselor, and they should have sent you to me."

I couldn't understand why somebody not sending me to Kramer was a big deal. I was greatly relieved that this was all this meeting was about. He just wanted to meet me, maybe to counsel me a little. "We are going to change your class schedule." What could be wrong with my class schedule? "You can't just fill your schedule with electives. You are here to get an education, not just to play your horn and go to gym. We've had troublemakers like you before. Starting tomorrow, you will be taking the sophomore-required classes. You will take English, history, and math. You will choose between gym and swim, but not both. You may keep one only of the music courses, so choose which two you want to drop."

Boy! My "electives" bubble burst with a bang. I now foresaw high school as an adversary to be confronted just as kindergarten had been.

> News Break
> December 30, 1947 KVOR radio
> Prison Break at State Penitentiary
>
> 12 dangerous convicts from maximum security escaped using a water culvert. The prison is in complete lock down. Residents of Cannon City are told to lock doors.

Back at the orchestra tryouts, I was given a minuet solo which wasn't too difficult. I thought I did pretty good since I had never seen this score before. The other three trumpeters were each given different music to play. Two of the guys sounded very good to me. As it turned out, I was given the second chair. The first chair assignment went to Jack McColl, a junior, who well deserved the slot. He was far more accomplished than I.

Learning the Stock-Boy Trade

After school when all the really cool kids were heading for Davis's, I went down the alley and opened Lorig's back door. The cowbell loudly heralded my arrival. The alteration ladies looked up and greeted me and went back to their alterations. I found Vern in the front of the store sorting and hanging some suits. I waited till he noticed me.

"Well, hello, Jack. Are you ready to go to work?"

I nodded.

"Let's go to the basement."

Down among all the stored dry goods in the dimly lit basement Vern introduced me to the strangest machine; "This is the marking machine that makes all the price tickets you see on all the garments." It was a complex looking machine and it seemed large for making the small price tickets. "This roll of tickets is fed into the machine." He then pulled open a drawer which held metal stamping dies which were embossed with letters and numbers. "You fit these numbers in here indicating the price of the garment you are marking. You will get the price from the bill of lading." He showed me a piece of paper that listed shirts and jackets and numbers. 'This number is the quantity we received. This number is what each piece cost us. Hand written right here is the price we will sell the item for. DON'T EVER MIX THEM UP." He punctuated. The letters you see here on the price ticket are the cost code." He explained that the cost to the store was coded onto the ticket by having letters represent numbers. The code letters were: IN GOD WE TRUST." I equaled 1, N equaled 2, G equaled 3, and so on.

"After you set the number and letter type, you turn the crank and a ticket comes out. One turn of the crank will spit out one ticket."

We tried it a few times until I got the hang of it. Vern told me that each day when I arrived at work I would first check at the office for anything to be mailed. "After you return from the post office, you will find open boxes of goods in the basement that will have a bill of lading on top."

These garments will need price tickets. This was to be my daily routine for the next six months. I especially liked going to the post office in inclement weather of all kinds because I could take a rain slicker or a hooded parka or other items depending on the weather. Also it got me out of the cramped basement. Saturday mornings it was my job to sweep the front walk and crank down the big awning that extended over the side walk. I would see other guys doing the same thing up and down Tejon Street. It was also my job, at lunch time on Saturdays, to go around the corner to the "Chink's" to pick up Chinese carry out. One Saturday morning I was up on the sales floor putting a new roll of wrapping paper on the roller beneath the wrapping table,[42] when Mr. Lorig called me up to the front of the store.

"The leather jacket I just sold was mismarked. I told the man the jacket went for twenty-five dollars. He looked at the price ticket which read $15.44. I had to let him have the jacket for $15.44 I'll let it go this time, but if that ever happens again, you will have to pay for it."

I told him I was sorry.

"Just don't let it happen again."

He was walking away when I said, "I won't, I promise." I felt dumb and miserable. I went to the basement and tried to stay out of Mister Lorig's sight for the rest of the day.

"I want to look at some saddles," a customer said to me one Saturday. I led him back to the shoe department and told him to have a seat.

---

[42]   All garments, other than suits, were wrapped in green paper and tied with string. No plastic bags in those days.

"What size shoe do you wear?" I asked him.

"I want to see some saddles, not shoes," he emphasized.

"Oh, I'm sorry. I thought you wanted saddle shoes," said the dumbest, most embarrassed stock-boy alive. "The saddles are up in the loft. I'll show you."

"No, thanks. I'll find them."

Tormented

It was March 1948. The last few weeks I had missed more classes than I had attended. I had quit my job at Lorig's because I wanted to hang out after school at Davis's with the other guys and go out for sports.

I had missed out on getting a letter jacket for basketball, but baseball was coming up soon. This new lifestyle was fun for a few days until reality set in: I now didn't have any money. Looking back on the school year, in the beginning I thought it was going to be a real fun time. I pledged the Chiselers club and knew a lot kids. On weekends I sometimes double dated with Edgar Howard who borrowed his brother-in-law's car. A date in those days would cost about two dollars; fifty cents each for the movie, fifty cents each for a desert afterwards and if you had to take the bus you needed twenty cents each for the round trip. More than once I would go to Lorig's and borrow two dollars from Uncle Walt. After I got off work at five I would head up to Davis's to see who was there; hoping some of the girls would still be hanging around, but usually most everyone had gone home.

I would order a fountain coke and sip it hoping someone would show up. I walked the ten blocks home and had dinner with Mom and/or Betty. One or both of them might be working the three-to-eleven shift. I would eat, maybe bathe and shave. Mom had bought me a Norelco electric shaver and a bar of Mennen deodorant. She was trying to ease me into manhood. I dabbed some stuff on my face that kind of covered up the zits and gave a lot of attention to my then dark wavy hair. I headed back to Davis's. After about seven o' clock, a few kids would be there. If someone had a car we would chip in for some gas, at twenty-five cents a gallon, and cruise around downtown. We often parked to "people-watch" down at Busy Corner for a while. We would make up scenarios about the people we saw, like, "That's not his daughter, that's some young chick from the office that he's running around with," or, "Look at her. She's so happy. She just ate a box of chocolates."

Sometimes we'd go into their imagined home life: "Man he looks so tired. I bet he's got six kids and a nagging wife at home and holds down three jobs."

And somebody would add something like, "And his roof leaks, and his dog is sick."

When we tired of scenario creations, we would go down south on Nevada Avenue to a drive in restaurant where a lot of kids hung out. We tried to make it with the carhops without any success. We might follow this with a return to Davis's and hang out listening to records on the jukebox and making up lyrics to songs; when singing Frankie Laine's "Jealousy," we substituted "Leprosy." and "In the Mood" was sung as "In the Nude." There were many more songs we applied our creative artistry to. Sometimes a girl or two might be in Davis's who we would spend the evening trying to impress. Once in a while it worked and we could give them a ride home and maybe even get a date. On the nights when we had no wheels, we would go down town and sneak into the last show at movie theatre through the alley emergency door which had no alarm and was always unlocked. We would file in one at a time so as not to be noticed by the ushers.

One Saturday night at the Ute theatre midnight show three of us walked slowly into the lobby backwards mixing in the leaving crowd from the previous show was coming out and paying customers were going in. The ushers didn't work the midnight shows, so the only person we had to avoid was the ticket taker who was busy punching tickets.

This life didn't allow time for homework which then led to my skipping a class or two for a while. I wound up just skipping all the classes. I hung out at the Pike's Peak Bowling Alley and Recreation Billiards, where I made a few dollars racking balls for twenty-five

US Forest Service

"Your first real man job."

The want ad read, "Forest service hiring. No experience necessary." The ad went on to indicate that applicants should come to the post office to sign up. I got down there early, so did some other guys. My cousin Duane was there with a couple of his Westside buddies. I teamed up with them in the queue waiting for the Forest Service people to get set up.

"This is my cousin the pool shark I was telling you about."

One of the guys I had seen around the bowling alley where we used to play the pinball machine for real money. If you could get a certain score on the machine, the house would pay you ten bucks. The police vice squad called this gambling and made the owner stop. I told the two West-side guys that I wasn't a pool shark and that I just played for fun, not money. A Forest Ranger asked for our attention and explained what the job was all about: "We'll be planting trees up in the Deckers area of the Pike National Forest. We will be living in tents, 4 men to a tent. The pay is seventy-five cents an hour. Thirty-five cents a day will be deducted from you're pay for meals. The job will last about two months." A couple of guys walked out. The rest of us signed up. The Ranger said he would meet us at eight o'clock at the Busy Corner restaurant Wednesday which was two days away. I parted with Duane and his buddies and went up to Davis's. I told the guys what I was going to be doing. "Man, Doak, that's neat." And, "When school lets out maybe I can get a job there."

I was basking in admiration for having bagged such an uncustomary job for a high school–aged guy. I was about to put a nickel in the jukebox when a couple girls came over and begged me to play a Frank Sinatra song. Girls all over the country really loved Sinatra. I was a Bing Crosby fan. All the magazines showed the bobby socks girls swooning over Sinatra. I really wanted to play the new record that had recently been put in the jukebox, a Count Basie record, but I dropped my nickel in the slot and said: "pick your tune." They told me I was wonderful. The next three minutes we were entertained by Sinatra's rendition of "Mam'selle."

I told Mom of my forest service job, and she was pleased. She knew the Deckers area. "It's real mountainous up there on the South Platte River. There's nothing up there but a bar and curio shop. Where will you stay?" I told her the Ranger said we would live in tents. "Take a lot of warm clothes. It gets cold up there. You get down to Lorig's and have Walt fit you up with some work shoes, socks, and some warm gloves." Which I did. The next couple days I hung out at the pool hall and Davis's.

As I went out the door Wednesday morning, Mom kissed me and said: "This is your first real man job." I showed up at the Busy Corner Restaurant about seven thirty. Some of the older guys I had seen and talked to at the Post Office lineup were sitting in two booths. I walked over by them.

"Hey, kid, you can sit here."

I put my canvas satchel down and slid into a booth. They were all drinking coffee. The waitress came over.

"Coffee?" I normally would have ordered a coke.

"Yes," I said.

I was sitting with coffee-drinking men, and I wanted to be like them. From that day on black coffee and Coca Cola have been my non-alcoholic beverages of choice. The Ranger came in and said the truck was outside. Duane and his buddies were waiting outside. We all climbed up into a stake bed truck that had a canvas canopy over the bed. There were long wooden benches on either side of the bed for our comfort. There were about twelve of us in all. The ride was kind of hard. We had to hold onto the bench on the curves. The bouncing up and down on the wooden planks was hard on the butt, and conversation was difficult what with the sound of the truck motor which wasn't muffled much through the exhaust system. We were nearly suffocated with exhaust fumes every time the truck stopped. Except for Duane, his buddies, and me, the rest of the guys were older. Three or four looked to be as old as fifty or so. The faces of these men grabbed my interest; I saw faces that were sad, forlorn, tanned, pale, wrinkled, dirty, clean, shaved and unshaved. Some eyes were bright and some deep and dulled. A couple of them didn't smell too good. Some of the men were quiet and some talkative.

"I thought I'd never ride in the back of a fucking truck again when I got out of the army," said the guy next to me.

Some of the other guys joined in with remarks about army life. The four older guys sat solemnly with sad looking faces. The old guy next to me had a stubble beard and a strong smell of whiskey on his breath. His flushed face was as vacant as the Bonneville Salt Flats. I wondered; what was on their minds? Why were they doing this? The fact that they were here said that life had not treated them very good. I had the uncomfortable feeling that maybe I didn't belong here. On the other hand, I felt a certain excitement. The ex-GIs kept up their banter over the truck noise. It was fun listening to them and exhilarating knowing I was going to be working with guys who had actually been in war. The truck left the paved highway and turned onto a dusty graveled road. Now the dust was nearly choking us and the ride got bumpy and our butts took a beating. After several miles of this we reached Deckers where, looking out the back of the truck, we saw two fishermen in wading boots standing in the stream casting their lines.

There was one building in sight with a Coors beer sign in front. We turned and started climbing up a winding dirt road for about three miles. We had to hold on to the benches to keep from sliding to the rear of the truck. Pulling into camp I saw a wooden building and two rows of white tents with what looked like smoke stacks planted in the ground next to each one. There were a lot of civilian guys and some Rangers milling around the camp. Some were putting up more tents, while a couple guys were chopping wood and stacking it. A guy in a forest service shirt and Levi's met us as we were unloaded.

"Welcome, men. I'm Ron Hudson."

He was an average-size guy with a tanned face that wouldn't give up his age. In my sixteen-year-old perception, he looked young, and he also looked old. His deep voice was one of authority, which I was an expert on. I figured he was the honcho here.

"The tents hold four men each. The empty ones are down at the end. Find one and park your gear. The latrine is over there," he said, pointing at a lone tent in among the pines. "We'll meet back at the building in an hour."

We four juniors stayed together and moved into our new digs. The tent was eight feet by ten feet with a plywood floor on top of a two-by-four frame. There were two bunk beds with mattresses and army-colored blankets. We flipped coins to see who slept where. I lost and took a top bunk, which turned out OK because guys couldn't use it as seating. The two westsiders and I exchanged names. The tall thin one was Rick, whose nickname was Boney. I was tall at sixteen, right around six feet, and thin, but Boney was taller and thinner. His shirt looked three sizes too big except at the cuffs which were too short. With the exception of the cuffs at his forearms, I think the only place that shirt touched his body was where it hung on his shoulders. His shoes must have been size twelve. He appeared to be awkward, but he wasn't. His movements were catlike. Gabe, the husky one, was on the short side and muscular. He had a crew cut. His hair was as short as Bone's was long, and his shirt fit as tight as Bone's hung loose. He walked like many boxers I had seen. They kind of walk with a bounce on the balls of their feet which comes from hours of jumping rope to develop speed.

Later I learned he was a club boxer who learned his sport at the Boy's Club. Over in the corner of the tent the floor had been cut out to hold a black metal box.

"What's that?" Gabe said, pointing at the black box.

"Must be some kinda stove or something," I said.

"I saw some smoke coming out of a smoke stack down the line. I'll ask them how this works," said Duane.

He took off and went down the line of tents and returned with instructions on the stove. We all went over to the wood pile and each carried an armload of chopped wood back to the tent. We got a fire started. At first the stove emitted so much smoke it drove us out of the tent. Duane went back in and poked the wood around some and it stopped smoking. The secret was we learned later was to heat the flu a little to start the warm air rising up while opening the grate in the door of the box to create a draft.

The latrine was no more than a large out-house in a tent; two long pits covered with long wooden benches, each with three toilet seat holes cut out. It made for truly sociable bowel moving.

The camp building was a large room filled with long tables and benches. The smell of something good cooking came from the double doors in the back of the room. There were about fifty of us waiting to see what we were here for. Some of the guys sat on the benches and some of us just stood around. From the conversations I overheard, a group of them from Denver had arrived the day before. They had put up all the tents and did all the chopping for the wood pile. The guys from Pueblo had arrived about two hours before us. Hudson came out of the kitchen with three rangers in tow.

"Have a seat, men."

We all scrambled around and filled the benches. Hudson explained that most of us would be planting trees, but he wanted five guys to help around the camp.

"Any volunteers for camp duty?"

Nobody volunteered.

"Okay, you, you, you, you, and you will work in camp."

The four of us missed the camp duty assignments.

"Supper will be served here at five. Don't be late the kitchen won't be open much longer after five. Breakfast will be served at 5:00 am. One of the Rangers will come around 5:00 am to wake anyone who needs it."

At supper the rush for seats was such that my tent-mates and I were unable to sit together. I squeezed in between two older guys where there was an empty metal tray, the kind with divided compartments. Each table had a large pan of mashed potatoes, a platter of sliced ham, and a big bowl of mixed vegetables. There were pitchers of water, pots of coffee, and a plate stacked with bread.

In a quick moment reality grabbed me: the food was not going to be passed around the table. The guy on my left half stood up and reached over beyond me with his fork in hand and returned to a sitting position with a fork full of ham. He looked at me with one of those shit-eating grins which said, "I got mine." The table was furious with reaching arms. It lasted only a minute or two. When the fury quietly ended, I went to help myself, only to find the only thing left on the table was half a bowl of canned vegetables, not even a piece of bread. The guy on my right, chewing on a piece of ham, made a sound somewhat like speech, which, I thought, told me to tell one of the kitchen guys to bring some more. I did catch one of the guys and told him what happened. He took my tray out to the kitchen and retuned it with generous helpings of everything.

When they brought the apple pies out, I was quick to get a piece. From that time on, I was among the quickest "food-forkers" and "spooners" in the camp. My six-foot height gave me advantage over some.

Daylight was the only light source in our tent. We let the fire burn out and lay on our bunks in the dark and talked and laughed. We didn't even have a flashlight to guide us to the latrine at night. Of course we could just step outside the tent and pee on the ground, which we did. The morning came with a loud wood-on-wood knocking on the tent floor and a loud voice, "LET'S GO. IT'S FIVE O'CLOCK," followed by more floor banging. God it was cold in that tent. I got dressed sitting up in my bunk. My jeans were ice cold, I was shivering, I had to pee, I dropped down off my upper berth and almost landed on Gabe. I hurried and got my shoes on, grabbed my jacket and ran for the latrine. (I didn't want to pee on the ground during the daylight. It might be against the rules.) The latrine was busy, I shared a hole with another guy. As I walked briskly toward the building, I noticed most of the tent smokestacks were smoking. Those guys must have got up early. I wished one of my partners would get up early and start a fire. Breakfast was pancakes piled high on a platter, whole pounds of butter, large bottles of syrup, pounds of bacon in a metal pan, and a large pan of powdered eggs. The coffee pots were constantly being filled by the guys on kitchen duty.

After breakfast we were herded into the beds of two stake-bed trucks and hauled off into the mountains on a gravel road. The road wasn't dusty yet, I guess the early morning dew held the dust down. After winding up and around mountains and valleys for about thirty minutes, we pulled over to the side of the road.

The gates were dropped and Ranger Flynn said, "Okay, men, here's where we start."

The pickup truck, which completed our three-truck convoy, was filled with what at first looked like picks.

"Get a Mattock and a bag of trees."

A Ranger at the pickup was issuing the tools and bags of small pine trees. I guessed Mattock was what the pick-like tool was called. A guy standing next to me referred to it as "mad axe." He said he had used the tool often in a turf farm in California. I got my mad axe, which was like an axe only the blade was horizontal at ninety degrees to the three-foot long wooden handle. I heard the Ranger tell some guys up the line: "Take the straps and tie them around your waist so the trees in the bag are easy to reach." He told us there were about fifty trees in the bag and that they were three years old. The bag of trees at my hip weighed about three or four pounds and the mad axe another four or five. We were split up into three different groups with a ranger in charge of each. I was in Ranger Flynn's twenty-man group. He walked us up a mountain slope away from the road to a spot near a small stream. "Here's how we plant the trees." He borrowed a mad axe from the nearest guy and with a strong blow sunk the axe blade into the ground.

He pulled back on the blade leaving a small hole in the ground. "Hand me a tree."

Somebody pulled a tree from their bag gave it to him. He placed the roots of the small tree in the hole and while he held the tree upright, he withdrew the axe blade, which released the dirt back to the hole which now also contained the tree roots. The Ranger tamped the hole with the axe, he then stepped forward and stood with his feet close together with only the tiny tree trunk between them. "That's how it's done. After you have planted a tree you then step forward about three feet and do it again. Flynn picked out this giant muscular ex-GI Sawyer, whose buddies called him Moose. "Stand here." He told him. "The rest of you, form a line from here over that direction about three feet apart."

Once we got into position, Flynn said, "We'll plant trees every three feet heading up that direction. Sawyer will start off, then the next man, and so on. I want all of you to keep up. We may have to adjust the lineup later to put the slower men at the end. Sawyer will set the pace. Okay, let's begin."

Then I realized why he picked the biggest, strongest guy to be the pace setter. This guy could probably outwork any four men.

I was number four in the line working between an ex-coal miner from Walsenburg and a former GI who had fought in North Africa, Sicily, and Italy. We talked as we worked—that is, they talked, I listened. Some talk was about the war, some about coal mining and John L. Lewis and the coal-miner's strike. There was talk of the easy virtue of the Italian girls towards their liberators. There was nothing in my sixteen years' experience that could interest such worldly men. We all plugged away moving up the mountain planting trees every three feet. It brought to my mind the picture of the spike drivers on the railroad and "John Henry," the "steel-drivin' man." Moose's pace kept us humping. We took a five-minute break every hour. During the breaks most of us lit up cigarettes. A bag of water was strapped to a guy's back. There was a spigot at the bottom of the bag, the "Water-boy" had paper cups and went from man to man turning his back to the man to present the water spigot. This was a good job. After he served each guy he went to fill the bag again and returned to a spot where he thought we might reach by next hourly break. He then just waited for us to trudge up the mountain swinging our five-pound axes. We stopped at noon and were given covered metal canisters of hot food which the water boy had lugged up the mountain. The food cans had been trucked from camp to arrive hot near lunch time.

I had taken off my jacket and tied it around my waist. The temperature had risen from near freezing at breakfast till now when the heat was getting to all of us. We worked like this the rest of the afternoon and nobody had to be moved to the end of the line. I noticed during the day sometimes when Moose would get too far ahead, Flynn would subtly motion for him to ease up so that our lineup would remain relatively straight. It was midafternoon and we had been climbing ever higher at a pretty good pace when one of our guys, the Texan stopped and sat down on the ground. "I feel dizzy and sick to my stomach."

The work stopped. Flynn came over and knelt down and talked to Tex a minute. I heard the words "altitude sickness." The ranger stood up and said, "Somebody bring me the water bag. You, men, keep on working. Tex and I are going back down by the stream."

Tex held onto Flynn's shoulder as they began the descent. While they were gone, Moose and another guy were talking about there being no jobs in Denver. "My Fifty Two-Twenty[44] ran out, and still the only job I could find was day labor. A lot of people believe we all returned to the jobs we left to go fight, but most of us didn't have jobs to return to. We went in the army right after high school. I can't go to college on the GI Bill because I joined the army before graduating. I stay in touch with a Negro buddy in Mississippi, who couldn't even get the twenty bucks for fifty-two weeks. He said the GI Bill in Mississippi was for whites only."

"How can they do that?" I asked.

"I don't know for sure, but I think the GI Bill is managed by each state."

Flynn returned without Tex and announced, "I'm pretty sure Tex had high-altitude sickness. He's feeling much better down by the stream."

We got back to camp around 4:00 p.m. I climbed up into my bunk tired and sore. My right hand was rubbed raw and red from the axe handle. My partners were worn out too. The welcome sound of the dinner bell rang while we washed up at the water barrels outside the building. We all ate like horses and went back to the bunks. We didn't even make a fire. I crawled under my two army blankets and read. I had brought a paperback copy of *I the Jury*, a Mike Hammer private-eye story, a hugely popular book at that time.

---

[44] A postwar GI bill providing returning GIs unemployment benefits of twenty dollars a week for fifty-two weeks.

News Break
May 14, 1948
State of Israel Comes into Existence

David Ben Gurion, head of the Jewish Agency,
proclaimed the establishment of the State of
Israel. President Truman recognizes the new
nation.

Next morning, the tent is freezing again. My back and my shoulder are screaming hurt. I feel sore all over. I was the last one out of the tent. I was sorely dragging ass to breakfast. Pancakes, bacon, and powdered eggs again. My reaching arm wasn't as fast, but my height got me a decent meal without having to wait for the kitchen guy to bring more. One of the older guys (actually they were all older than me) sitting across the table, said: "Slim, pass me the sugar, will ya?"

"My name's not Slim."

"Well, what is your name?"

"It's Jack." I was having second thoughts about correcting this guy. He could have slammed me to the floor with one hand.

"Well, my name's Roy. Now how about you passin that sugar can over here so's I can sweeten my coffee?" he said this in a kindly manner like he didn't understand the issue. Even though I thought he might be making fun of me, I thought it best to hand him the sugar. "Thank ya, Jack."

I felt something had happened here, but I didn't know what. I turned this over in my mind, "Did he make a fool of me by not using my name until he got the sugar. Or did I win by getting him to eventually call me Jack?" Nobody in the camp, for the rest of my stay there, called me Slim again, but I have relived the Slim-Jack scenario several times over the years with other men and with other results. More than one guy said words to the effect of: "You're a touchy bastard."

"You're goddamned right I'm touchy. My name's Jack. It's not Slim." I always thought Slim was some dumb hayseed name.

While getting our axes next morning Flynn reported that Tex decided that high altitude work wasn't his cup of tea. He decided to stay in camp until the truck went to Colorado Springs Saturday.

The first tree I planted that morning brought pain from areas of my body I didn't know existed. I hurt so much I was afraid I was going to live, but as the morning wore on, the pain wore off. By noon I was alive and well and the job went okay. After supper that evening Duane suggested we walk down the road to Deckers and get a beer. It was a three mile hike down the mountain road. I was the youngest in the group, but none of us were old enough to legally buy alcohol. There was one other guy at the bar; the old guy from Colorado Springs who smelled like whiskey that first morning. He had a shot and a beer in front of him. I don't know if that was his first drink or third or fourth, but he just sat there breathing heavy stroking the beer bottle. He didn't even look up when we entered. I sat next to him and said "Hi." He barely turned his head and grunted something. I know it wasn't: "Well hello young man. Glad to see you. Can I buy you a drink?" I really felt for him. I know he had a story all locked up behind that empty face.

We ordered beers and no ID was requested. Up in these mountain tourist communities the law is relaxed. This place even had a one armed bandit that took quarters. This was definitely illegal. We asked the bartender about the slot machine and he told us: "It's funny, ya know. It's illegal to have one in the place, but you must pay a tax on it." Man, I thought that was crazy. I've since heard of many laws around the country that were just as crazy. It was illegal in Colorado to drink alcohol while riding a horse because back in the day, a horse was considered a vehicle. When I was in Texas, it was illegal to have more than three sips of alcohol while standing. There's hundreds of goofy laws on the books. Lawmakers are not the brightest people of our society. We drank beer and dropped quarters in the slot machine until closing time. We stumbled three miles back up the mountain road in the moonlight, stopping once to watch Boney throw up. We chorused into camp giving our rhythmic rendering of "Ninety-Nine Bottles of Beer on the Wall."

One of the audience commented, "SHUT THE FUCK UP," and some other like endearment. On waking after three hours' sleep, I was all head and it all hurt. My tent-mates had similar symptoms. I barely ate anything at breakfast. Hot coffee was my only friend. Several remedies were offered: "hair of the dog, Dill pickles, drink water, eat tomatoes, etc. The only remedy available was water. I felt better after lunch, but the morning was painful: each blow of the axe vibrated up to my head like Moose had sunk his axe into my skull. By suppertime I was ready for another night in the city lights of Deckers. However, I hadn't the means to finance it, nor did my partners. I spent the evening reading my Mike Hammer book till it got too dark.

Thirty-five cents a day was deducted from our pay for meals, which was a real bargain. I guess that was set up in case someone lived close enough to drive home, or for some reason some might just want to buy their own food. Our crew had such a guy. He had about a quarter of a gunny sack filled with walnuts. He took a lot of vitamin pills and ate berries, wild onions, and other roots. We called him "Vitamin". He was probably in his fifties. His hair was long and dull with dust, but his brown sun tanned face was clean shaven each morning. His pants were at least two sizes too big and were cinched up tight with a long belt which, after it was buckled, hung down to his crotch. He wore an army surplus shirt and GI boots. His clothes had not felt any water but rain for who knows how long, if ever. We used to joke that Vitamin's clothes only got changed when they rotted off. He didn't smell too good either. During lunch break when he wasn't rooting around in the earth looking for something to go with his walnuts, he would sit with us and preach. "I'm a messenger of God," he would proclaim as he crushed a walnut shell between two rocks. "You fellas should repent to save your souls you know." He wasn't really obnoxious with his preaching. He would just lay out a proverb or two and let it go as his message for that day. ("In all your ways acknowledge him, and he will make your paths straight.") I found him interesting and used to engage him in conversation: "Vitamin, what church do you belong to?"

"I belong to the Church of the Universe, the only true church."

"I've never heard of the Church of the Universe.

"That's why I'm charged with spreading the message."

"Where is the church?"

"It's in man's heart." I saw this line of questioning was headed south. His argument for the existence of God was this: "What else could create the universe?" He didn't give me multiple-choice on that one, so I let it go.

At lunch one day one of the ex-GIs asked Ranger Flynn, our foreman what his regular job was. He told us he and his wife lived in a forestry fire lookout station on top of a mountain called Devil's Head they worked there day and night all year long. The road was a mile and a half away so they had to back pack all food and supplies up a 960-foot climb and they were often snowed in for weeks. Their job was to watch for forest fires. While he slept, his wife was the lookout and while she slept he was on duty.

After nearly four weeks of this back breaking labor, the four of us decided to quit. It was Friday I told Flynn my mother needed me at home and that I wouldn't be back to work Monday. A truck left for Colorado Springs each Saturday morning and we were on it.

Working for the Admiral

I told Mom the tree planting project was winding down and they laid off a lot of us. She was glad to see me looking so tanned and healthy.

"Well, you'll have to start looking for another job."

A lot of the guys at school got summer jobs with the Interstate Gas Company. I applied, and the man who did the student hiring told me that since I was no longer a student, he couldn't hire me. I put in an application at Douglas Jardine's, a big contactor whom Kenny had worked for.

I handed in the application, and the young woman said, "Wait just a minute."

She took the application and disappeared behind a large door which sounded like it opened to a shop of some kind. She returned shortly without the application which made me think that either the application was in the trash back there, or some decision maker was holding it. I expected to hear "We'll keep your application on file and call you if something turns up." But what I heard instead was, "Mr. Jardine will see you now. Follow me."

Jardine's office was just off the shop where two guys were bending sheets of metal into what looked like air ducts. Another guy was doing something with a grinder that was throwing sparks and I remember seeing a welder with a helmet-like mask pulled over his head. He was wearing long gauntlet-like gloves and leather sleeves that reached clear up to his shoulders. He was welding pipe together. The sparks from that welding rod flew everywhere. There were other activities taking place in that huge space. I followed the young woman around the corner and through a doorway into an office. There was an older man sitting behind a desk talking on the phone.

"Have a seat. He'll be with you soon."

I sat. She left. It wasn't hard to picture the man on the phone in a naval officer's uniform. I knew he had been an Admiral in the Navy "Sea Bees" (CBs, Construction Battalion). The room was filled with Navy stuff; there was two large photographs, one showed guys in white Navy caps building an air strip the other photo was of sailors working on a frame building. He put the phone down and turned his chair quickly to face me. He offered his hand and said: "Hello." Before I could respond he had my application in his hand.

"So you were working for the Forest Service."

I didn't know whether that was a question, or a statement.

"What kind of work did you do there?"

"We planted trees in the mountains."

He asked how that was done, and I explained that we used a mad axe and planted a tree every three feet.

"That's pretty hard work, isn't it?"

"Yes, I guess so."

He also wanted to know why I left the forest service. I stuck to my story that I was laid off.

"What makes you think you would like to work here?"

"My brother Kenneth Lankard worked here, and he liked it."

"Lankard, yeah, he was a navy man. Worked in the shop. Good man."

If I remember correctly, this was the end of the interview. Without asking me when I could start, he ordered me to report for duty the next day at 7:00 a.m.

At 6:45, I entered the shop door. There must have been fifty or sixty guys standing around over near Jardine's door. They appeared to be kind of lined up in three crooked rows. I walked over near them and caught the attention of the guy nearest me.

"This is my first day. Where should I go?"

"Just stay right here. When the Old Man comes out, we line up in straight rows." He then asked, "What department are you in?"

I told him I didn't know.

"Are you in the trades?"

I didn't know what the "trades" was, so I said, "No."

About that time Jardine came out of his office. The lines of men quickly straightened as if the mechanism that opened Jardine's door also straightened the lines of men. All conversation stopped. The men didn't exactly stand at attention, but nobody slouched either. Jardine stood in front of the lineup with a piece of paper in his hand. He read from the paper various assignments of men to projects: "All of you working on the road job in Knob Hill will stay there." He then asked one of the guys in the front row, "When do you expect finish out there?"

I didn't hear the answer. Jardine went on to assign projects to roofers, plumbers, carpenters, laborers, welders, "tin benders," etc. Somewhere in the middle of his assignments, I heard, "Walker, you will go with Johnson." Jardine ended the muster with, "Let's get to it"

The assemblage broke up, and guys headed all different directions. I asked the guy next to me, "Who is Johnson? I'm supposed to go with him."

He scanned a moment, then pointed and called out, "Johnnie, your guy is here."

Johnson and I walked toward each other. Johnson was a big guy in his forties, I would guess. His big belly pushed tightly against his bib overalls. He was what Grandpa would describe as "big enough to eat hay." Johnson had a thick shock of red hair large dark eyes, heavy red eyebrows, a big ruddy colored nose, and a good smile.

"What's your name, kid?"

After I answered his question, he told me we were going to replace a sewer pipe over on the west side. "Wait here. I'll bring the truck around, and we can load it."

He brought the truck and we went to the shop tool crib where Johnson handed the guy behind the cage a list of the materials he wanted. "Going honey dipping today, huh? Who's the new guy?"

Johnson introduced us. He had one of those Mexican sounding names like Carlos or Miguel or something. I don't remember. He went in the back and came out through a set of double doors next to the cage pushing a cart loaded with about six or eight lengths of big black metal pipe. Johnson was to teach me later that this was six-inch cast iron. Also on the cart there were several ingots of lead, a burner of some kind and a bag of something Johnson told me was "oakum," whatever that was, I didn't know. And he offered no explanation, like he thought everybody knows what oakum is. We loaded the truck and took off. Johnson was a jolly fat man who joked and laughed all the way over to "Colorado City," as it was once called, but in 1948 it was just "the west side."

I asked Johnson, "What did Carlos mean by 'honey dipping'?"

"That's what they call it when you're workin' on sewer pipe clogged and backed up with toilet waste. It gets messy."

He turned into an alley and backed up to the back end of one of the old commercial buildings on Colorado Avenue. From the back of the truck Johnson pulled out a steel rod about three feet long which was bent to make a hook at the end. He walked to the alley and pulled a manhole cover off with the hook. "Bring me two of those red cones," He placed them on opposite sides of the open hole. We unloaded the pipe and shoved it down an old coal chute to the basement. We each carried a brick of lead. Johnson carried the burner and I had the bag of oakum. We entered the back door of the place and went down to the basement. The odor in the basement was not good. Johnson told me that not only did the sewer back up from some clog somewhere in the line, but one of the lengths of pipe had a hairline crack which had not been noticed for a long time and the crack is where the odor is coming from. "Go back up to the truck and bring the buckets."

I returned with six galvanized metal buckets.

"These are "honey buckets. We are going to replace all the sewer pipe in the basement. These pipes have been here since the building went up seventy five or eighty years ago. I'm going to start loosening these pipe joints, and I want you to put a bucket under each joint to catch the spill. These are called 'hub and spigot' joints. See the circle of lead in the joint?"

"Yeah."

"The lead holds the oakum packing in the joint to keep it from leaking. First, I'll loosen some joints, and we'll let them drain. He took a chisel and hammer to the lead circle. As piece by piece of lead popped loose, the joint began to drip. "Put the bucket under it." Johnson began poking at the soggy mess the lead had concealed. "This is the old oakum," he said as the joint began releasing more fluid into the bucket. He then moved to the other end of the pipe and repeated the lead/oakum removal. Once three or four joints were loose and draining Johnson said, "Now we'll cut the pipe. Get more buckets to put under the cuts." He used a tool that looked like a big bicycle chain with cutting wheels and a ratchet device. As he tightened the ratchet eventually the pipe broke in to. Fluid and toilet waste splashed all over me. The stench was gagging. There were about five or six additional cuts and splashes before he said, "Take the buckets up to the alley and dump them in the manhole."

On the way up I slopped more waste on my pant leg. (Before this I'd never heard of shit, piss, and toilet paper referred to as "waste.") While pouring the "honey" out, I splashed my shoes. God, I smelled bad. This procedure was repeated several times that day and each time I spilled human waste on my hands and clothes. While I was dipping honey, Johnson cut the pipe up into manageable sizes so we could carry them away. We went up to the truck for lunch.

"Get one of the clean buckets and go fill it at that spigot and clean yourself up." After washing with three different changes of water in my bucket, I still didn't smell too good. My nostrils were filled with the stench. I sat on a trash can and ate my sandwich which was wrapped with wax paper. I tried not to touch it with my bare hands. In the afternoon I watched Johnson pump up the blow torch and melt an ingot of lead in an iron pot. I dragged a length of new pipe from the coal chute and watched the big guy join the new pipes together. The oakum was packed into joints with a chisel then, using a rope looking thing, He wrapped it around the joint and with an iron dipper he ladled molten lead in behind the rope so that the lead flowed into and sealed the oakum. When we knocked off for the day Johnson hoisted the pipe pieces up through the coal chute to me, we then loaded them onto the truck bed. He took off his bib overalls and threw them in the back of the truck. He had pants on underneath. He gathered up the tools and told me to go rinse out the buckets. We both then cleaned up at the outdoor spigot. On the way back to the shop Johnson said, "Kid, you need to get yourself some overalls for these dirty jobs so you don't get your clothes dirty."

I couldn't agree more.

I asked him, "Do you do this every day?"

"No. That's the first honey dipping I've done in maybe seven or eight months."

When we reached the shop, he stopped the truck before going into the garage.

"Why don't you get out and go on home and change your clothes. The guys inside will really make fun of your odor."

I was planning on going to Davis's to brag about my new job, but I smelled so bad I walked home taking streets I thought to have the least amount of pedestrian traffic. When I got home I changed clothes and took the dirty shirt and pants down to the yard and turned the hose on them and hung them on the clothesline. I even hosed my shoes off. And went back upstairs and took a bath. The smell still lingered in my nose. I stayed home that night, thinking I still must smell. I told Mom my story.

She advised, "Blow your nose good and put a little Vicks on your upper lip. The smell will be gone in the morning."

She was right. The next day after work I went to Lorig's and charged a pair of coveralls.

Hanging Out

My routine for after work continued to be to drop by Davis's to see who might be around. I might stay for one Coke, no matter who was there. If one of my close friends was there we might make plans for the evening, like sneak into the City Auditorium to see the Globe Trotters ball game. We did this by either going through the unlocked restroom window backstage, or by paying for one ticket then the ticket holder would go up to the second balcony and let us in from the fire escape. Or we might go shoot pool. Also we might take in the last movie at the Peak theatre. One of the guys worked part time as night ticket taker there. After the box office closed and he was locking the doors, he would let us in to see the last movie. On our way in we'd stop at the lobby refreshment machine and get a bottle of Orange Crush and a bag of peanuts to empty into the Orange Crush.

Movies of the day were shown by means of reels of film projected on the screen by a projectionist up in a room above the balcony. Full run movies usually took more than one reel of film. So as not to have a long delay removing the used reel and installing the continuing reel, there were two projectors so when the first reel was used up, the second projector was turned on and the movie continued. If there was a long delay, the movie crowd would start stomping the floor and whistling, thinking the projectionist was asleep, which probably was the case sometimes.

On a night that someone had a car we would go to the drive-in movie. They charged for each person so we would have two guys pay and the three we put in the trunk were in free. We pulled the same kind of thing during state basketball tournaments in Denver. We'd have two guys check into a hotel room and five or six of us would occupy it with our coat pockets filled with cans of beer. There was teen common knowledge that if you drank beer warm, you could get high much faster, so we put beer cans on the radiator. I don't remember what effect that actually had. Also with a car we went to a drive-in restaurant down on South Nevada Avenue. It was a big High School hangout. Maybe we could get some girls to come get in the car and neck a little, and if lucky maybe go park at the Garden of the Gods, or Austin Bluffs where there was no traffic. Many a romance started at that drive-in, and maybe a marriage or two. From time to time a carload of us would make the seventy-five-mile drive to Denver to ride the roller coasters at Elich Gardens, or at the Lakeside Amusement Park, Sometimes two or maybe three of us guys would just go to this one all-night restaurant, drink coffee and exchange teen age wisdom. The conversation might be sex, sports, ambitions, philosophy and coolness in people, cars, and clothing. The subject matter was only limited to the extent of our imaginations. On the subject of sex: "Girls have it really good. They can get screwed anytime they want." Then would come the almosts: "I almost made out with [her] last night, but her dad made her come in." We had a lot of almosts to talk about. For most of us the extent of our sexual experiences was on that rare occasion when the girl consented to letting you "feel her up" and maybe she would also be into "French kissing." We would pass around dog eared type written pages of pornography. I never knew where these originated. And there were "Eight Pagers" or "Tijuana Bibles," little graphically illustrated eight-page booklets of famous cartoon characters in hard core sexual situations. These documents are where we received a lot of our sex education erroneous as it was. Dirty Speedy Gonzales jokes were shared for a time. Our talk on sports was mainly confined to high school heroes. We rarely talked politics. Once in a while, one of the guys would introduce an esoteric subject like genetics: "My older sister says that in one of her classes, they were studying how certain genes in our body determine hair color, eye color, and even when a white person mixes with a colored person there are genes that determine the color of their children."

Now, here was a subject to hold our interest for a whole night. There would be many questions and many theories founded in and supported by our ignorance. We often spoke of the taboo of racial intermarriage and how it was widespread in Germany with our colored soldiers and the German girls.

"Man, are those girls in for a surprise when they get back here and find out how the colored live."

Then someone would introduce, "Yeah, and you know, from pictures I've seen of those German women, they are all ugly."

Ignorance wins again. And in the same breath, we praised the accomplishments of the city's best all-around athlete, James "Sonny" Bell, who was probably the only Negro[45] man in town holding a white-collar job. Bell excelled in all sports. He was our Babe Ruth, Jim Thorpe, Jesse Owens, George Mikan, and Joe Louis, all in one. The stories of Sonny's accomplishments were many. I would tell the guys how Sonny would come in to Lorig's when I worked there. This was true. "What's he like in person?" and I would tell them what a nice guy he was, which was also true. What was not true was that I sold him a shirt or a pair of shoes and how he was so nice to me and called me by my name. I never once waited on Sonny, usually Mister Lorig, himself, had that privilege. I didn't have much interest in cars, so I was left out of automotive conversations. Boxing was big with us. Joe Louis was home from the army and defeating all comers.

> News Break
> June 25, 1948
> Russia Blockades Berlin, Allies Airlift supplies
> Russian commanders have tightened the blockade around the Allied sectors of Berlin. Western powers say they are determined to fly in enough supplies to keep the Germans from starving.

> News Break
> June 25, 1948
> Joe Louis Retains Title against Jersey Joe Walcott
> 42,000 people in Yankee Stadium see the aging champ KO Walcott in eleventh round.

---

[45] "Negro" was now replacing "colored" and was used with pride.

Not a Teamster

At muster one morning the Old Man ordered, "Walker, take truck number three, and go to the hot mix plant, load up and go out to the Knob Hill paving Job."

After muster I approached him: "Mister Jardine you told me to get a truck. I don't have a driver's license."

"You can drive can't you?"

"Yes, sir."

"Well, get to it."

I went out in the garage looking for truck number three. There was a long semi flat bed with an International Harvester tractor, three or four pickups and a few dump trucks of different sizes. I had never driven any vehicle except Aunt Edith's DeSoto but I was pretty confident I could drive a pickup truck. I looked for a number three on the pickups. There was no number 3. I thought maybe one of the other guys took it by mistake. I checked with the garage mechanic. "Number 3 is that three-ton dump over there." He pointed at the dump trucks. I walked over to the huge trucks with fear in every part of my being.

Sure enough, there was a big number three on the door. It was the smaller of the dump trucks, but to me it might as well have been the semi. I climbed up into the cab. I checked out everything in this strange place. I recognized the steering wheel, the keys in the ignition, the brake pedal, the clutch and the gear shift. Right away I noticed there were markings on the gear shift knob. "Oh man!" The markings indicated the location of each gear. There were four numbered in the H pattern and a R off to the right and down which

I took to mean reverse. There was another position off to the left of the H and down. I knew only the three forward gears and a reverse gear of a passenger car. I stepped on the clutch, turned the ignition key and the big engine responded. The truck was pretty new so the sound was not loud. I wrestled the gear shift to the R position and slowly let out on the clutch. I was nervous as can be. The big vehicle began to move backwards. There was no rearview mirror in the cab. I hit the brake pedal and put the gear stick in the H cross bar which I hoped was the neutral position. It was. I didn't know how I was going to get this truck backed up without a rear view mirror, then I saw the mirror was mounted on the side of the truck, better yet, there was a mirror over on the other side also. I started backing up slowly again carefully watching the left mirror to be sure to clear the garage doorway.

Crash! I heard. I hit the brake and looked in the direction of the sound. The mirror on the right side had hit the wall of the door opening and was hanging loose. My heart was pounding. My first reaction was to look around to see if anyone saw me. There was no one in sight. I turned the steering wheel so as to maneuver the truck away from the wall and continued backing out into the street. I figured I'd stop somewhere on the way and check out the damage. I slowly drove to the hot mix plant. I don't think I ever got up enough speed to use the fourth-gear position. I followed the signs at the hot mix property and drove up to a big metal structure as tall as a three-story building. Steam rose up from the structure, and the smell of hot tar invaded everything. There were two conveyor belts running to the top and what looked like an oversized coal hopper directly above where the guy was standing waving me to drive under the hopper. I slowly approached until he signaled Stop. Within a minute the truck bed violently sunk as three tons of asphalt hot mix was dumped in it. The guy told me I was loaded and could go. The truck stalled on me twice until I put it in a lower gear. I was cautious and up tight driving out to the job.

I saw the signs: "Road Work Ahead, Road Closed, Detour." I turned onto the gravel road and met a Jardine dump truck coming from the direction I was heading. I drove up to the work site. A bunch of guys were working with rakes and shovels on a layer of hot asphalt which I assumed had been left by the truck I saw leaving. Behind them was a guy operating a big roller. I slowly approached and waited for instructions. I didn't know what I was supposed to do. Finally a guy, I guessed to be the foreman, came over to me: "Back your truck up to where those guys are workin'." I turned the truck around and started backing up at a creeping speed. The foreman was in my rearview mirror directing me. He signaled Stop and jumped up on the running board. He pulled a lever just behind the door which I later learned was the tail gate release.

"I want you to drive away slowly while the bed is raising so that you leave an even bed of mix about six inches deep."

"Okay."

I searched frantically for some lever or something that would raise the truck bed. There was a box on the floor board next to my right leg that had what looked like a gear shift stick with knob on it. The markings on it said "raise" on one end and "lower" on the other end. I pulled the stick to the "raise" position and was in the process of putting the truck gear shift into a forward gear when all the guys yelled, "No, No, No." I heard an "OH SHIT," also. I had dumped the entire three tons of hot mix right in one spot. The foreman jumped up on the running board.

"WHAT IN THE HELL ARE YOU DOING? YOU DUMPED THE WHOLE LOAD RIGHT THERE WHERE WE NOW HAVE TO MOVE IT ALL BY HAND. JESUS CHRIST, WHO IN THE HELL TAUGHT YOU TO DRIVE? ARE YOU FUCKING DEAF? DIDN'T YOU HEAR ME TELL YOU TO SPREAD IT EVENLY?"

He jumped down and threw his hat on the ground and said, "GET THE HELL OUTTA HERE." I drove away about a hundred yards and stopped when I realized the truck bed was still up. I pushed the control stick to "lower" and waited for the bed to come down. When I heard it lock, I drove off. I wasn't looking forward to my second trip out to the paving site. An hour later when I pulled up to try again, I knew every man working there hated me and who knew what epithets were used to describe me. I'm sure I could guess.

This time the foreman jumped up on the running board and calmly asked, "Have you ever done this before?" He sounded like he really wanted to know.

"No, I haven't."

He then told me to move over and that he would show me how. He explained everything that was taking place as he moved away slowly until the bed was empty. "It takes some practice, kid. I'll see you on the next trip."

On my third trip out there, he sat on the passenger side and talked me through a successful spread. Before he got out he said, "What happened to your rearview mirror?"

"I don't know," I lied.

"Don't leave. I'll tape it up for you."

He left and came back with a roll of friction tape and made that mirror look good as new, almost. I hoped nobody would notice it for a long time. I made one more trip that day and without help did a creditable job of spreading. All the guys cheered. I know the story of the dumb kid who dumped 3 tons of asphalt on the ground spread throughout the shop.

The next morning before muster, Johnson, the plumber, said to me, "Hey, kid, I understand you had a little trouble at the paving site yesterday."

I sheepishly nodded.

"Well, don't worry about it, worse things than that have happened here. Everybody has to learn. Hell, you didn't injure anyone."

He patted me on the back and again said, "Don't worry about it."

Johnson made me feel really good.

Not a Brakeman

About two weeks after my paving performance, I was again assigned to truck number three. The shop foreman directed, "There's a rail car of crushed rock down on the tracks near Las Vegas Street. Go down there and load up three yards of rock and take it to the Naval Reserve Building at Prospect Lake. The Chief out there will show you where to dump it." I asked the mechanic in the garage: "How much is three yards of rock?" He told me it would fill my truck. I drove down to Las Vegas Street and found a cross road that reached a dead end at the rail tracks. There was an alley that ran parallel to the tracks I saw a lone rail car parked on the tracks about a hundred yards up track. The tracks were on an incline and the rail car was at the higher elevation. The adjacent alley was level, which meant to drive closer to the rail car would put me too far below to reach it with the truck. How can I get close enough to that rail car? I backed the truck up as close as I could get it on the railroad embankment and walked up to the rail car. It was a small open hopper car. I climbed up the ladder and looked in. It was filled with crushed white quartz.

This information didn't solve my problem. While up on the car, I surveyed the area searching for a route the truck could take to get closer. I saw nothing that would work. I was standing on the ladder right next to a turn wheel that I figured was maybe a break since the car was sitting on an incline, something was keeping it from rolling down, or maybe this was to open the hoppers underneath the car and something else is the brake. I climbed down and looked at the two hoppers. They each had a turn wheel. I checked the car wheels to see if anything was blocking them. Nothing. I climbed back up the ladder. This must be the brake. I grabbed the big iron wheel and started to turn it. It didn't give. I pulled with all my strength and it slowly gave a little. Nothing happened. I pulled on the wheel with both hands gripping one of the wheel spokes and my foot pushing against the side of the rail car. The wheel gave a little more. I felt the car move a little. It was moving at a hardly noticeable pace. I felt smart.

As the car rolled down the track, it began to pick up speed. I pulled on the brake wheel; the car kept on rolling faster. I panicked and pulled and pulled on that wheel and the car rolled on faster. I was frightened and jumped off the ladder, hit the ground and rolled down the embankment. I got up, dusted myself off and watched the car roll down the track. It was not rolling fast, but then in slow motion it jumped the track and slowly kept on moving forward until it started to go down the embankment. It slowly tipped to the right side and gradually turned over on its side. Tons of white rock were spread all over. I walked down the track with butter flies in my stomach. I thought I was going to throw up. Down where the car jumped the rail I found there was a derail installed on the track. With trembling fear, I drove back to the shop.

"Tell me again, what happened?" the shop foreman asked.

"I went down there and found a rail car tipped over on its side with white rock spilled all around it."

He asked me a couple other questions like he couldn't believe it. I stuck with my story and said no more.

The rest of the day I worked in the tool crib stacking shelves with tools, mechanical parts, pipe, and sundry other things that had been delivered by a semitruck. I never heard more about the derailed car.

On my last day at Jardine's I carried rolls of tar paper from a truck in the parking lot to the roof of a big new building of some kind. Luckily there was a staircase to the roof. It was a hot day in June and the tar paper rubbed on my neck till my skin was raw and beet red. The rolls were what was known in the trade as "thirty-pound felt." Each roll would cover a "square" (one hundred square feet) and the rolls weighed nearly thirty pounds each. During lunch I found an old rag in the truck and wore it around my sore neck for the rest of the day. Why I quit Jardine is a mystery to me. My pay of one hundred fifty dollars a month, was not bad for an unskilled sixteen-year-old laborer working forty-eight hours a week. It was the first job I had that I saved any money on. Maybe my savings of two hundred dollars gave me a sense of freedom from work. Anyway, I quit and after giving Mom fifty dollars (which I paid her every month), I had a $150 plus two weeks' pay. This allowed me to sleep in a couple of mornings till Mom started waking me and telling me I better find a job. I would get out of bed and just kind of mosey around using the bathroom, getting dressed, and fixing breakfast, stalling till she left for work. I didn't go back to bed, but I didn't go look for a job either. The freedom of not going to work was fun for a few days, but there was nothing much to do. I spent my mornings at the pool hall, took lunch, and hung out with my friends at Davis's.

My afternoons were spent back at the pool haul until school let out, at which time I went back to Davis's. Jerry, a school drop-out like me, was one of the pin setters at the bowling alley next to the pool hall.

One day he let me come back where he worked setting up bowling pins after they had been knocked over. His work was hard dangerous labor. After resetting the pins, he had to quickly jump up and balance himself on a perch up behind the pins waiting for the next bowling ball to come barreling down the lane knocking pins everywhere. His perch didn't always protect him from the flying pins. Immediately after the ball collided with the pins he had to jump down, pick up the ball roll it back on the ball return track, reset the pins and jump back up on his perch. I watched all this first hand from a perch near his. He did this for hours. The only breaks he got were when his alley was not in use. He said that sometimes when it was slow, he worked two lanes at the same time. He worked for the minimum wage of forty cents an hour plus tips. "Usually we only get tips when there is league play." I hoped I'd never have to do this.

Coke Head

I started scanning the help wanted ads. It wasn't long till I saw an ad for help at the local Coca Cola Bottling Co: "No experience necessary." I walked over and put in an application and was hired right away. I started work the next day. The owner, a Mr. Brown, a short man in suit and tie was one of those people that are easy to forget. He had no distinguishing features or mannerisms that would set him apart from anyone else in a crowd. He took me out in the back to the bottling plant. There were two young guys sweeping the floor of the plant. Brown called one of them over and introduced us.

"Get the bottle washer started, and show Jack how to feed it."

The guy was near my age. He wasn't fat, but he was bulky. He was built like a square box. He needed a haircut, and his ruddy face was sprinkled with pimples. His shirt and pants were long overdue for washing. When Mr. Brown returned to the office, the guy flipped a switch to turn the big bottle washer on. The machine was a large stainless steel thing with a big roller at one end that had slots in rows. After the machine ran for a while, from a stack of pop cases, the guy picked up four bottles; two in each hand with the bottle necks held between the fingers, one between the index and middle fingers and the other one between the little and ring fingers. He lifted the four bottles up and pushed them forward into four slots on the slow-turning roller. He then reached down to the pop case and pulled up four more bottles and repeated.

"You do it," he said.

He wasn't too interested in teaching me. I tried it; the bottles felt kind of awkward. I swung them up like he did, and one of the

304

bottles didn't match up to the slot, and it almost slipped out of my hand. I looked at the guy.

"You better do better than that," he said with no expression on his face at all. "When you finish this stack, there's more over there." He pointed to case upon case of empty bottles. That was the only thing he said to me all day. When he departed, he walked over to the other guy and told him something, and they both laughed and looked at me. I pumped those bottles into the roller till noon or after. My fingers were blistered. I stopped for a moment to see what time it was. The two guys were at the other end of the plant sitting on some boxes eating.

I walked over there and asked, "Is it lunchtime?"

"Yeah," one of them said.

Then they both snickered. These guys didn't like me. I had brought a sandwich, and Mr. Brown had told me to help myself to the Coke in the machine. I got a Coke and walked back to the washer and ate lunch sitting on an empty bottle case. When I saw the guys get up and start to work, I got up also. By midafternoon the blisters had broken, and by quitting time, two or three of my fingers were seeping blood. Before going to Davis's, I stopped off at the Johnson-English Drugs to get some Band-Aids. The druggist saw my sore fingers and asked what had happened. I told him about the bottle-washing operation. "You're working with those Atkins brothers, huh?"

"There's two guys workin' there. I don't know their names. I just started today."

"I know them. They're not the kind you want to be hanging out with. They'll get you in trouble. I don't know why Brown even keeps them around. They're a couple of bums."

He never did tell me what his opinion was based on. So these two guys were brothers. I always shared my day's experience with the guys at Davis's and made plans for the night, maybe to go either up Ute Pass where there was a night spot near one of the small tourist communities of either Woodland Park, Green Mountain Falls or Cascade, where they didn't ask for ID, or a place we had heard about down near Fountain where it was said that no questions were asked.

Sometimes on a Saturday night I was paid a couple bucks by Uncle Walt to babysit my little two-year-old cousin Mike.

"There's some horse[46] in the refrigerator if you want a sandwich, and you can drink a beer if you want."

It was an easy two bucks. Mike usually slept the evening away while I ate a sandwich, some potato chips, and drank a beer while listening to "You're Hit Parade," "Truth or Consequences," and/or "Gang Busters" on the radio. Most households didn't have television at that time, even though the appliance stores were beginning to display them. We had heard about the "radio with pictures" for years, but never really thought it would happen.

At the Coke plant next day, I was back at the bottle washer till lunchtime when I ran out of used Coke bottles to wash. While eating lunch, the big overhead door of the plant opened, and a truck came through. Mr. Brown came out of the office and spoke with the driver, then he told the two guys something and on his way back to the office told me, "After you finish eating, help load the truck. The truck driver introduced himself to me as Ben.

He added, "Glad to have ya. This place can use some good people. Those two," he said, pointing at the brothers, "are worthless."

We started loading. The brothers brought dollies full of pop cases. I lifted them up to Ben on the truck. The loading took most of the afternoon.

When Ben left, he told me, "Don't let those fuck-offs take advantage of you."

I washed bottles for the rest of the week. The following week, by some small degree, my bandaged fingers stopped hurting. I was taught to inspect uncapped bottles of Coca Cola moving down on a conveyor belt to be capped. My job was to look for bottles that didn't get a full amount of Coke in them. And pull them off the belt and put them aside. This was one long, boring day, but it was good to get off the washing machine.

[46] "Horse" or "horse cock," a GI euphemism for bologna, so called for the long tubular shape it's packed in, which the army and navy guys thought symbolized a large equestrian penis.

At Davis's that evening I ordered a Coke even after drinking about four or five at work. Fountain Cokes always tasted better than bottled. There were new records on the Wurlitzer. I put a quarter in and selected some old standards like "Sentimental Journey," "When the Saints go Marching In," and "One O'Clock Jump." I tried one tune I'd never heard before, "Sunny Side of the Street" by a singer I'd never heard, Frankie Laine. This Frankie Laine we really liked. He had one more record on the juke; "Shine." It was great too. Four of us in the booth tapped our feet and drummed the table to the beat of these songs.

We played them over about three more times each before leaving.

I had been at the bottling company about two or three weeks when it finally happened; I was pulling cases of Coke off the conveyor roller belt and stacking them eight high nearby. The cases were being shoved down the conveyor to me by one of the brothers. He intentionally kept shoving the cases faster than I could pull them off. "Hey slow it down a little. I can only pull them off so fast." He just gave me a blank look and kept on shoving them at me. He shoved one case down that smashed my hand in between two pop cases. The brother was about six or seven feet from me on the opposite side of the conveyor. I reacted by moving toward him as fast as I could. I reached across the conveyor, grabbed his shirt with my injured hand, and the fist of my other hand smashed hard straight in his nose.

Blood spurted from his nose, and he fell backward, knocking over a stack of empty cases. My heart was beating fast as I stood waiting for him to come after me. He got up holding his hand over his nose and stumbled into the office. A little later the girl from the office came out. "Mister Brown wants to see you." I went into browns office. Brother was sitting in a chair holding a Kleenex over his swollen nose. The areas around his eyes were swollen and darkened. "Tell me what happed here Jack." I told my story and showed him my now, swollen hand. Mister Brown sent me back to work. The brother was not seen the rest of the day. I guess he was sent home. I thought I might get fired, but I never heard another word about the incident and the brothers from then on tried their best to avoid me all together.

Ben the truck driver came out of the office early one morning and told me I'd be working with him on the truck from now on. Man, this was good news. I hated working in that plant with those two shit heads. "Brown said I could pick any man I wanted for the job. I picked you. I wouldn't work with those two idiots if they paid me double." From that time on, the job was good. I even got a 5 cent raise. I now was paid forty-five cents an hour. Traveling on the Coca Cola route with Ben was a happy time for me. We delivered to the few big grocery stores and the many small neighborhood stores. There were the drug store stops where sometimes we'd stop and have a taste at the soda fountain. We delivered to liquor stores, restaurants and even out to the Knob hill auction lunch counter of my early childhood. Ben was welcomed at each stop with a lot of fun banter. Everyone liked him as I did. Ben was a talker and I enjoyed listening to him. He was an ex-GI and told me of all his adventures in Italy and Germany.

He told me of the horror of D-Day at Normandy where he was shot in the leg. I didn't want to leave Ben, but I ran into Al Hollingsworth in Lorig's. Al was a former neighbor of Kenny and Nancy. His trade was plastering. He was a tall guy and I don't think I ever saw him out of work clothes; white pants and shirt, both splattered with plaster. I'm looking for a helper. If you know someone have them call me." He went to look for a pencil to write down his phone number. When he came back I asked how much the job paid. He told me sixty-five cents an hour. Right away I said: I'll work for you. I told Ben I'd be leaving at the end of the week. I also told Mr. Brown. Both treated me kindly. Ben said he would miss me. And Mister Brown said he would have my final pay check ready on my last day.

Mixing Mud and Carrying the Hod

A l picked me up Monday morning. He drove an old 1935 Chevy sedan and pulled a four-wheel flatbed trailer that had been constructed from an automobile chassis. Behind the trailer was a concrete mixer which had lost any color it might have had. Where it wasn't rust, it was white with plaster. The trailer was loaded with long wide boards, wood frames, ladders, buckets, tubs, tools and bags of something I guessed to be plaster. I saw the word "Gypsum" on one stack of bags and the word "Portland" on another. All this was tied down with rope. This little caravan looked like a travelling scrap collector. We drove out to one of the new subdivisions to a home still under construction. All the way there Al asked about my life, my family, and my ambitions. He asked if I had heard from Kenny. He seemed to be a genuinely caring person. Al told me he had grown up with a trowel in his hand. His father was a Plasterer as were his three brothers. He had struck out on his own after the war.

"My brothers are still workin' for Daddy," he said.

Although spending most of his life in Colorado Springs, his words and the way he put them together in sentences was pure hillbilly.

"The last guy I hired wasn't worth a hoot and a holler. He was lazy and dumber than a box of rocks."

Al was a big blond-haired guy with rough chapped and cracked hands. We drove on to the construction site. A couple guys were up on the roof nailing shingles. The yard of the house was all mud and was littered with construction debris. There was a pile of sand up near the house. On the ground there were tire ruts and caterpillar

309

tracks filled with rain water. I followed Al walking on a plywood boardwalk up to the front door. The flooring was sub-floor plywood. I followed him as he toured every room in the new house. All but two rooms downstairs were covered with what Al called "metal lath."

"Well, I'll be, they told me they'd be done with these walls by last Thursday. They're slower than molasses in January. Let's go upstairs."

The second floor rooms were all completely lathed. "We'll start up here." Back down at the trailer we started unloading. The fifty-pound bags of gypsum plaster and Portland cement. The big wooden frames, Al told me they were leaning scaffolds. There were five-gallon white buckets galore and miles of garden hose, electrical cord and a wheel barrow. Two canvas bags were filled with tools. And there was a V shaped wooden tool with one end closed and it had a long handle attached at the bottom of the V. This tool and I were to be constant companions for the next week or so. First Al found an outside electrical outlet on the house, for the mixer.

"First, I'll show you how to mix mud for the 'scratch coat.' Get the shovel and put enough of that sand till it comes up to about here." He held his finger on the mixer barrel. When I finished the sand, he said, "Now we put a bag of I don't remember the recipe, but I think we put a bag of the gypsum and a bag of cement. While I was shoveling sand Al had hooked up the hose which he held pouring water on the sand/plaster/cement. Just before he pulled the hose away he showed me by a deep scratch on the mixer where the water should reach before pulling the hose. "Throw the switch right there." The old mixer blades started turning over the ingredients. "Grab the saw horses, and let's go upstairs."

I took a saw horse in each hand while Al carried one of the tool bags and a sheet of four-foot square plywood which had remnants of plaster on and about its edges. Upstairs he arranged the plywood atop the saw horses and we went back to the mixer.

"Get the wheel barrow and put it right here." He tuned mixer off and grabbed a handle on the mixer barrel and rolled in down till it dropped its load into the wheel barrow. "Get the hose and wash out the mixer. You do this after every load." I wheeled the load into the house carefully, afraid I was going to tip it over. "Take it over by the stairs."

He then picked up the Triangle of wood with the long handle attached and leaned it against the wheelbarrow. "This is a hod. It's what you use to carry the mud. Get your shovel and shovel mud from the wheelbarrow into the hod. Don't put in more than you can carry. Full, the hod weighs near two hundred pounds." He showed me how to cradle the hod on my shoulder and where to hold the handle. "You can load it now, and we'll go upstairs." I loaded the hod to less than half full and followed Al upstairs. The hod was painful against my shoulder. Up in the room where the sawhorse table was Al showed me how to get out from under my load and dump it on the table. "This is a "Hawk," he said as he picked up a tool that was a flat metal surface with a handle coming out of the bottom of it. "I'm sure you know that this is a trowel," which he held in the other hand. He pushed an amount of the plaster mix from the table with the trowel onto the hawk. I asked: "Why do you call this a "Scratch" coat?" He explained it was the first of three coats he would be applying and that he'd let me help him scratch it later on. He then stepped up onto a plank supported by two buckets turned upside down and started to plaster the ceiling. "Go get another hod full and just keep the board full a mud. When the wheelbarrow gets low mix another batch. We don't want to run out till the ceiling is finished." I carried hod after hod all morning and mixed about three batches.

About eleven thirty Al said, "Don't mix no more. I got enough to finish with. Hose off your hod, and we'll eat lunch directly." Before lunch he pulled two tools from his tool bag. They looked like big combs with thin round metal tongs. "These are Scratchers." He showed me how to use them to scratch gooves in the plaster he had just applied. "The scratches give the second coat somethin' to hold on to."

We ate sandwiches in the shade of the house. "Well, wataya thinka the job?"

I told him I liked it except that the hod was hurting my shoulder. After lunch Al pulled a big sponge from his car and told me to put it on my shoulder.

"When we get down stairs you can use the wheel barrel instead of the hod."

The sponge helped some, but I still went home with a sore shoulder that evening. That job lasted the rest of the summer. I worked on two smaller jobs with Al; a stucco repair, and a room addition. He taught me much about the plastering trade; the use of certain floats and sponges for textured walls. A hot water bottle with a handle Al had attached was used at times to texture ceilings with the design on the rubber bottle. He would let me trowel some scratch coats, and once in a while a brown coat (second coat) but never a finish coat which was very exacting. I mixed all the different coats for him, even mixed quick lime in a mixing box with a hoe. "Wear these goggles and gloves with this "hot lime," it'll burn your skin and blind yer eyes." The powdery white lime, used for finishing coats, got hot and bubbled like it was cooking over a flame.

Al gave me his car keys and sent me to the neighborhood grocery to buy a couple of Cokes. When leaving the store, I backed out and scraped the car parked next to me. The grey haired driver got out of the car to inspect. I was scared. I still didn't have a driver's license. I got out and went around the car to see the damage. His black car had a grey streak about a foot long on the back fender. I told him I was sorry and that I would pay him. He was nice about it. He said: I think ten dollars would take care of it." I told him I didn't have the money and the car wasn't mine, but I would get the money from my boss and pay him.

He asked, "Who is your boss?" I gave him Al's name, address, and phone number, which he wrote down on a piece of paper he pulled from his wallet. He closed with, "I'll take this up with Hollingsworth." I waited for him to back up and leave first. I told Al what had happened and asked that he hold ten bucks from my pay. He agreed and all was forgotten.

It was mid-October. Uncle Walt and Eileen had a second son about three weeks earlier. He was named John. I hadn't met him yet, but I was anxious to meet Mike's little brother. I always wished I had a little brother. As years went by I grew closer to my uncle until our relationship came to feel like we were brothers and his sons, Mike and John, I always thought of as nephews.

One Saturday afternoon Sally Green showed up at Davis's with a group of girls. My heart jumped a beat. She was just as beautiful as I remembered her in Junior High, only now her body had matured to young womanhood. I had long regretted ever breaking up with her, but didn't have the courage to risk being rejected. Her group took up a booth and a half. She was in the half filled one. Her hearty laugh filled the room.

I went over and said, "Hello, stranger."

She greeted me warmly with that familiar big smile of hers and asked me to sit down. One of the girls with her I knew from school, the other was a classmate of Sally's at North Junior High, where she and Sally had just graduated. They would be starting high school in the fall. One of her friends in the other booth looked over and asked: Sally, you know Doak?" Sally was confused with the nickname but they got her straightened out. I asked Sally if I could talk to her a minute. We went out by the back door and I asked her: "Would you like to go to a movie tonight?" I really didn't think this would happen, but she said "yes." We made arrangements for me to come to her house. She went back to her friends and I went cloud walking like I had fallen in love again. I walked down by Sutak's peanut shack on Nevada Avenue and turned the corner and walked down Pike's Peak Avenue past the Ute Theatre, and the Miller Music Company where we used to pick out a record to hear and cram four guys into the listening booth made for single occupancy. Some of rock and roll's lyrics are really dumb: "You ain't nothin' but a hound dog," or how about, "My vibe is too vibelicious for you, babe." In my day we had deathless lyrics like, "Mairzy Doats and Dozy Doats and Liddle Lamsy Divey," and "I've got a lovely bunch of coconuts."

I ambled on over to Tejon Street where I bought a coffee to-go at the Busy Corner Grill and walked north on Tejon up past the JC Penny department store and the Kress five-and-dime. I was excited about my upcoming date with Sally. I was just walking off my nervousness. Actually I was floating. I stopped to look at the windows at Giddings Department Store. It was rumored that Ralph Giddings was "queer." All I knew was that the store had the most artistic show windows in town. I walked on up to Bijou Street and cut through Acacia Park and made my way home.

I arrived at the Green household a few minutes early. Sally opened the door and asked me to have a seat in the living room while she gathered up those things that girls gather up. We talked for a bit until Mrs. Green came in. "I thought I heard your soft voice Jack. Most of her friends are loud and rowdy."

I'll never forget the movie we saw that night; "The Casbah" with Tony Martin and Yvonne DeCarlo. The beautiful ornate chief theatre with its thick plush luxurious carpeting, two-balcony vaulted cathedral like ceiling, opera boxes and colorful indirect lighting was never so beautiful as it was that night. The usher seated us about half way down on the first floor on the aisle. We settled into the soft velvety seats and held hands. I put my arm over Sally's shoulder. This was like old times. We took the bus home and held hands walking to Sally's house from the bus stop. At the door Sally faced me, raised her head, and we kissed. It was a long lingering passionate kiss like no other. I wished it would never end.

I walked home on a cloud visualizing how great it will be going with Sally again, holding hands, hanging out at Davis's together, going to movies, and most of all, kissing and hugging again. After work the following Monday, I called Sally. Her mother said she wasn't home.

"I'll let her know you called, Jack."

I tried to call back that night, but I kept getting in on someone else's conversation on our party line phone. The next day I called and Mrs. Green gave me the same response. The rejection hurt, and I didn't know why this was happening. Another case of La Donna E Mobile. I thought, "Just like with Mary Jean Oliver at the Stratton Home and the waitress at the Blue Spruce."

As I looked back in later years, I surmised that I had changed too much from our junior high days; I was a school dropout, a smoker, a drinker, and I had a tattoo and had a ducktail haircut. This was probably too much outlaw for Sally.

One of my best friends during this period was Ozz (Dwight Ostrowski). He and I pledged Chislers Club together.

One evening down at Davis's, he told me, "An old buddy of mine, Fred Schmidt, will be coming in from California tomorrow."

I told Ozz, "I once knew a Freddie Schmidt in fourth grade before I went to the home."

The more we talked about Fred, the more it seemed like we might be talking about the same guy. The next evening when I went by Ozz's house, he had a visitor.

"Doak, this is Fred."

We talked a few minutes in Ozz's living room, and sure as hell, this was Freddie Schmidt from fourth grade at the Lowell School. He was the one who lived above the downtown store with the entrance in the alley. He was the one who could draw cartoons and do an impression of Donald Duck's voice. Fred remembered me and my sister and Billy, the boy next door who tap danced. This was a real reunion. Fred at this time was now eighteen years old, wore a small mustache and hair in the ducktail fashion. He was about as tall as me and wore intentionally-never-washed Levi's with the cuffs turned inward to reveal white sweat socks and penny loafers. I guessed that all this was pure West Coast fashion which hadn't arrived in the higher elevations yet. He also told me he was married and had a child.

Fred had been in town a couple weeks when he asked me if I'd like to go up to Casper Wyoming for the week end. He said his Father lived there and he hadn't seen him since his parents were divorced some years back. I agreed and that Saturday we took a bus to Casper. It was cold and windy when we got off the bus. The pale winter sun was setting behind the low lying mountains in the distance. Casper didn't strike me as being inviting at all. Fred had his Father's address on a well-worn envelope folded up in his wallet. The envelope had once held the last communication he had received from his dad. How long ago he didn't say, but that dog-eared envelope looked to be plenty old. Fred had lived in Casper when his parents were together, so he knew roughly the whereabouts of the envelope address. We set out on foot. Fred had the impression that Dad would have a place for us to stay. However, it turned out Dad rented a room in his brother's house. Nobody knew we were coming, and I had the impression that nobody was pleased to see us, including Dad.

Fred's Aunt did feel obligated by Christian decency to fix us something to eat, and Dad said, "Since you're only going to be here one night, I guess we can all three fit in my bed."

It was a crowded, sleepless night.

In the morning Fred turned down the offer of breakfast. We took off walking toward the downtown area. The temperature had dropped and the wind was biting. Fred said: "I wanted to get out of there. I don't think they wanted us to stay." I didn't know if he was hurt or angry. For sure he was disappointed. We found a restaurant and had breakfast. I couldn't believe the menu; there was an item called "Brains and Eggs."

I asked the waitress, "Is this really brains?"

She said, "Sure, they're calves' brains. Lot a people eat 'em."

Fred said he would try them. The thought turned my stomach. I opted for bacon and eggs. Our bus back to Colorado wasn't scheduled to leave till late afternoon. We walked around town some, bought some cigarettes and chewing gum in a drug store and took a couple chances on a punch board lottery game.[47] Punch boards were considered gambling devices and were outlawed in Colorado. Fred won a free punch. It didn't win any cash either. We wandered into a pool hall that was in the basement of a storefront long forgotten. We shot a few games of pool. Fred and I were about evenly matched on each game we played.

He got the idea to look up some girl he had gone with when he lived here. He went to the phone booth, looked up her number, dropped his nickel in the phone and dialed. I didn't hear the conversation, but he was on the phone long enough to have to put in another nickel.

"She's home. Let's go see her. We've still got time before the bus leaves."

---

[47] Punch boards were game boards with holes punched in them. Each hole had a rolled-up piece of paper or ticket stuffed in it. You bought a chance and were allowed to, by use of a stylus, punch out a ticket. If your ticket had the winning number, you won cash.

Her name is beyond the reach of my memory, but I remember her well. She lived with her parents, who were both at work. She was home taking care of her baby. She had quit high school when her pregnancy began to show. The father of the child was not in her life. We sat in her living room and talked for about an hour. Mostly it was them reminiscing about their schooldays. On the bus back to Colorado, Fred suggested we move to Casper. I don't know what he had in mind, but the idea excited me.

Mom's response when I told her I was planning on moving to Wyoming was, "What in the world would you do that for?"

She went on, "It's winter, you don't have a place to stay, and you don't have a job."

"We're going to stay with Fred's dad," I lied. "And we've lined up jobs with the railroad up there," I lied again.

She finally gave in.

Casper Wyoming

It was evening when we stepped off the bus. The light snow fall was being blown horizontally. We walked a couple blocks to a hotel in downtown Casper.

When we went to check in, the clerk advised, "All the rooms are occupied. We can rent you each a cot in the mezzanine if you wish." He advised that with all the oil drilling going on in the area, the oil workers had taken all the available space. We told him we would think it over. Back out onto the cold street, we walked a couple more blocks to another hotel. We were told they were booked full.

"There's another hotel around the corner, but it's probably the same story."

We walked back to the cot offer.

The clerk told us, "We set up the cots at 8:30 p.m. and remove them by 8:00 am. We can check your baggage."

It was about seven forty-five when we checked our bags and sat in the lobby waiting for the cots to be brought out. Our numbered tickets gave us each a cot for the night. The canvas bed of each cot was stenciled US Army. We were assigned our cots and told we could pick up a pillow and a blanket each at the linen closet down the corridor. We were expected to use the public restroom down in the lobby. Surprisingly, I slept really well.

Early next morning we stepped out into an inch or two of snow and a bitter wind. The restaurant was two very long cold blocks down the street. At the restaurant door we had to squeeze in and wait shoulder to shoulder for seats. After a long hot wait (there wasn't enough room to take your coat off) smelling garlic, liquor, sweat and oil, we wound up taking separate seats. Fred took one where he shared a booth with three other guys. I got a stool at the counter.

We left the restaurant and went to the pool hall and got a newspaper for the help wanted ads. I don't remember the ads, but I can still see us trudging around from place to place putting in applications. At the hotel we had to pay for our cots each night. Towards the end of the week, we were running out of money. I got a day labor job unloading a box car of cased pop bottles at a bottling plant. The eight dollars I earned kept us going a couple more days.

We finally had to leave the hotel and shoulder our bags and seek warmth elsewhere. The guy at the pool hall let us store our bags in his back room. We kept looking for work during the day and sleeping in various places at night. The pool hall was home base for us, but the guy didn't want us sleeping on the benches. Between us we had but very few dollars and we had no hint of what we would do when there was nothing. At times we slept in parked cars in residential areas. (People didn't lock their cars or their houses in those days.)

Even in a car it was freezing cold. The only thing the car offered was protection from the wind and snow. It was hard to get to sleep in the cars, but eventually extreme exhaustion would kick in for a few minutes of shallow sleep. In between cars we would go to the pool hall to warm up. We met some young guys there who would pay for a game or two, just to see if they could beat us. Usually they didn't. There was a small cafe where they served a bowl of oyster crackers with their chili. We would fill our pockets with crackers and ask for more. The hotel lobbies were good for a little shuteye until the night clerk realized we were not hotel guests. We asked at the police station if we could stay overnight in the lockup. They turned us down.

I tried to pawn my Zippo cigarette lighter, but the guy said he already had thirty Zippos. This was our lifestyle for about four or five days and cold miserable nights. Down to our last three dollars, we met a guy in the pool hall who wanted a game. We told him we didn't have any money. "I'll pay." Fred lost a couple games of straight pool to him. I racked the balls for them. He was very good. They kept playing and the guy, whose name was Paul Scott or Scott Paul, kept paying for the games. "You guys wouldn't be looking for work would you?" We responded in unison: "Yeah."

"I work for a pipeline company that's always looking for men." He told us about the big oil pipeline they were laying out in the Powder River Country. "I'll take you over there in the morning. I'm sure you'll be hired. It's cold out there. I hope you guys have some warmer clothes."

We told him of our homeless, moneyless situation.

"Tell you what. I'll get you a place to sleep where I stay, and tomorrow I'll tell the boss I need to take off. We'll get you some warm clothes. You can pay me when you get your first paycheck. Have you guys eaten today?"

We told him we had a bowl of chili at noon and were now eating the confiscated crackers.

Scott said, "Let's go get something to eat."

We all went to the restaurant and he treated us to hamburgers, fries, and coffee. Scott told us his story: "I'm from Chicago. I was unemployed for a year after I got out of the army in 1946. My folks wanted me to finish college, but I wasn't interested. After all the bloodshed I had seen, the buddies I had seen killed, and the killing I had committed, I felt that everyone and everything was irrelevant. I finally took a job driving a cab and saved up a little money and though, What the hell. I'm going to go out west. I'm twenty-five years old and wasting my life here. So here I am."

He took us to the second floor of a rundown old building off the main drag. There was an outside entry door to a narrow dimly lit staircase. Before reaching the top I could see a wall of exposed two-by-four studs with cardboard nailed to them from floor to about six feet high. Chicken wire was attached from where the cardboard left off up to the ceiling. I thought the place must be getting a new wall or something. At the top of the stairs was a desk where sat an emaciated looking little man with a cigarette hanging out of his lips. He smelled like cheap whiskey. "Johnnie I brought you some new customers." Johnnie put his magazine down and his eyes scanned us up and down. "Where ya workin'?"

"They're going to be working with me on the pipe line. Have you got a room with two vacancies?" What did Scott mean by a room with two vacancies? "I got two cots but not in the same room." I was soon to find out that there was a number of cardboard and chicken wire walled off spaces which held four cots each renting at fifty cents a day. Scott explained that all the guys in here had jobs in and around the oil drilling industry, but couldn't find housing elsewhere. Johnnie showed us our bunks and told us the bathroom was down at the end of the room. Scott said we'll meet in the morning and go get you guys some winter work clothes. "I told Johnnie to wake us at five."

The Pipeline

I was up and had met my three roommates by the time Johnnie came around. They were guys in their forties, I guessed, and all worked for the same oil drilling company. Scott treated us to a breakfast of pancakes, sausage, and hash browns, then Fred and I returned to our new home to wait for Scott who had gone to the pipeline office to see about getting off work for the day.

On his return he took us to a store that sold work clothes and army surplus. Fred and I were outfitted with blanket-lined jeans, used army field jackets, combat boots, wool socks, gloves, and a sweater for Fred whose wardrobe was cool-guy-from-California. After we stored our new gear under our bunks, Scott asked us to sit down with him on the ratty sofa up by Johnnie's desk. "I'll tell you guys, I don't have much money, but I've worked out a plan that I think will get us through till pay day (which was about seven days away). We can buy weekly meal tickets at the restaurant and if we each eat just a stack of pancakes and coffee for breakfast, get a carry out of a bologna sandwich and a piece of pie for lunch and the house daily special for dinner. If we stick to this, we'll be okay. We're paid up with Johnnie for a week. You can pay me back when you get paid.

"Scott, how do you know they will even hire us?" This question had been nagging me ever since we met Scott.

He said he was sure we would get jobs because the foreman was always asking them if they knew of anyone looking for work. Of all the kind acts I have been the beneficiary of, this act of Scott's rates as the kindest. "You might wonder why I'm doing this. To tell you the truth, I don't know myself." I will always wonder. The rest of the day we just hung out. I wrote and mailed a penny post card to Mom telling her I was doing well and was soon to go to work for a pipeline company.

Our new winter wear was well appreciated in the cold walk to the pipeline office. "The foreman asks everyone if they are "work-wise." Just say yes," Scott advised.

Sure enough, when we were introduced to the foreman that was his first and only question. We were loaded standing up into the back of an open stake bed truck along with about thirty other guys and driven nearly thirty freezing miles to the work site. Just stopping the truck was a relief. I was so cold from that ride that I didn't know how I could work at anything. I could hardly walk. The work site was out in the middle of nowhere. There was a yellow caterpillar with a boom attached sitting beside a trench that stretched for a mile or more. Beside the trench were these wooden skids built up like Lincoln Logs about four feet high. They were spaced about twelve to fifteen feet apart. Lying across the skids was black pipe twelve or fourteen inches in diameter. The pipe and skids stretched as far back as the trench. I was shivering cold. A couple guys started some fires in two oil drums and we all stood around smoking and warming. The foreman showed up in a pickup followed by what looked like a school bus.

"Who's in the bus?" I asked one of the older guys.

"That's the welders. They're the prima donnas here."

The foreman said, "Let's hit it. Walker you'll work with the skid crew. They'll show you what to do. Schmidt, you'll work as helper on the skid truck." He pointed at a flat-bed truck parked nearby. He put his hand on Fred's shoulder. "The last guy was fired. He was a fuck-off."

Fred took off for the truck. I saw him get in, and they drove away. The skid crew's function was to build the Lincoln Log structures out of four-by-fours about four feet long. Coming behind us was the caterpillar boom with a twenty-six feet length of the black pipe. The pipe was lowered onto the skids. A welder was waiting to attach the pipe to the length previously place the same way. All of this was done outside the trench. I was curious as to how the pipe got down in the six-foot deep trench. Up ahead of us about a quarter mile was a trench digging machine and about a half mile behind us was, I was told, was a wrapping machine which wrapped the pipe in paper and coated it with tar. You could smell the cooking tar. That's where Scott was working. It was freezing cold and the wind never let up. The welders (there were several of them) would spell each other. While two of them were welding a joint, the others remained in the heated bus. Even during lunch they would not share the bus. They were union Welders working with a contract. We were considered lowly scab laborers. Some of the guys ate lunch by the fire drums. I ate my frozen sandwich and pie standing next to the caterpillar engine which was left running. The hard labor and the freezing cold made standing by a diesel engine eating a frozen bologna sandwich almost reverent. Fred and his truck driver came by while we were eating. His truck was loaded with the four-by-four skids. He told me they picked up the skids after the pipe was lowered into the trench by another caterpillar with a boom. It worked about a quarter mile behind the wrapper. Fred's job looked a lot easier than mine; at least he got to get in a warm truck once in a while.

One morning a group of us were taken back to get a load of skids. It was then that I saw the pipe being put in the trench. The pipe appeared to be flexible as it gradually curved up from the bottom of the trench to rest on skids four feet above the ground. How this huge steel pipe could be bending, I still don't know.

The work for the day ended as daylight was waning. We had been at it for ten hours. It was still miserably cold and the ride back to town in the back of the open truck made it worse. My three roommates had already had dinner and were laid back in their bunks.

"How'd it go Jack?" one of them asked.

"Okay, I guess, but I'm frozen."

"What'd they have ya doin?"

I explained my work to them. They sympathized, and each one said he had done skid crew work in their early careers. There was talk about their work history. They were from Texas and had worked for several different oil companies. They spoke of the various jobs they had held.

I heard jobs described as "roustabouts, roughnecks, and derrick-hands." I didn't know if they were pulling my leg or not. The oldest of the three said that he was a Driller. One of the others was a Tool Pusher. The years since have impaired my memory as to what the third guy did.

At the end of the week we were paid by check. I had never asked what the pay was, but my paycheck was the largest one I had ever received for seven days' work. I don't know the exact amount, but the check was for more than one hundred dollars. It was explained to me by one of my skid crew mates that for our seventy-hour week, we were paid a dollar and a half an hour with time and a half after forty hours and double time on Sunday. This was more than enough to pay back Scott and meet my expenses for the next week. Next week I could send Mom some money.

There was a bar and grill in town that made a practice of cashing oil hands checks. Scott, Fred, and I celebrated pay day at the bar. I had turned age seventeen. Fred was only a year older, but we were not asked for ID. The bar was crowded almost shoulder to shoulder with oil men and some cowhands.

I talked with a cowhand at the bar who was also an oil man. He told me ranched with his dad, but the oil money was too good to pass up. "Is this place always this busy?" I asked.

"Every time there's a big pay day somewhere. There'd be more, but some guys cash their checks and head down to the Sand Bar."

"What's the Sand Bar?"

"There's some bars and some whorehouses down there."

"Where is that?" He told me it was on the west side of town.

"You guys wanta go down there?"

We said, "Yeah," and he led the way. Scott opted out.

The Sand Bar was a mixture of run-down vacant—what our cowhand said had been—prostitute's cribs. There were bars and assorted businesses, including a couple of nice restaurants also. A building called Van Rooms was where the girls were. Some were at their windows waving at us. Our cowhand "Ev" (short for Everett) asked, "You wanta go in?"

Fred looked at me. I shrugged my shoulders. I didn't have nerve enough to try this activity, and anyway, I was freezing. Fred turned to Ev. "Maybe some other time. You go ahead." We bade Ev goodbye and walked on down First Street. The Sand Bar was down by the river,[48] and from what I learned later from some old timers in the bar, it had a rip-roaring history of lawbreakers of all kinds from pickpockets to murderers.

We had been working but two weeks when Scott said he was quitting and heading out for Alaska. Fred and I pooled our money and bought a 1936 straight 8 Pontiac Silver Streak. The hood was long to accommodate the in-line eight cylinders. It was old, but it ran well. The foreman gave me a new job.

"Walker, I want you to take this marker and tape and walk down the line and measure and mark the middle of each length of pipe with a big X so the boom operator knows exactly where to clamp the pipe." I walked down the line measuring thirteen feet to the middle of each pipe and put a big white X on the black pipe with the marking stick. I got about a mile ahead of the crew and lay down on the leeward side of a big pipe to get out of the ceaseless cold bitter wind that howled across the flat, monotonous prairie where there was nothing but sagebrush, tumbleweeds and dirt, and the most pale winter sunshine. The landscape was dead and gray. The wind out here was an entity, no less than a tree or a mountain. It could not be ignored. You could touch it, hear it, taste it, smell it, and you could almost see it. It swept the ground free of all debris because there was no geologic interruptions for as far as you could see. As the tumbleweeds rolled by me, I often wondered how many miles they had traveled to reach this spot and how much farther must they go to reach their final destination.

From time to time there would be a small dust devil stop by to dance for me then move on. This was a lonely job, but it beat lifting skids all day. The aloneness made me aware of how my mind constantly hopped, skipped, and jumped from one thing to another. Some thoughts were seriously sad, some hilariously funny, some

---

48   The North Platte.

were stupid, and some were pure fantasy. Sometimes I would be so involved with my rambling thoughts that I couldn't remember if I had marked the last pipe, or maybe two. I would go back to check, and each time, I found out I had, in fact, marked them.

> News Break
> Nov 3, 1948
> "Dewey Defeats Truman," read the erroneous banner headline of the *Chicago Daily Tribune* after President Truman had, in fact, won an upset victory to be reelected.

California or Bust

Fred and I had worked on the pipeline for about six weeks when the pipeline's destination was reached. All, but a skeleton crew, were laid off. We were offered jobs in Oregon where a new pipeline was scheduled for construction. Fred and I decided to go to his home in Monterey, California.

We drove our big Silver Streak down to Colorado Springs where I told Mom of my California plans. She wasn't happy about my being gone so far away. "It's bad enough your brother moved to California, and now you want to move there. That leaves just Betty and me here. I won't let you do that."

I couldn't argue those facts, but I didn't see how they were reason for me to change my mind. She also came down on me for my long ducktail-styled hair, aka a California DA, or just plain duck's ass. The hair, I told her, was what all the cowhands wore. That placated her a little.

On the big issue, I told her I was going to California and I would like to leave knowing I had her blessings. Betty interceded on my behalf, "Let him go, Mother. He's not a child."

Mom said we'd talk about it later. I learned much later that she had conferred with her brother and he had told her, "Let him sow his wild oats. You're not losing him."

We weren't planning on leaving for a couple of days. I kept the car. I don't remember where Fred lived when he was in Colorado Springs. I think his older sister lived there. Even though I had no driver's license, I drove the Pontiac downtown and at an intersection I misjudged the closeness of another car and I clipped its back bumper. I reacted out of fear and drove away. I had gone a block from the accident when I decided to circle the block and return. No sooner had I turned than there were flashing red lights in the rear-view mirror. I pulled over and waited for what was coming. As the policeman approached I rolled down the window. "You were leaving the scene of an accident." He had seen the whole thing.

"I was turning around to go back," I told him.

"Let me see your driver's license."

"I left it at home."

After asking where I lived, he said, "Get in the patrol car, and we'll go get it."

I came clean and told him I didn't have a license.

"Whose car is this?"

I explained that it was in Fred's name, but that we both owned it. I didn't want to get Fred in trouble. He asked for the registration, which I pulled from the glove compartment. He read it and pulled a tablet from his pocket and started writing. "I'm giving you a ticket for driving without a license. The other driver is making no charge against you, and I'm going to forget that you were leaving the scene. This ticket requires you to pay a twenty-five-dollar fine. You can pay it at the courthouse. You're getting off easy," he said as he handed me the ticket. I had been sitting there scared I was going to be locked up or something. I managed to push out a weak "Thank you."

"Don't drive this car any farther until you get a license." He drove away, and I walked home. I was glad I had the twenty-five dollars so I wouldn't have to tell Mom. I did tell Fred. His concern was with damage to our car. There was only a small scrape on the left front fender.

> News Break
> December 13, 1948
> America Startled by Sex Report
> Professor Kinsey of Indiana University has pub-
> lished a report called "Sexual Behavior of the
> Human Male." Men were asked about frequency
> of masturbation, orgasm, 'petting,' marital and
> extramarital intercourse.

On the day of our departure for California, Mom had prepared a box of fried chicken for the trip. It was mid-December, and armed with a road map and a full tank of gas, we were off. I had packed all my belongings, except my trumpet, in a duffle bag I had acquired in Wyoming. The trumpet was in its own case. Heading west on Colorado Avenue, we drove through Manitou Springs which was dead as ever, it being winter and all. Climbing Ute Pass we ran into a light snowfall as we passed through the little tourist towns I was so familiar with: Cascade, Green Mountain Falls. I could see the old midland railroad bed on the other side of the canyon, a road bed that once delivered gold from Cripplecreek, Aspen, and Leadville. On up to Woodland Park we traveled Highway 24. It was a pretty steep climb up the canyon, but it leveled off some as we approached Woodland Park and drove on up to the summit at Divide. Where a sign read, "Divide, Elevation 9,165 Ft." We had climbed three thousand feet from Colorado Springs. The road leveled off and we rode through South Park, a vast grassland flat within a basin surrounded by mountains.

We crossed what is the headwaters of the South Platte River which flows to meet up with the North Platte in western Nebraska and goes on to empty into the Missouri River and on to the Mississippi. Leaving South Park we climbed Trout Creek Pass (9,487 feet). The pale winter sunlight had set deep behind the mountains. The snow had accumulated to three or four inches and was falling thick and heavy. We came upon a road grader at work on the snow as we descended the pass. We came to an intersection with a sign pointing South to Salida and pointing North to Buena Vista.

"That's where my brother did time at the reform school!" I exclaimed.

This bit of news didn't impress Fred; he was busy negotiating the roadway to Salida. It was beginning to get dark when we pulled into Salida. The snow was heavy and getting deep. At a little gas station the old attendant asked, "Where you boys headed?"

Fred told him we were going to California.

"I wouldn't try to take that road over Monarch Pass in this snow if I were you."

As all smart teenagers would do when receiving good adult advice, we stuffed it in our mental trash can and put the lid on it. We drove through Salida. Lights of the town were on, and the snow kept falling. We found Highway 50 and headed west. The windshield wipers moved sporadically. We passed through two or three small communities that couldn't be identified in the near blinding snow. Starting the climb up over the continental divide by way of Monarch Pass was now our challenge. Our map indicated the pass summit to be over eleven thousand feet. The wipers became so sluggish against the wet heavy snow it was useless depend on them. Fred drove with his head out the window and once in a while reaching out to wipe off the windshield with his left hand as he steered with his right. Electric motor wipers hadn't been invented yet. The old Pontiac was equipped with a vacuum system that was not able to keep the wipers at a constant speed. Their speed was determined by the speed of the car's engine, and as we were going so slow they had died. We were moving about five miles an hour. From where I sat I could only see out the side window.

"Man, it's dark as a well digger's ass. I don't know how you can even see the road." His head was out the window, so he didn't hear me. There were no other cars on the road luckily. The car would slide a little sideways, and then the tires would find purchase, and we'd inch ahead. I wasn't as scared as I should have been. I just had memories of Wyoming trying to sleep in the freezing cold of a car, and I don't know why, but my mind also went to thinking about our benefactor, Scott, and how he took us in off the street in Casper. I hoped he would find whatever he was looking for.

"We gotta go back, Jack. We're g'tting nowhere."

The descent was about as precarious as the climb. Fred kept the car in the second gear, all the way inching down, slipping and slid-ing. We rented a room in Salida and went to a cafe and filled up on hamburgers and fries. Mom's fried chicken didn't last beyond South Park. The snow had stopped some time during the night. The streets of Salida were being plowed and the sun was rising as we drove out of town toward Poncha Springs where we turned and headed south hoping to avoid high snow covered mountain passes. Not far south of Poncha Springs, we were faced with Poncha Pass. The climb was mild and the road had been plowed. The south ascent was a moderate 5 percent grade. We had a nice easy drive straight down the San Louis Valley to Alamosa where we turned west to again get over the Rocky Mountains. We encountered only one significant ascent; Wolf Creek Pass. The climb was steep, but the road was good, a sign at the summit informed us that we were more than ten thousand feet above sea level. The trip down the west incline was just as steep. It was second gear a lot of the way down to Pagosa Springs then the road skirted the foothills of the San Juan Mountains, where the Rio Grande River begins its journey to the Gulf of Mexico.

The splendor of the mountains and valleys we had traveled was wasted on my young, unappreciative values. We arrived in Durango about noon and had lunch. There was a Hockshop on the main street where I sold my trumpet. My memory has jumped the rail as to why I did this. It's hard to believe now that we needed money only two days out of Colorado Springs, but we were impetuous young men, so who knows? But I do recall I got twenty-five bucks for it, and actually I hadn't played the horn more than a handful of times since leaving school.

Leaving Durango, we hoped to spend the night in Salt Lake City. However, nightfall found us on the side of the road with a dead motor and the Pontiac's radiator blowing steam. We could see city lights glowing in the sky in the distance. After the steam stopped and the motor cooled off, Fred started up the motor. It hummed like new for about two hundred feet then died again. We went through this one more time. On the third try the motor wouldn't even turn over.

Fred said, "We could pee in the radiator. That might be enough to get us to that town."

One at a time we stood on the bumper and peed into the thirsty radiator. It wasn't enough to make that motor move. It only created the odor of steaming pee. Finally a driver stopped and gave us a lift to the next town, Price, Utah.

We found a gas station still open, and Fred told the guy our plight. He said he would send a tow truck and bring it in and look at it in the morning. We found an all-night café and had dinner before checking into a nearby cheap second floor hotel. A tall, pretty mid-dle-aged woman checked us in. Shortly after we had gotten settled, she came by the room. "Would you, boys, like to see a girl tonight?"

Before we could answer, she said, "It's five dollars."

Fred said to me, "Why don't you go ahead. We can afford five dollars." Then he turned to the woman. "He's a cherry." I was embar-rassed. My face felt like it was burning.

"He's blushing. Isn't that sweet." I turned her down. After she left, I promised myself again that the next time I get an offer like that, I'm going to accept.

After breakfast, we got the diagnosis of the Pontiac's illness. "Your car has a cracked block. I doubt if I can find a used block any closer than Provo. If someone has one there, I don't know what it would cost. I'd have to drive up there and get it, so it would proba-bly take two or three days maybe to get it done. I could try to patch the crack just to get you by. I see you have Wyoming license plates. Where ya headed?"

Fred told him our destination was Monterey, California.

"If I were you, I wouldn't try to make that trip with a patched block."

After some discussion about the patch and its cost, Fred said, "Let us think it over."

We left the garage and walked back to the hotel. My fragmented memory wouldn't give up the conversation we had, but the upshot of it was that the price of patching the block and the risk of it giving out as we made our way across the Salt Desert, the sparsely popu-lated desert across Nevada and then climb over the Sierra Nevada Mountains, was not worth it.

We kissed the Pontiac goodbye and bought two Greyhound tickets for Monterey, California. Of that trip I remember seeing the Great Salt Lake and the vast salt flats, where John Cobb of Great Britain had broken the land speed record at 394 miles per hour. The Great Salt Lake Desert is so vast and so flat there are absolutely no surprises here.

I next remember Reno, Nevada. The sun had set when the bus pulled into Reno. I had never seen so much neon lighting. The whole downtown was lit up. There was a large lighted arch over the street that proclaimed that Reno was The Biggest Little City in the World. Another large sign reading Harold's Club. This was the gambling capitol of the country and Harold's was the most famous casino. Quick divorces were granted here. We were always reading about this or that celebrity had "gone to Reno." It meant only one thing; divorce. It was rumored that newly divorced women customarily threw their wedding rings off the Virginia Street Bridge into the river below. Nevada was also notoriously famous for its legalized brothels. This was all exciting to me. I had heard of Reno all my life, but never dreamed I would be here. We had a short layover to use restrooms and get a new driver. I would like to have toured this carnival like town, but there wasn't time. Fred and I each got a candy bar and a pack of fags and stood outside the bus terminal smoking and taking in all the colorful lights of the Biggest Little City.

Not too far out of Reno we were going over a pass of the Sierra Nevada Mountains. "This is the Donner Pass. Back in the pioneer days a wagon train of people got snowed in here and couldn't get out. They became cannibals to survive."

"THEY WHAT?" I didn't believe what I just heard. "You gotta be bull shitin' me, right?"

"No, we studied that in school. When somebody died, they ate 'em to keep from starvin'." I let it go.

Fred was a bullshitter sometimes. I didn't listen to the rest of the story about rescue efforts and survivors. I remember nothing of the trip from the Donner Pass to the San Francisco Bay area. We crossed the bay on the double-deck Oakland Bay Bridge. The bay itself is not in my memory, but what sticks in my head is that I bought an apple at a coin machine in the bus terminal. By the way, I did learn much later that Fred was telling me the truth about the ill-fated Donner party.

Monterey

Leaving San Francisco, it was a short trip down to Monterey. We caught a city bus to Seaside where Fred's mother lived with her teenage daughter. Mrs. Schmidt fixed us a good dinner, and Fred and I made a bed on the living room floor.

The next day Fred took me to downtown Monterey. This was a really old town. There were a couple of buildings which looked to be over a hundred years old. They were built in the old Spanish/Mexican style with stucco exteriors and wooden doors and they were still in use now in 1948. Fred led me to a second floor apartment above a store where I met his wife, Lauren (pseudonym), and child. I don't remember the child's gender. She was a pretty young girl. We sat around and talked for a while then we left her. Fred said he had never lived with her.

"I knocked her up when we were in high school. I didn't want to marry her, but between her folks and my mom, they wouldn't quit badgering me, so I gave in. I drop in on her once in a while to see how she's doing." I thought he was treating her badly. I'd been with him nearly four months, and he'd never mentioned her.

I would bet he didn't even know the child's name. But I figured that was his business. I guessed her folks were supporting her. We went next to a store front building on Alvarado Street which had its large widows painted from bottom to about halfway up, just high enough to prevent pedestrians from seeing in. Inside was a large room with tables where some guys were playing cards. As I looked from table to table I noticed that most of the players were older grey haired guys. Fred stopped and looked around the room like he was looking for someone. "I'm lookin' for a guy that owes me some money, but I don't see him."

"What is this place?" I asked.

"It's a card club."

"Are they actually gambling for money?"

He explained, "It's player against player, not player against the house like in Reno." He told me the dealer at each table worked for the house and took a rake of the pot from each hand.

I followed Fred to a wide double door opening. The back room was a pool parlor. There were five or six pool tables, but only two were being used. We walked to the back table. One player was lining up a shot and had his back to us, the other was chalking his cue.

"Hey, Freddie, how ya been, man? Rick, look who's here."

There were handshakes all around as Fred said: "This is Jack."

"Man, we thought you were bustin' broncs in Wyoming."

"The only thing I been bustin' was my back workin' my ass off."

"Jack, I'm sure you know by now Freddie's a big bull shitter."

"You can't tell Jack anything about me. We go back to fourth grade in Colorado."

After all this banter slowed down, Fred hit on a serious note, "Have you guys seen Cabello lately?"

"Does he owe you money too?"

Fred nodded.

"Good luck, man. I heard he lived over in Pacific Grove. He hasn't been around here for a couple of months. He owes everyone in the county." Then he asked, "Whata ya gonna be doin' now that you're back?"

"I don't know. I gotta find a job."

"Frank got a couple more cabs since you left. He's lookin' for a nighttime driver."

Frank's Taxi Service was owned by an unusual guy. Frank, a disabled war vet, had two completely paralyzed legs and got around in a wheelchair. He was a fun-loving guy, just full of life and laughter. He even drove his own specially equipped cab with hand controls replacing the clutch, the brakes, and the accelerator. Fred had driven part time for Frank before. After some talk took place, Fred was hired and to begin that night. "Does Lynn still work for you?"

"Yeah, she's doin' real good too."

They explained to me that Lynn was a single mom going to college.

Fred offered, "She's a prostitute. She rents a cab each night and heads for Fort Ord."

Fred started to work at five o'clock that night. His hours were five to midnight. After midnight Frank took all the calls till the morning. On his first night I hung out at the pool hall for a while then went to spend the evening with his mom listening to the radio. It was Christmas Eve. Fred's fifteen-year-old sister was going with a thirty-year-old soldier who invited all of us to go to the Fort Ord Christmas dance party. I danced too little and drank too much. I spent Christmas day nursing a real good hangover. The morning after Christmas I walked down to Cannery Row to see about a job. One of the guys in the pool hall said the canneries were always hiring. Down by Fisherman's Warf I got my first look at the Pacific Ocean.

It was like looking at the Great Plaines covered with water, only there were small white capped waves coming in and you could hear them lap the shore. There was a noticeable smell at the waterfront that was foreign to my nose. It wasn't good nor was it bad. It was just a smell I had never encountered. As I approached Cannery Row I thought out loud, "So this is the famous Cannery Row from John Steinbeck's book." I pictured some of the book's characters in my mind: Doc, Mack, Lee Chong. I looked around for Doc's Biological Laboratory and Lee Chong's Grocery and the Palace Flophouse, but they were nowhere in sight. Cannery Row was a group of old buildings, some sided and roofed with rusting corrugated tin. The buildings faced the street and extended out over the water. There were long piers extending farther out. There was a boat lashed to one of the piers which I took to be a fishing boat. The names of the different canning companies were boldly painted on the face side of each building. I don't remember any of the signs but the image of the Del Monte logo remains vividly. The first building I came to just didn't look too inviting; Paint was chipping off the windowed door and the window couldn't be seen through due to grime, dust and dirt. I walked on by and entered the Del Monte doorway.

"What can I do for ya?" asked a tall, oily-haired guy with a face that I'll never forget: it was almost a perfect square with corners and all. His pants looked like maybe they once were part of a suit. He wore a once-white dress shirt with the sleeves rolled up to the elbows. His forearms were covered with tattoos of what I couldn't make out.

"I wanted to apply for a job," I blurted.

"Here," he said, handing me a piece of paper and a pencil. "Gimme yer name and address." I gave him the Seaside address. "We don't have no fish to can right now. When ya hear the whistle blow, come on in, and we'll put ya to work." I left the place wondering, *What kind of place is this? Where am I supposed to go to wait for a whistle to blow? How long will I have to wait?* I should have asked him. I noticed on the hillside nearby several little tar paper shacks that reminded me of the cribs on the Sand Bar in Casper. They evidently were lived in. I saw some women go in and out of them. I walked up the hillside a short distance and sat on the ground and lit a cigarette. I sat waiting for about an hour before I gave up on hearing the whistle. I headed back to Alvarado Street and thought, "I bet those people in the shacks on the hill are the cannery workers."

One of the guys back at the pool hall said, "Ya gotta be there when the sardines are runnin'. We don't have the fish we used to have. Not many boats bringin' fish these days. When the fish are runnin, there's plenty of work." He indicated that if I got down there very early in the morning I might catch one of the night boats coming in with fish. Back at Seaside I hung out with Fred. He fixed me some lunch of left-over mashed potatoes mixed with a couple eggs and fried in butter. "Ya wanta come ride with me tonight?"

"Yeah, I guess. Does Frank care?" He assured me it would be okay with Frank. I rode with him on a couple trips. "This cab doesn't have a mileage meter. How do you know what to charge people?"

"We charge by zones." He showed me a map of the bay area with zones marked off.

"You mean if I only go two blocks, I have to pay the same as ten blocks?"

"Yeah, if you stay in the same zone. It's five bucks a zone." I left him and went back to Seaside to get some sleep so I could get down to the cannery early.

I got down to Cannery Row about five thirty. The place was dead with silence. The early morning fog veiled everything. It reminded me of a London horror movie. I walked around waiting and smoking. I saw my square faced cannery guy come and unlock the door and enter. I walked and waited. I don't know how many cigarettes I smoked until I gave up. Nearby I walked out on a long pier and saw a guy busy doing something on a boat. As I approached the guy looked up, smiled and said: "Good morning."

"Hi," I said.

The guy was average height, had full head of coal-black wavy hair. His skin was brown, and he had smile a yard wide showing a mouth full of white teeth. He was coiling some rope on the deck. His shirtsleeves were rolled up revealing biceps the size of my thighs. He had on Levi's and rubber boots.

"Nice morning," he said. I hadn't really noticed the climate in my remorse over not hearing any cannery whistle. The fog had lifted. It was a nice sunny morning. The sky was blue with but a few big fluffy clouds. The seagulls were all circling, swooping and squawking. I thought that maybe they were waiting for the whistle to blow also. "Yes, it is." I confirmed.

He finished with the rope and lit a cigarette with a kitchen match pulled from his pocket; striking it with his thumb nail. Stepping toward me he lifted one of his boots up onto the boat's gunwale. "Just enjoying the waterfront?" he asked.

"No, I was waiting for the whistle to blow, so I could get a job."

"The whistle's not going to blow this morning. I was the only one out last night. You might be lucky enough to get something tonight. I could use another hand on the boat. It maybe wouldn't pay any more than the cannery, but I give you a dinner every night. You interested?" Man, going to sea working on a fishing boat. That sounded neat. "Yeah, I am."

"You ever work on a seiner before?"

I told him I hadn't.

339

"That's okay, we'll teach you the ropes. The way you get paid is you get a share of the catch. The more fish we get, the more money you get. If we don't catch fish, none of us get paid. The sardines aren't running like the old days. There were so many when I was a boy on my dad's boat they used to call it the 'silver tide.' You like Portuguese food?"

I told him I didn't know.

He laughed and said, "Be down here at seven tonight. We'll cast off at seven thirty. Come aboard and let me get some information from you. What's your name?"

I told him my name.

We shook hands as he said, "I'm Joe DeJulio. The guys call me Skip. It's short for Skipper."

I stepped on the gunwale and dropped down to the deck. I followed him as we walked across the rocking deck. Even though the boat was secured to the pier, it still rocked back and forth, requiring some attention to balance. Joe opened a small door which led to the cabin below.

"After you," he said.

I bent down and stepped down through the opening and down three steps to the cabin.

"This is the kitchen, dining room, living room, and bedroom. Nobody sleeps here, but the bunks are here just in case." This was a place of wonder. There were small round windows on each side. I saw four bunks folded up against the walls, two on each side. There were benches at each wall. "Have a seat, Jack."

I sat on a cushioned bench, and Joe raised a table which was hinged to the wall. He opened a cabinet door and pulled out a note book and pen without leaving his seat. While he was thumbing through the notebook looking for the page he wanted, I took in the sights. There was the smallest refrigerator I had ever seen as was the little two burner stove. After he gleaned all the information he wanted from me. We sat and drank coffee. No potential employer had ever invited me to coffee.

"I've got some old doughnuts, if you want one?"

"No, thanks."

He pulled a hard doughnut from a coffee can and dunked it. We shared some small talk for a while. I gave him some of my background. He asked if I had seen any wild horses, which I hadn't.

"The Rocky Mountains must really be a sight!" he exclaimed.

I assured him they truly were impressive. It excited him that I had been to the top of Pike's Peak.

"God, what a view there must be from there."

I assured him of his preconception of the grandeur of the vista from the Peak. He told me he had lived in Monterey all his life. His folks were immigrants from Portugal. His father had been a fisherman. Joe had worked as a deckhand and his wife had worked in the canneries until their first of four children was born. They had saved enough money for a down payment on a used seiner (as the boat was called), and with his father giving a cosignature and a second mortgage on his parent's home, the bank gave him the money. "My three longtime deckhands are Portuguese also. You'll meet them tonight. I think you guys will get along good." Then he added, "I gotta get to work."

He lowered the table and let me slide out ahead of him.

"Okay, I'll see you tonight." As I walked back on the pier, I thought, *What a neat guy*. He was so friendly, and he didn't even know me. I could have been a serial killer. How would he know? I figured he could either read people really well, or he was one of those people who trust everyone.

The sun was now shining bright. There was no trace of the fog which had so hampered vision earlier. Back on Alvarado Street I walked through the card room. Even at this early midmorning hour, every card table was filled with players. Back in the pool hall there were a handful of guys. I ran into three guys I knew.

"Hey, it's Farmer Jack."

That was a nickname given me because these self-acclaimed supercool California cats thought all people from such square places like Colorado were farmers. I took it. They didn't intend it as an insult. They were all nice guys who had treated me like a longtime friend. After a couple of games of pool, we all went for coffee. That's when I was introduced to the coffee float, a scoop of ice cream plopped on top of the cup of hot coffee.

I separated from them as we came out of the restaurant. I wanted to go by Lauren's. For some reason, I just wanted to see if she was all right. Fred didn't seem to care about her much, and I wasn't really sure anyone cared. I walked up the narrow stairs and knocked. Lauren welcomed me. We sat on her nearly threadbare sofa while her little one-year-old amused itself in the play pen. I asked her how things were going.

"Oh, Jack, I'm so worried. I lost some food stamps and can't get any more for three more days. After today I won't even have baby food. There's nothing in the house to eat except one sweet potato, and I don't know how to cook it." She finally let it all out and broke down in sobbing tears. I put my arm around her shoulders until the tears subsided.

"I'm sorry, Jack. I shouldn't have dumped this on you."

I tried to assure her it was all right.

"Where's the sweet potato? I'll cook it, and while it cooks, I'll go to the grocery and buy some stuff if you'll give me a list. She scrounged up a piece of paper and made out a small list. Baby food and milk are the only items I remember, but I do remember buying more things than she had asked for. I still had seven dollars from my trumpet proceeds, which would translate to about seventy dollars in 2017. "Oh, Jack, this is so kind of you." When I returned, the sweet potato had boiled enough. I fried a couple hamburgers that we laced with lettuce and tomato. Lauren almost broke down in tears again as she spoke words to the effect of, "Jack, I have been praying to God for some miracle. I believe you were sent by God, and I am so grateful."

We finished our hamburgers and sweet potato, and she washed dishes as I dried. We sat back on the sofa, and Lauren told me she had gotten pregnant in high school and had been forced to quit. Her parents kicked her out of the house, and Fred was no help at all. I knew Fred was not a compassionate guy, but I didn't figure him for a complete bastard. I told her about my going to work on a fishing boat and that I would drop by once in a while. I left and went for a walk around downtown Monterey just window shopping, as Grandma used to call it. I wound up back at the pool hall where I hung out till time to go to the boat.

The sun had set. The stars were out, and there was a full moon easterly. The night air was cool, but not really cold. I was comfortable in my leather jacket with a navy surplus sweater underneath. I wore Levi's and rubber soled oxfords. And not to forget my cool argyle socks. I walked out on the pier and saw some guys working on the deck of Joe's boat. One was doing something with some rope and the other two were working with the huge net. "Is Joe here?"

"He's down below. You the new guy?" said the rope handler.

"Yeah."

"Come on board," I stepped on the gunwale and jumped down. The guy offered me his hand and said, "I'm Neves. They call me Nev."

"I'm Jack."

The other two fishermen came over and offered their hands. All of them had the roughest hands I had ever shaken. "I'm Rocha, but I go by Rocky."

The third guy stepped up. "Benny, 'cause these guys can't pronounce Benedito."

Nev went to the cabin door. "Hey, Skip, the new guy is here."

Joe came up from the cabin and asked Nev, "Are we ready to cast off?"

"Yeah, Skip."

"Jack, I want you to cast off the bowline and get back on board."

I was glad he pointed to the bowline. I didn't know what a bow was. I jumped up on to the pier and unwound the rope from around a metal cleat on the pier. I now didn't know what to do with the loose end of the rope.

"Throw it here, Jack, and hurry and get aboard," said Benny.

I tossed the rope to him and scrambled to get aboard because the bow started to drift away from the pier and Nev was casting off the other line at the back of the boat (the stern line). Nev threw his rope fast and jumped aboard. The boat was drifting away from the pier. The skipper was up in a three-sided enclosure that had widows all around (pilot house). The motor kicked on, and we started to move seaward slowly.

"Jack, come up here," the skipper called out.

I went up the four steps to where he stood in front of a stool with his back to me. I went around to his right side. He had both hands on a wooden helm. In front of him, a large compass the size of a dinner plate dominated an array of gauges, for what, all I didn't know. "You stick with Nev. He'll show you what to do. He knows you're not experienced. He's my first mate. Do whatever he tells you. We're getting ready to leave the anchorage. Go now and check in with him."

"First off, we'll get you some wet weather gear," Nev said. He was all decked out in a yellow slicker, pants, and rubber boots, as were Rocky and Benny. From a locker beneath the stairs leading up to the pilot house Nev pulled out a hooded yellow slicker and a matching bib overall. He held the overall up to me. "Too short." He reached in and pulled out another. "A little short, but it'll work. The boots will cover your legs. Reach back in there, and find some boots that'll fit."

There were about four or five pairs of rubber boots on the floor of the locker. I pulled out a pair I thought would fit and they did.

"Okay, put these things on, then come over by the boom. You can put your shoes up on that shelf where the others are." He pointed to a shelf in the locker. Getting the gear on, I didn't know whether the slicker went over the overall or vice versa. I looked around. All the guys had their slicker on top. I also noticed the full moon and stars had been swallowed by heavy clouds and it now was dark on the boat. There was a dim orange light coming from a fixture on the rear of the pilot house. The heavy boots and the other gear felt clumsy and awkward to me especially with the deck rolling and heaving. "Skip tells me you're from Colorado, so I guess you've never been on a seiner before." Nev said.

"What's a seiner?"

"That's what this boat is. It's called a purse seiner. The seine is a type of net. The purse means we can pull the bottom of our net closed like the pull strings on a purse." He then took me to the stern of the boat where a small motor boat was lashed. Benny had a red gas can pouring gas into the out-board motor. "Benny, tell Jack what you do with the skiff."

"I put the skiff in the water and pull the net out and around the fish." Benny was a man of few words. He was younger than Nev, I would guess, by ten years, Nev being in his forties (another guess).

That was when Nev explained how purse seine fishing is done at night. "First, we have to find the fish. They swim close to the surface and put off a glow that you can only see at night. We then drop the skiff into the water and Benny pulls the net away from the boat and circles the fish and brings the skiff and net back to the boat. Those white blocks are floats that pay out on the net line Benny is pulling. We feed him the net slowly so it doesn't get tangled. That line over there"—he pointed to a large coil of rope nearby—"is the purse line. It runs through the rings at the net's bottom and pays out with the net. It will be drawn in by the power winch to close the net at the bottom to prevent the fish from sounding. Once the purse opening is closed. We start winching in the net. When the net full of fish is pulled up alongside the boat, it is hoisted by using the boom and dumped into the hold."

Nev then walked me all around the deck and pointed out and explained the function of each piece of equipment. "You and I will watch for the glow on the starboard side. Benny watches the stern, and Rocky is on the port side."

With Skip watching the bow, we got all directions covered. I felt a light water spray, which seemed to be coming from the bow each time it dipped downward. Water drops formed on and ran down my slicker. Not wearing my issued gloves, my hands were wet and cold.

The boat didn't move very fast. We had been underway for nearly an hour when we made a gradual forty-five-degree turn. "Why's the skipper turning?" I asked Nev.

"He's coursing the bay now that we have cloud cover. You can't see the glow when the moon is shining. There's an old fisherman's poem called 'The Moon Man Fishes Tonight.' Nev went on,

> The waves roll out and the waves roll in and the
> night wind blows

Why the Moon Man fishes the sea, only the
Moon Man knows.

At my request, he said he would write the poem down for me.
"Skip knows all the places where the fish are most likely to be. He'll
bring the boat about in different directions all night. Sometimes he'll
leave the bay and cruise up shore. You just keep watching on the starboard side of the boat no matter how many times he turns direction.
We sat and talked for a while.

I asked him, "What does 'Portagee' mean?"

"It's a dirty word ignorant Anglos use for Portuguese people. It's
like 'Nigger' or 'Wop.'" He stood up, took a long look out over the
dark water, and said, "Watch for the glow on the water. I'm going
below and heat up some food."

I stared intently into the darkness. At times I thought I caught a
glimpse of a glow, and then it wouldn't be there. I had never seen this
glow I was looking for so didn't know what to expect.

"Here's your supper, Jocko." Nev handed me what looked like
a large mixing bowl of something, the delicious smell of which rose
heavily into my nostrils, blocking out the fish/salt water smell of the
boat. The scent was rich and spicy. My mouth watered in want of the
taste. "It sure smells good. What is it?"

"It's Portuguese chicken." He told me the Portuguese name for
it, but even though I can still almost smell it, the name of it has faded
away. Nev broke me off a big chunk from a loaf of French bread and
handed me a table spoon. It tasted every bit as good as it smelled. It
was like a stew with chicken, sausage, potatoes, tomato, garlic and I
don't know what all. Rocky and Benny were served then Nev went to
the pilot house and relieved the skipper, who went below. After the
skipper returned from eating, Nev came and took my bowl. "Skip
said we'll make one more pass and go in if we don't see fish."

It was about eleven o'clock when we docked. I jumped off and
tied down the bow line. We had caught no fish so there would be
no pay. I walked to Mrs. Schmidt's house. She was just getting ready
to go to bed. "Jack you can sleep on the sofa if you like Freddie is
staying at Lauren's. I slept late and woke to an empty house. Mrs.

Schmidt had gone to work and her daughter was in school. It was about ten o'clock. I fried a couple eggs and made some toast. There was nothing on the radio except soaps, so I headed for the pool hall. The card players were up and at 'em. There was no one in the pool hall I knew. An old guy asked me if I'd like to join him in a friendly game of snooker, friendly meaning no money involved.

"I've never played snooker before," I told him.

He said he would teach me. Over five sets he taught me the game of Snooker. It's more complicated than pool. The table is larger, the pockets, called pots, are smaller, and there are twenty-two balls instead of the fifteen used with pool. He beat me soundly the first three games. I came close to winning the fourth game. In the fifth game, I was either tied with him or ahead on points. As I was so close to winning the fourth game, I thought I was on the way to winning until there were only six balls remaining and I only needed to sink two of them to win. I sunk one of them and missed on my second shot. Now I only needed to sink one out of the remaining five balls on the table. The old man methodically sank one ball at a time until the table was bare and left me sucking hind tit as they say. After I got over the brief shock of his five-ball run, I realized he had hustled me. It's a good thing no money was involved. He smiled and patted me on the back and complimented me on my skill. "Where did you learn to handle a cue like that?" I told him about Roland teaching me back home.

"Let me give you some advice: You're young and just good enough to think you can make some money at pool. You handle the cue well enough but one. You haven't yet developed the temperament or the patience to be a really good pool shooter. Those things will come in time. Two, you have no strategy for winning when you play. Pool is like chess: you must plan at least three to four shots ahead. Three, you must also be able to read your opponent; what is he likely to do if I do this? You must ask yourself. This, along with humility, you will learn with experience. And kid no matter how good you get, there is always someone better who will hustle you and take you to the cleaners. You thought you had me on that last game when it got down to six balls, didn't you?"

I nodded.

"On your last shot, you were so sure that you got sloppy."

I agreed.

"This town has some very good pool shooters, so be very careful. If you don't get greedy, you won't get conned."

With that he thanked me for the games, put his cue stick in the rack, and left. I never saw him again. I was thinking as I left the pool hall that I knew several pool shooters who were better than me—Billy Mudd and a few others back home, as well as a couple of guys I had played with in Wyoming.

I spent the afternoon just walking around town. In the drug store I bought a paperback copy of Tobacco Road, a story of a poor Southern family. The book was banned in various parts of the country, especially in the south. Southerners felt the easy sex, violence, ignorance and shiftlessness of the family was meant to describe southerners generally. Some northern cities banned the book because they felt it was just plain obscene and pornographic. I was attracted to the book because I had heard about the sexual passages from some guys in Casper and I had read about it being banned, which made it attractive. I couldn't wait to find the "good" pages. I pocketed the book and walked down to the pier. I was early. A good smell was coming from below I followed the smell and found Skip stirring a big pot of something. He greeted me with, "Hi, Jack. You like fish?"

I told him I had only eaten trout.

"You'll like this. How'd it go last night?"

I told him that I guessed it went okay.

"Nev says you learn fast. He thinks you'll work out all right." He put something else in the pot and stirred slowly. "Pour yourself a cup of coffee if you want. The cups are in that cabinet." He pointed to the cabinet. I sat, drank coffee, and chewed the fat with Skip for about half an hour before the other three crew members showed up. Our routine this night was the same as the night before. No fish, no pay. Wonderful fish stew. On the third night we left the pier as usual.

At about eight thirty or nine, Rocky yelled, "FISH ON THE PORT BOW."

I went over to see. Sure enough, I saw a faint greenish glow coming off the water at a distance of about the length of a football field.

Nev came to look. "It sure is. I'll tell Skip," he said. He went to the pilot house. The boat's motor slowed, and we began to pull about to the port. We had turned a full half circle which brought us closer to the glow. Then the motors became silent. Benny was lowering the skiff.

"Jocko, come over here." I went over where Nev and Rocky were tugging on the net which was folded over a big roller.

"Jocko, I want you to put on your gloves and pay out this lead line to Benny when he gets underway. Keep the slack out of it. We don't want it tangled and twisted." Benny had started the outboard motor of the skiff and at Nevs signal started moving slowly away from the boat. The skiff was moving in a direction to the right of the glow. I paid out the rope until Benny and the skiff were out of sight in the dark. Shortly after I lost sight of the small boat, Skip came down and took charge.

"Okay, Jack, move away from there the net will knock you down and pull you overboard. Come around here and help Rocky with the purse line."

From this point on I had lost the details of how they got the huge net off the boat and into the water where Benny's skiff was pulling it out and around the glow. I do have a firm visual memory of my paying out the purse line. I don't remember how long it took, but in time the skiff reappeared from the left side. Benny had made a full circle around the glow. The purse line was pulled by a power winch on the deck, "pursing" because, as I had been told, it is like pulling the draw string of an old time purse. The net was then pulled aboard by means of a big pulley block attached up on the end of the boom hanging above the deck. The net now lay alongside the boat filled with hundreds of squirming silver fish which were then scooped out by a smaller net and dumped into the hold. You could feel the boat sink a little deeper into the water. The net was folded back on board and we headed in to the cannery. I watched as Rocky scooped a baby squid out of the sardine catch. He shook it hard at the deck two times. The squid's eye balls dropped out on the deck, and Rocky bit into the animal and chewed off a chunk of flesh and ate it. "Jocko, you want some lula?" He offered the dripping squid to me.

"God, no!"

"It's good, you'll like it."

Benny came over and took a big bite. You'd have thought they were sharing a fried chicken breast. I shook my head in disgust and walked away.

As we approached the cannery pier, I could hear the whistle blow. It sounded like a steam locomotive whistle. Lights went on throughout the cannery and on the pier. The fish were scooped out of the hold and deposited into large wheeled containers on the pier and wheeled into the cannery. As I walked down the pier I could see inside the cannery. There were lots of people milling around; men, women, young and old alike. I thought: These people must have all come from the tarpaper shacks on the hillside. The next night I got down to the boat early again. Skip was working on one of his supper delights. He handed me an envelope. "Here's your share of last night's catch."

I opened the envelope. There was a ten, a five, and two ones. "Wow." Seventeen dollars, now I could rent a place of my own ($17 would be like $170 in 2017).

That night we came in empty. The next morning I rented an efficiency apartment in a building just off Alvarado Street. It wasn't a flea bag, and it was far from being five-star. I liked the place. It was the first time I ever had a place of my own. The small room had a day bed serving as both a bed and a sofa. A small refrigerator and stove were provided along with a small table and two chairs. I also had a closet and a bath room squeezed tight with tub, sink and toilet. The place was so crowded that while taking a bath, your head was almost in the toilet. There was a window overlooking the alley. I was happy. I spent the afternoon buying stuff for the room; sheets, pots and pans, a wind up clock, a percolator and a few groceries. My rent choices for the apartment were a dollar fifty a day or nine dollars a week. The monthly rate would save me four dollars, but not knowing if I would ever see another pay day, I opted for the weekly rate. Before going to work I went to Seaside to pick up my belongings. I left Mrs. Schmidt a note and thanked her for being so good to me. That night there were no fish again, nor the following next three nights. We had gone without a catch for five nights.

On the sixth I was really getting bored with watching for a glow which never appeared. I had thought about quitting and getting a job with regular paydays. I had torn an ad out of the paper advertising for dining room help with meals and sleeping quarters provided.

On this night it was me who saw the glow. At first I didn't believe what I was seeing. When the moon was swallowed by a cloud, I thought I saw a glow, then the cloud moved on and the moonlight made it hard to see a glow. I figured I'd better sound off just to be safe, "FISH ON THE STARBOARD!" I yelled.

Nev came over and looked. "It's a glow all right, and it looks like a big school. Good work, Jocko." He went to the pilot house, and the boat began to come about to the starboard side.

Benny started unlashing the skiff, and Rocky and I stood by the purse line. I went to my station of feeding the lead line to the skiff. The seining operation went as before, only this time there was enough fish to more than fill the hold. The surplus was stored in the scoop net.

The next night Skip again handed me an envelope. There was twenty-two dollars in it. That was a real bundle of money. "Hey, Jocko, whata ya gonna do with all that dough, buy a Cadillac?"

"Rocky, I'm going to buy a purse seiner and make you the skipper."

Benny chimed in, "You'll have to shake him down every night. He'll fill his pockets with fish."

We carried on like this every night. It helped relieve the boredom.

No catch that night. The following morning I opened a pass-book savings account and, after much thought, decided I would quit fishing and go to the Del Monte Lodge at Pebble Beach to apply for the dining room help job.

The Del Monte Lodge at Pebble Beach

I got directions to the lodge from a guy in the pool hall. I caught a bus which discarded me at an open gate. "Where is the Del Monte Lodge from here?" I asked the bus driver.

"Just follow that drive. It'll take you right to it." I hoped he was right because the drive was a two lane paved road leading into a forest of tall evergreen trees not like the pines at home. It was a sunny but cool damp morning. The sun beams coming through the trees reminded me of the forest scenes of Snow White, a movie Grandma took me to. I walked for about a quarter of a mile and came to a parking lot half filled with expensive cars: Cadillacs, Lincolns, Chryslers, sprinkled with some convertibles and a few foreign sports cars. This was not Model A country. The lot lay in front of a long elegant two-story ivory-colored building. I guessed this to be the Del Monte Lodge as stated in the help-wanted ad. It looked to me like a building straight out of F. Scott Fitzgerald's *The Great Gatsby*. I pulled the folded-up ad out of my pocket just to make sure I had read it correctly.

Dining room help wanted.
Meals and sleeping quarters included.
Ask for Ms. Henderson.
All inquiries in person at Del Monte Lodge.

I was glad I took this last look because I had forgotten who to ask for. I walked through the double doors and across the deepest plush carpet I had ever walked on. I had slept on surfaces much harder than this.

"I'm looking for Ms. Henderson," I told the guy at the front desk.

He pointed me toward a large open doorway. At the doorway was a small sign mounted on a pedestal which read, "Dining room closed. Room service only. Will reopen at 11:30."

It was about ten thirty when I stepped into the dining room. "Is Ms. Henderson here?" I asked one of the guys who had a stack of dinner plates he was placing on tables.

"That's her over there." He nodded toward a woman across the room with her back to me, talking to a guy dressed in a white tunic with knot-loop buttons and a tall chef's hat.

I walked over and stood behind her and waited for her. From that vantage point I could tell she was a taller-than-average woman with dark hair that was graying. She wore the standard high heels and shear nylon hose. From behind it appeared she was not thin, nor was she fat. Her hips from behind looked kind of wide. She and the chef came to an agreement on something and he turned around and walked back through some swinging doors which I assumed led to the kitchen. She turned around and was startled to find a stranger standing behind her. "Ms. Henderson?" I asked.

"Yes, may I help you?"

"I came to see about the dining room job."

"Well, come sit down."

She pulled out a chair from one of the dining tables and sat down. "Pull out a chair and let's talk," she said as she pushed dishes out of her way. "Have you ever worked in a restaurant?" I told her of my jobs at the Blue Spruce and Odone's. Her hair was almost shoulder length and parted on one side. She kept fluffing it for some reason. Maybe it was just habit. She had some other questions and told me I could have the job. I would be bussing dishes in the dining room and waiting tables on room service orders. "Do you need sleeping quarters?" I told her I had an apartment in town, but that I did want to move. She asked if I could start the next day, which I assured her I would. "Okay, come tomorrow morning at ten, and we'll get you started."

She stood and said, "One thing more, you'll need some dark trousers." I hadn't heard the word "trousers" since I worked at Lorig's clothing store. "Yes, ma'am, I have some." I still had the pants to the suit the home bought for me over two years ago. They were a little short on me, but they would have to do for now. On my way back to the bus stop, I wondered what kind of boss she would be. She gave no indication. She was polite to me, she was soft-spoken, but she never smiled. She was strictly business, but not stiff. On the bus ride back to town my thoughts went to "How do I tell Skip I'm leaving? And how do I get the stuff out of my apartment and tell the building manager I'm leaving?" Telling Skip was the bigger worry by far.

As soon as I got back to the apartment, I told the manager I would be leaving. He agreed to take my few pots and pans, dishes, sheets, and other things. The only food in my refrigerator was a few slices of bologna and half a loaf of bread. I ate all the bologna and two slices of bread and threw the rest in the garbage can behind the building. I kept my clock and a couple of books.

I walked down by the pier hoping to find the skipper. Of course the boat wasn't at the pier; it was anchored off about a hundred yards. I thought, "I'll just have to wait and talk to him tonight."

The rest of the day dragged as I struggled painfully through the things I should say to Skip. How would he take it? How would the guys take it? Maybe I should just not even go to the boat. I went to the boat early as always and broke the news to Skip, who was turning out another delicious supper for us.

"This feast and famine life is not for everyone, Jack. Don't apologize. I understand."

"I just feel bad about letting you and the other guys down."

"It's okay, the guys understand, and I got a cousin out of work. I'll start him tomorrow."

That night we came in with an empty hold again. After securing the bow and stern lines, the guys all wished me well.

Skipper Joe said, "My cousin may not work out, so if you ever need a job, check with me. If I don't have a spot for you, I may know another boat looking for someone."

I left them all and walked back down the pier feeling sad. I wasn't excited about being a busboy again, but the Del Monte job offered a steady pay check, meals, and sleeping quarters. It was one of the few times in my life I would choose security over adventure.

> News Break
> January 3, 1949
> Wyoming Strangled by Blizzard
> Eastern Wyoming, all traffic is stranded. People and cattle are freezing and snowbound. The National Guard is called out to aid rescues. Air Force planes are air lifting hay to cattle.

I arrived at the Lodge ten minutes to ten. I dropped my suit case by the cloak room and scanned the dining room. Across the room I caught Ms. Henderson's eye. She motioned me over. She then showed me around the dining room, an L-shaped room with a fully windowed bay view along one wall. As she was showing me the proper way to arrange the place settings, we were interrupted by one of the bus boys. While they were talking, I couldn't help, but see the beautiful view of Carmel Bay, the shore line cliffs and the famous Pebble Beach golf course. The 18th hole was just outside the windows and the cliffside seventeenth was in view. I could see the waves hit the cliffs and cause huge explosions of white water spray.

My visual tour of the bay was interrupted by, "Dale, this is Jack.

We shook hands and said, "Hi," in chorus. His fingers were short and chubby, but his hand shake was hearty. Dale was on the short side of average, but not short enough to be called shorty. He was not much older than me if at all. He was dressed in dark blue pants, white shirt, and a snow white five-button waiter's jacket with mandarin collar, buttoned to the top. "Jack will be your new room-mate. After the lunch period you can show him your quarters."

"Yes, ma'am."

He turned and walked away. Ms. Henderson and I continued our tour. I was shown the bus stations and the kitchen where she introduced me to the chefs and cooks. In the kitchen I also met a couple waiters. They were dressed in black tuxedo pants with a thin black satin strip running down each pant leg. They wore white Eton jackets, white shirts and black bow tie. Two Mexican-looking guys were washing dishes. She nodded toward them. "They don't speak English." I gave her my all-knowing nod.

"Did you bring any luggage or belongings which need to be put away?" I told her where I had deposited my suitcase. "Put your things to the rear of the cloak room for now. You can take them to your room after lunch." She motioned to another busboy. He came over and was introduced as John. "John is the head bus person. If you have any questions, ask John." With that, she left us.

John was not a boy; he was a tall, well-built young man in his midtwenties, I would guess. His voice was soft, and his smile was subtle.

He ran down the bus service routine to me and showed me where everything was kept—water pitchers, ice cubes, napkins, tablecloths, etc. He introduced me to a couple of waiters I hadn't met yet. The guests started arriving at about elven o'clock. "Go say good morning and nothing else unless you're asked. Pour the water and leave." I had learned all this from Sam at the Blue Spruce back home.

The lunch period went smoothly. I was mesmerized by the wine steward, or sommelier, as he was called. I had never seen the wine pouring/tasting ritual before. During a slow period nearing the end of the lunch hour while I was standing around with a water pitcher in my hand trying to look busy, I had the chance to watch. The steward, a gray-haired stout man of about fifty or more, was elegantly decked out in a black tuxedo, black bow tie, white shirt with black buttons, and French cuffs with black cuff links. He wore a wide black cummerbund around his midsection. Around his neck was a long, silver chain with a small silver cup attached. He first showed the bottle of wine to one of the guests. I don't know if the guy was reading the label or what.

The guest nodded, the steward then pulled a corkscrew from his pants pocket, applied the screw to the cork, pulled the cork out and placed it on the table. He then picked up the guest's wine glass and poured a small amount of wine in the glass and returned the glass to the table. The guest lifted the wine glass and swirled the wine around. After swirling the wine, he raised the glass toward his face. I thought he surely was going to drink the wine, but no, He put the glass to his nose and appeared to be sniffing it. Next he finally got to the tasting. The wine was held in his mouth for a while and then I saw his Adam's apple bob; he had swallowed it. He nodded to the steward, who then poured more wine in his glass and also the glasses of the others at the table.

By the time the last guests left, we had set up all the tables for the dinner crowd. If needed, we changed the white linen table cloths and brushed off all the chairs and vacuumed the carpet. We now had nearly three hours for ourselves until dinner. If we wanted to eat we had to go to the kitchen an hour before the dining room opened. There was an employee's menu for each meal; nothing like the gourmet menu of the guests. Even so, I thought our menu to be especially good.

During the afternoon break, Dale took me over to our quarters which were in a low ceilinged wood frame white building. We entered to a narrow hallway. Two interior doors were spaced about 12 feet apart along the side wall. An open door at the end of the hallway presented a shiny white commode, leaving no doubt as to the room's use. Dale led me through the first door.

"This is our room. John has the other room."

The room was not large, nor was it small. There were two metal cots, one made up tightly with a grey blanket tightly tucked in all around with a white incased pillow at the head. The other cot was all messed up with blanket and sheet all intertwined. I didn't need to be told which bed was mine. There was a window with a rolled-up shade placed between the cots and above the bedside table, on which was a radio, a wind-up alarm clock and a couple copies of *Western Story Magazine*. I plopped my suitcase on the bed and scanning the room I found the closet. We were also furnished a chest-of- drawers.

"There's some hangers in the closet, and you can have the top two drawers of the chest. I'll take the bottom two."

I thanked him and put my few belongings away. We sat on our bunks and talked for a while. Dale was from Pacific Grove and had never been more than a few miles from there. His reaction on learning I was from Colorado was, "Are there still wild mustangs there?"

"Yeah, there are." I didn't tell him I had never seen one.

"Can you go and just capture one for yourself?"

I told him yes, but in fact, I didn't know. He indicated that someday he wanted to go get a mustang and ride it back to California. Man, I thought I had some crazy thoughts, but this one topped most of mine.

"Do you ride a horse when you go home?"

"Yeah." This lie was rationalized by the fact that since the only place I had ridden was back home. I felt I was helping Dale create the image of me as a true pulp Western citizen. I figured that was the kind of roommate he hoped I would be. "Do you own a six-shooter?" I now figured I'd better end this fiction he was creating. I told him I had never carried a gun.

Dale's response was, "There's a US marshall I read about who never carried a gun, but everyone obeyed him."

This guy was incurable. He went on, "Did you bring your boots?" I told him no. He asked a few more questions about Western life and then said he was going to go over to Pacific Grove and would see me at dinner.

I now had about two hours to myself. After putting my stuff away in the top drawer, I put my leather jacket on and went to explore the premises. I walked around the lodge and went down beyond the eighteenth green and a white sand trap to the water front and stood watching the waves driving at the cliff and causing a spray straight up. Across Carmel Bay I could see homes. I stood scanning the bay taking it all in. This was a beautiful place. I walked along the shore marveling at the twisted wind beaten Cypress trees which looked like they were growing right out of the rocks. I came to a small cove where below the cliff there was a tiny sand beach.

I climbed down the cliff and stood on the sand, the water was no more than 15 feet away. The calm waves of the cove just lapped the sand very gently. There was no evidence that any humans had ever been here. I threw a few pebbles in the water and then sat in the sand for a short time before climbing back up the cliff. I headed back to my room walking by some cottages on the Lodge property. I learned later they were guest cottages for those not wishing to be quartered in the Lodge rooms. Back in the room I dug out Tobacco Road, which I hadn't begun to finish. I still hadn't found the "good pages." I read for a while till Dale returned and we went for our supper. The dining room dinner went about like lunch. The room was closed at 8:00 p.m. Ms. Henderson asked me to stay late so John could show me the room service duties. One bus boy was held over each night to take care of room service calls. This was John's night.

The most interesting thing about room service was that there was an uncommonly narrow, almost secret stair case at the rear of the building for the service staff to use. There was a closed door at the top which opened to the second floor corridor. I walked through one order with John, I soloed on the next order and he took the third. That was all the action for that night. We walked out of there at 10:00 p.m. I got a one-dollar tip which was quite generous for those days. From that time on, I took the night shift in rotation with John and Dale. Breakfast the next day was not that much different from the other meals so far as bussing dishes was involved. There was about an hour break for us between breakfast and lunch. Dale and I walked back to our quarters.

"Do you like Bing Crosby?" he asked.

"Yeah, why?"

He told me Bing was on the radio every morning about this time and that he never missed a show. And from that day on Dale and I listened to Bing Crosby open his show with "Where the Blue of the Night Meets the Gold of the Day."

"Bing Crosby lives right over here just off the golf course. He comes here once in a while."

"Oh yeah. You've seen him?"

Dale said he had poured water for Crosby a few times.

"What's he like?"

Dale said he had never really talked to him. "In a couple of weeks, you'll see lots of celebrities. That's when we have the Bing Crosby Golf Tournament."

Later that week one of the waiters asked if I played golf. I told him I had caddied at the Broadmoor but hadn't played much. He advised me that employees could play the course for free.

"I've got a nearly complete set of clubs and a bag you can have for five dollars."

I took the deal, and the next day, he brought the clubs. The bag was canvass with leather reinforcements. I'm sure it was as old as me. There was a wooden handled putter, two drivers (numbers two and three). There were four irons: numbers two, five, seven, and nine. Further examination of the clubs revealed that this bag of clubs had been cobbled together and not bought as a set. There were three or four different signatures on them. Two of the irons were signed Gene Sarazen. One wood was signed Ben Hogan; the other carried the name of Bobby Jones.

Regardless of the mongrel nature of my clubs, they were treasured by me. The next afternoon I took my clubs and went to the club house, gave the man my employee pass, and prepared to tee off. The bag had contained about six balls and a big handful of tees. It was kind of misty so I wore my US navy wool sweater. I had no golf shoes, or even "tennis shoes," as we called sneakers in the day. After pulling the two wood out of the bag, I lay it on the ground. I pulled out a ball and a tee and set them for my drive down the long fairway. I was about to address the ball, when a voice behind me said, "Do you mind if I go out with you?"

I turned. *OH MY GOD, it was Bing Crosby*. I was choked up and couldn't speak for what seemed like an hour. I had been an avid fan for as long as I could remember. I finally stuttered words to the effect of: "I'm-Mis-Mister Crosby, I'm just a beginner. I have never played before. I would hold you up."

He was all smiles and said, "Okay, go ahead, I'll follow you."

"No, you better go ahead. I would just hold you up," I repeated.

He teed off and drove the ball straight down the fairway almost out of sight. He pulled his golf cart down the side of the fairway. I waited until he had taken his second stroke toward the green which was dog-legged to the right going around a grove of tall trees. After slicing my drive into the trees twice, I finally got a ball to stay on the fairway. It didn't go far, but it was a straight and true drive. I was proud. It took me two more strokes with my two iron to get to where Crosby had gotten with one stroke. Now I could see the green. Crosby had already holed out and gone on. He was nowhere in sight. Two more strokes and I was on the green. Three putts and a gimme. I was down in eight on the par-four hole. Crosby had already cleared the second fairway. I would never see my singing idol for the rest of the day. I played the course about twice a week after that. I got a little better, but not much.

The Annual Bing Crosby
Pro-AM Golf Tournament

The tournament professional golfers and celebrity amateur guests began to arrive. I knew but one professional on sight, Ben Hogan. I had seen his picture on the sports pages often. I started going to the front desk each morning to see what celebrities had checked in. One morning a young, good looking, tanned man was checking in. The bell hop was waiting to carry his two suit cases. As the man finished at the desk and turned, the bell hop bent to pick up the luggage. His left arm could not lift the case. He stood looking puzzled.

The young guest said, "Here, I'll get that one. My weights are in there." He picked it up with ease and walked to the elevator, followed by the still-confused bellhop.

I asked the desk clerk: "Who is that man?"

"That's Frank Stranahan, probably the best amateur golfer in the world. He's also a world-class power weightlifter and heir to the Champion Spark Plug Company."

The first amateur golfers I recognized were Forrest Tucker and Randolph Scott. I had seen them in a Western movie together where they were bitter enemies. Scott was one of my favorite movie cowboys, so therefore I had a certain disdain for Tucker. When I saw them together laughing and joking and wearing slacks and sport coats, my images of them became confused. I saw Leo "The Lip" Durocher, baseball's bad boy manager of the New York Giants. Durocher, long-time manager of the Brooklyn Dodgers, friend to pool hustlers and acquaintance of mobsters, had been suspended from baseball for "association with known gamblers" He was an unlikeable big mouth, but to his credit, as manager of the Dodgers, he helped pave the way for the first black player in the major leagues: Jackie Robinson, who joined the team in April, 1947. Durocher is to have said to his team prior to Robinson's arrival: "I don't care if the guy is yellow or black or if he has stripes like a fucking zebra. I'm the manager of this team, and I say he plays. What's more, I say he can make us all rich. And if any of you cannot use the money, I'll see that you are traded."

Actor Dennis O'Keefe came to dine and had to be provided a jacket. It was a dining room requirement that all gentlemen wear a jacket. There were several jackets stored in the cloak room to help gentlemen with this requirement. O'Keefe was greeted time and again with "Hi, Denny," as he walked across the dining room. What made him so popular, I don't know. I recognized character actor William Frawley.

At the time I didn't know his name, but I had seen his face in many movies. Opening day of the tournament, during the morning break, I walked over to the first tee to watch professional golfers tee off. There was a big crowd of people around the tee area which was roped off to keep them back from the players. I found a good spot on a knoll where I could see as well as hear the golfers. It was a lucky time for me because Bing Crosby and professional Lloyd Mangrum were to start. Mangrum drove the ball very close to the woods on the right of the fairway and about as close to the dog-legged green as one could possibly get. The gallery of fans really applauded the perfect drive. Crosby, tongue -in-cheek, said: "You're going to have to do better than that." He then stepped up to drive. His ball soared true and far, but nowhere close to Mangrum's drive. I didn't have time to watch any other golfers. I had to get back to the dining room.

I was filling water glasses one evening when for some reason, I can't say for sure, I turned with a glass of water in my hand and splashed it on a man's shirt. In a split second I instinctively turned back to the table and grabbed a napkin, turned back to the man. It was Randolph Scott. I started to nervously brush him off with the napkin while babbling: "I'm sorry, I'm so sorry." My cowboy hero smiled and said:

"Don't worry about it, son. It's okay."

I thanked him and picked a napkin off an empty table and gave it to the guest I had taken from.

Working room service one night, I had the opportunity to serve Frank Stranahan. He greeted me with a warm friendly smile and said, "You can put the tray right here." I placed the tray, and he said, "Thank you." Many guests wouldn't even look at you, let alone thank you. As I was leaving, Stranahan said, "Could I impose on you to get me more butter?"

"Yes, sir. I'll be right back." I filled a soup bowl with butter packets and returned.

"Thanks much. What's your name?"

I told him.

"I'm Frank. I like a lot of butter with my meals, as you can see." He thanked me again. For the remaining days of the tournament when he wanted room service, he asked for me. I always took him plenty of butter, and he always gave me a three-dollar tip. I don't know how he placed in the tournament, but I do know I'll never forget him. Late one night a room service call came from Durocher's room. I took the order up and was received by Durocher and Frawley, both of whom reeked with the smell of booze. I put the tray down, and Durocher asked me to bring him a bottle of whiskey. I told him I was too young and not allowed to serve whiskey.

"If you get someone up here to take the order, there's five bucks in it for you, kid."

I scampered down the service stairs and went to the bar. I told the head bartender that if someone could take Durocher's order, there would be a big tip in it for him. I took one of the bartenders to the room. "Mr. Durocher, this man can take your order."

"Thanks, kid. We won't need you anymore."

As I was leaving, silently I was screaming, "Where's my five-dollar tip?"

I'd hated Leo Duocher ever since. After the tournament, I worked a cocktail party serving hors d'oeuvres. I just walked around the room with a tray of little crackers with stuff on them. The golfers gobbled them up and I'd go back to the kitchen for more. I ate a few myself. The host, Bing Crosby, was pretty high. His words were slightly slurred. So I can't truthfully say I attended a cocktail party with Bing Crosby, because he really wasn't there. I could say though that I was invited.

Ms. Henderson invited me, "Jack, you'll be working the cocktail party in the banquet room this afternoon."

Ms. Henderson, from time to time, advised me to get a haircut, which I did, but what she really wanted me to do was get rid of my Pachuco-looking ducktails.

One damp, cloudy, misty afternoon out on the links, I just teed off at the eleventh hole when it began to rain. About halfway down the fairway was a pavilion. From where I stood, I could make out three people in silhouette. As I got near I saw that it was Bing Crosby and two boys. He greeted me like an old friend even though he didn't know my name, he remembered me from our first meeting on the tee. He introduced me to his sons. I remember only Gary. Crosby asked how my game was going. We had a few minutes of small talk before the rain stopped.

They took off down the fairway, took their second strokes and were out of sight by the time I reached the green. That was the last time I saw Bing Crosby. That same day after I finally holed out the seventeenth green I stood and watched as successive waves loudly crashed against the rocks below and send water spray wildly gushing up and then see the water calmly and quietly return to the sea. There was a hypnotic rhythm to it. The green was so close to the cliff that I'm sure that many a golf ball had been given up to the deep.

Dale told me the Lodge owned horse stables and if no guests were scheduled to ride, we could ride for free. That afternoon he took me to the stables and we checked out two very nicely groomed mounts. They were saddled and ready to ride. We took a trail which led across some sand dunes and down along the beach. I asked Dale if he wanted to leave the trail and go down by the water and race.

He said, "I think we should stay on the trail, or we'll get in trouble." He was obviously half scared of the horse, let alone try racing it.

I stayed with him on the trail. I asked him if he still wanted to go to Colorado and get a wild Mustang. He didn't answer. Dale was truly a tenderfoot when it came to horses.

On my weekly day off, I often caught the bus to Monterey and hung out with the guys at the pool hall. "Hey, Farmer Jack, how's your buddy Bing Crosby?" We'd shoot some pool, go for coffee, maybe a movie. These guys must have worked nights. They were always in the pool hall during the day and they seemed to always have spending money.

One night a car load of us went over to Pacific Grove to crash a high school sock hop. We pulled up into the parking lot and saw two guys fighting, actually only one guy was fighting, the other guy, seemed helpless down on his hands and knees while he was being hammered on the head with a flashlight. A small crowd of guys and girls were watching. I don't know why, but I went over and pushed the top dog as hard as I could. He fell away and landed on his butt. I didn't know what he might do next. I was relieved when he picked himself up and walked away. The guy on the ground got up. Blood was running down the side of his face. A couple of his buddies who had been watching him be beaten stepped out of the crowd and helped him walk away.

A girl stepped out of the crowd and said, "Thank you. That Luke [pseudonym] is always beating up on someone. Everybody is afraid of him."

I don't remember if we went to the hop, but I had acquired a reputation as a tough guy. To tell the truth, I was about half scared that Luke would come looking for me. We did crash a big party over in Carmel one night. The party was held in a residential area of large beautiful homes with manicured lawns. Cars were parked on both sides of the long driveway. We parked on the street. The party had been underway for about two hours. The house was all lit up and the familiar tune of "San Antonio Rose" was being tendered from within. The front door was open. We figured to go in one at a time so as not to be conspicuous. I went in second and moved around the edge of the crowd till I got to the open bar. I ordered a Lucky. Lucky Lager was a popular California beer. On the bar was a Mason jar marked Tips, I dropped two quarters in. My two companions arrived at the bar and ordered beers.

We watched the dancers and checked out all the chicks. The band was small but good. Our beer bottles empty, we had proven our point. We had successfully crashed an upper crust party in Carmel. We exited the same way we entered: one at a time. Back in Monterey one of the guys said he was going to the tattoo parlor for another tattoo. He already had both his forearms covered with a peacock on one and a Vargas girl on the other.

"You wanta go with me?" he asked.

I went with him and watched as he got a skull punched into his shoulder skin. It looked painful, but my friend's face didn't give that impression. He laughed and joked all during the procedure, even though it bled a little. The tattoo guy just kept dabbing the blood with a tissue. When he finished he put a bandage on it.

"You ought to get one, Jack."

I picked out a small blue bird with a red breast and had it placed on my left upper arm. It didn't take long, and it didn't hurt much. In time the tattoo wound scabbed over and began to itch. The scab peeled off little by little and the full colors of the tattoo were exposed. This would really get attention back home at the Davis Sweet Shop, if and when I ever returned.

The Native Son Comes Home

"Jack, we won't be needing your services after Tuesday."

For a moment I didn't know what she meant, then it sunk in: I was being fired. I was stunned. I really couldn't figure why. Maybe it was because my hair was still too long. I went through the grief steps of shock ("I don't know what's happening"), denial ("This isn't happening"), blame ("It's because she never did like me"), anger ("I'm the best bus boy she ever had in this place. Where does she get off firing me?"), and finally, I reached the serenity of acceptance of the fact I could not change what had happened. I started making plans to go home. I had nearly a hundred dollars in the bank. I fantasized a triumphant return home with the word going around: "Doak is back."

On Tuesday after dinner, Ms. Henderson handed me my little brown pay envelope. I spent the night in my quarters and left in the morning for Monterey. I had to wait for the bank to open to close my savings account. I put my suitcase in a locker at the Grayhound station and walked over to the pool hall. It was closed. I went back to the bus station, bought a one-way ticket to Colorado Springs. It was about seventeen dollars and change. I waited in the terminal about an hour, went to the bank, closed my account and bought twenty-dollar traveler's checks. I got back to the bus terminal just in time to catch my bus. We had a layover in San Francisco. I had a sandwich and coffee at the terminal lunch counter and went for a walk. I saw the Golden Gate Bridge and Alcatraz Island. Back on the bus we traveled through Reno, Salt Lake City, then up across Wyoming to Cheyenne and dropped down through Denver to Colorado Springs.

It was a two-day trip. I caught a cab home and called Mom at work. I took a bath and just hung out in the apartment listening to music on the radio. I counted out fifty dollars of my wealth to give Mom. I had been sending money home while I was gone. It helped with the rent and things.

Betty came home with a guy she introduced as "Clarence, we're married." Like any young brother who had been bullied by his big sister, I couldn't believe a guy found her attractive. He seemed like a nice guy. They were staying in the apartment with Mom. Betty said that Clarence worked at the hospital as a histologist. I had no idea what that was, nor did I care. To me the medical field was a large group of people with all kinds of titles I didn't know anything about.

After dinner Mom and I were clearing the table. "You've grown, Jack. Come over here, and we'll measure you. I stood erect up against the doorjamb while she put a book on my head and marker the doorway. With her yardstick, she came up with, "You are six foot three. What were you before?" I told her the last time I was measured was in gym class in high school a year ago and I was six foot. "Well, I thought so, you've grown three inches."

Betty and Clarence went out. I stayed home with Mom. I always enjoyed the times we spent together. She told me about the birds and the bees and about all her boyfriends, some she liked and others were just fillers till a good one came along. We laughed a lot about those guys. Her last marriage up to that time was to Doctor McCracken, who she said she didn't even know had a wooden leg until one night, before they were married, he took his pants off. "At first I was shocked, then, I said, 'What the hell, who cares? He's a nice guy. This will be an interesting experience.'"

I slept in the next morning. Mom left me a note on the refrigerator door: "Coffee is made. There's eggs, bacon in the fridge, and cornflakes in the pantry. There's lunch meat and cheese for a sandwich. Glad to have you home."

I ate a bowl of cornflakes and got dressed in my midsleeve Hawaiian shirt, never-washed Levi's, white sweat socks, and penny loafers. I carefully combed my ducktails and presented myself to the world. Thinking myself to be a perfect Beau Brummell, I walked with a certain cocky gate down to the post office where jobs are posted. The Forest Service was recruiting laborers again. Applicants were instructed to take an application and return it the following Monday, which was three days away.

Armed with a job application, I went to the pool hall to kill some time till noon when the high school gang would be at Davis's for lunch. There were a couple guys playing pool on one of the back tables and a couple old guys playing three-cushion billiards. I played a solo game of straight pool then went to watch the billards players. The experience and finesse required for that game had all my respect and appreciation.

I hoofed it up to Davis's and entered the back door. The minute I stepped into the room there was a burst of "DOAK" from a few voices both male and female. There was a small group around me.

"When did you get back?"

I took a seat in the nearest booth where three of my closest buddies were sitting.

A couple other guys hung over the back panel. I ordered a Coke and a hamburger from a guy in a white apron who I had never seen before. "Who is that?"

"That's Ed Colt. His brother Sam is over behind the counter. They bought the place from Davis. They call the place Colt's Corner. Sam is the boss. They have a younger brother too, named Al."

The place hadn't changed. The jukebox was rendering songs of the day. The pinball machine was sucking up nickels. I told the guys of my adventures in Wyoming and California. "No shit. You met Bing Crosby?" I told them of Cannery Row, the fishing boat, Pebble Beach, movie stars, and pro golfers. They were greatly impressed when I pulled up my left sleeve and showed my tattoo. Everyone had to get a closer look.

One of the guys called a booth full of girls over. "Come and see Doak's tattoo."

The girls "Ooed" and "Awed, did it hurt?"

"No, not much."

"That is neato, Doak."

"Doak, a bunch of us are going up the pass. You wanta go?"

I told him, "Yeah."

"We're going to meet here at six."

All right, my social life was back on track. Even though my life in the working world and the life of my friends in high school were diametrically opposed, we still held the same recreational values.

Saturday afternoon I was enjoying hanging out at home alone listening to music on the radio, when the phone rang. Who could that be? I picked the receiver.

"Hello."

A male voice on the other end asked, "Is this Jack Walker?"

"Yes."

"This is Sheriff Sullivan. Can you account for your whereabouts on January 17?"

"Yes, I was in Monterey California."

"Can you prove that?"

"Yes, I was working at the Del Monte Lodge at Pebble Beach."

"Where's your father?"

"I don't know."

"That's a good answer."

"My parents are divorced."

"If we need you, we'll be in touch. Don't leave town." I was confused and scared. I wondered what had happened. Mom got home right after I hung up. I told her of my phone conversation.

"I'm going to call Earl Sullivan and find out what this is all about." While she searched the phone book for the sheriff's number, she was mumbling something about some unsolved crime that had taken place in January. She found the number and sat down by the phone. While she was getting settled on the sofa lighting up a cigarette, she said, "I'm not going to let them pin that on you." Pin what, I didn't know. The phone rang. Mom answered it. Listening in, I overheard, "Well, you sure scared him. I was just getting ready to call Earl Sullivivan. You want to talk to him?" She turned and handed me the phone. "It's your uncle Walt, the sheriff." I took the phone and said, "Hi."

"Hey, I'm sorry." He chuckled." I had second thoughts and had to call you back. I'm really sorry." He was still laughing.

I said, "That's okay."

We talked for a while he asked me to drop over when I got a chance.

Monday morning I was down at the post office with about fifteen or twenty other guys waiting in a meeting room for the forest service guy. The guy that showed up was my old boss from last year, Ranger Flynn. He collected the applications and started the interviews, which was not much more than making sure he had your name spelled right and asking if you had any disabilities that would prevent you from physical labor. He remembered me from a year ago, so we had a nice little talk.

When he finished with the last guy, he told us, "Those of you whose applications I kept are hired. We will meet at Busy Corner on Wednesday at 8:00 am."

This was just like last year. I looked around to see if he had kept all the apps. One old Mexican guy who limped still had his app in hand. I felt very sorry for him. On the way out, I patted him on the back. I didn't have the words to console him. He looked up and gave me the slightest smile.

I told all the guys at Colt's I was going back to work for the Forest Department. The next days I spent either in the pool hall or at Colt's Corner. After 3:00 p.m. when school let out, I would hang out with the guys till they went home. Only a very few could come back out on a school night. We would sit around and share our common ignorance: "Chicks have it good. They can fuck whenever they want to. If I was a chick, I'd get fucked every night."

When Ozstrowski, who was on the short side, learned I had grown three inches, he exclaimed, "When I graduate I'm going to California to see if I can grow three inches."

I didn't believe that would work, but I kept my mouth shut. We all at one time or another lied about how far we had gotten with our last date. We never really claimed to have gone all the way, because we only dated "nice girls." We were all cherries, and we knew it. We did, however, brag about getting to feel them up or we might brag about the passionate French kisses we received, or how high up a thigh our hand had gotten before it was intercepted. None of those guys had ever gotten their hand all the way up. We couldn't name a single bone in the body, but we could run off innumerable slang terms for vagina, penis, anus, and sexual intercourse, even some in Spanish.

Back to the Forest

This year we were working up around Bailey, Pine, and Buffalo Creek. We started off in a tent town in the mountains between Pine and Buffalo Creek. The first day in camp we were welcomed by the project boss, Ranger Johnson, a short, blond haired, sun tanned guy with half the index finger on his right hand missing. He wore a kaki shirt and faded Levis. His voice was soft and deep. I liked him right away. The big cook tent sat in the middle with the smaller tents surrounding. I was assigned a tent with three older guys: two ex-GIs from Denver and a guy from Pueblo who had been laid off at the steel mill. I don't remember even seeing anyone near my age in camp. The two GIs looked to be in their late twenties or early thirties. One, I'll call Tom, the other, Dick and the steel worker, Harry. Tom was a personable, outspoken, well versed guy who had dropped out of college to join the army. He still hadn't found anything he wanted to do. Dick, who had learned book keeping in the army, had served in General Eisenhower's headquarters in England. He was quiet but very witty and funny. Harry was salt-of-the-earth, blue-collar, union-working stiff, divorced after twenty-six years and now unemployed. Everybody was his friend. I had hooked up with a good crowd. We were all assigned to Ranger Flynn's tree planting crew. I volunteered to be water boy. It was a good job.

On the second day I started packing a paperback book in my pocket to spend the time while waiting for the crew to take a break. There was no place near camp to go get a beer after work. Tom had come with a bag full of books. He read constantly and he let me read two of his books, Richard Wright's *Native Son*, a book which brought home to me the harshness of racial bigotry, and Ernest Hemingway's *For Whom the Bell Tolls*. I had seen the movie of the Hemingway book, staring Gary Cooper and Ingred Bergman. Up until that time I didn't even know there was a Spanish Civil War.

Dick wrote letters every night to old army buddies. We had a rural mailbox number out on the road. Harry hung out in the cook tent which served as a recreation center after the supper clean up. Guys played cards, checkers and dominoes. Some just sat around and drank coffee. The coffee drinkers were my crowd. I liked listening to all the men talk about politics, the war, women, guns and cars, subjects of which I knew diddly squat. Some told dirty jokes and sang dirty songs. Some of the war stories were ugly. I learned the hard lesson that even our soldiers committed atrocities. I still have the vivid picture described by one of the ex-GIs: "This Krout would respond to every order by saying 'Heil Hitler.'" I slammed my rifle butt in his mouth. He spit out blood and teeth. My buddy kicked him in the balls. He screamed and bent over and went stumbling away. That son of a bitch didn't say 'Heil Hitler' after that." This story ran contrary to all the wartime propaganda I had come to believe during the war.

I naively thought we were the good guys and they were the bad ones. Growing up is hard.

On pay day once in a while Dick and Harry hosted the camp floating crap game in our tent. This was my introduction to the fascinating world of the ivory cubes and the law of probability. I learned that the odds for rolling most number combos are about seventy-two to one. For the six, the seven and the eight, the odds are better. "Once in a while Lady Luck interferes and a guy has a good run." I learned how to palm and throw a crooked pair of dice.

"Jack, don't ever shoot craps on a soft surface. You'll be taken to the cleaners by the 'blanket roll,'" Dick cautioned. "What is that?" He explained and demonstrated the controlled roll on a soft surface. HE rolled the dice over and over till his arm got tired and a seven never came up. "I lost plenty in the army to the blanket roll till a guy pulled my coattail. Always play on a hard surface and make the rule that each throw of the dice must bounce off something hard or it's "No dice."

We spent about three weeks planting trees then we went over near Pines and spent a couple weeks spraying trees to get rid of some kind of beetle that was killing the forest in that area. Two nice guys who used to come to our tent just to hang out were Doc and Shorty. Doc was a recovering drunk dentist who had lost his practice and his family due to his drinking. He had been straight for four weeks. His partner, Shorty, was a six foot six inch giant, a failed farmer. To offset Shorty's height and bulk, Doc was short and skinny. They had become the best of pals, though they were nothing alike. Doc was deep and erudite whereas Shorty was just a plain old country boy. Doc was soft-spoken, and his vocabulary was that of an educated man.

Shorty was big, jolly, and loud. It was fun and interesting to spend time with them. You really got the full spectrum of thought on any idea they brought up. Shorty wore bib overalls and Doc, who probably didn't own any work clothes, wore pleated dress pants and white dress shirts. His only shoes were his dress oxfords. They were two of the nicest guys I had ever met.

Once the tree spraying was completed we broke camp, packed up our tents and threw them on the truck and moved over near Baily, where we set up camp and built barbed wire fence. Each morning we were trucked out to the fence site, where a mountainous pile of rough-hewn seven foot posts were stacked. Leather gauntlet gloves were issued. We were issued picks and each of us slung a post up on our shoulder and hiked down the fence line that had been previously marked with red paint spots on the rocks every so often by the surveyors We dropped our post ten feet beyond where the guy in front of us dropped his.

The terrain was rocky and steep in places. It reminded me of pictures I had seen of the Great Wall of China. We chipped away at the rocky soil until a two-foot post hole was achieved. Where there was solid granite that refused to chip, we moved to the nearest forgiving spot. Doing this sometimes made the fence jog away from the original line and sometimes the ten-foot interval between posts was extended or reduced. Two guys were pulling two reels of barbed wire between them on a piece of pipe, laying out two strands of wire.

Behind them was a guy with a wire stretcher pulling the wire taunt, while another guy had the dangerous job of stapling the tight wire to the posts. Those of us not working with the wire stretching were told to stay our distance. "If this wire snaps, it could cut your throat wide open or take out an eye," Flynn told us.

The camp had its share of genuinely goofy characters: Lafayette Lincoln, the only black guy in camp, was a friend who when I turned down the opportunity to take a swig from his wine bottle, told me, "A man who won't drink wine is a sissy man." I think he was about the oldest guy in camp. His very dark skin and snow-white hair gave me the impression of Uncle Remus from the movie *Song of the South*. I could picture him singing "Zip a Dee Doo Dah." Joking with him one day over coffee in the cook tent, I told him of my Uncle Remus impression of him.

"That show was bad," he said.

"How was it bad?"

"It showed colored folks as a bunch of clowns."

I told Lafayette, "I didn't mean anything bad. I was just joking."

He forgave me. I now wanted to see that movie again, but never did.

Another older guy told me, while we were taking a piss break in the woods, "Boy, when I was your age, I could piss a stream through four inches of concrete."

One goofy old guy with a gold tooth told me he picked up radio transmissions through the tooth. These old guys seemed to store up stuff to drop on me, the dumb kid.

The town of Bailey I don't remember much about. It was no bigger than a postage stamp, but I do recall it had a post office and a bar with a dance floor that really jumped on Saturday night. I was sitting watching the Polka dancers one night and a buxom middle aged lady asked me if I would like to dance. "I don't know how to do this" I told her.

"I'll teach you." She pulled me out of my chair and began to show me all the jumps, bounces, twists, and turns of this nineteenth-century European dance. The dance called polka is an activity enjoyed by millions, but my clumsy feet and body couldn't get a fix on it. I was also introduced to vodka that night. I became less self-conscious with the polka after each vodka boiler maker, so much so that they sent me back to camp. I don't know what all I did, but they didn't want me to dance with them anymore.

The next day I nursed the worst hangover I had ever had. It was Sunday, and I didn't get out of my bunk till afternoon. I couldn't remember even coming back to camp, let alone how I found the right tent and the right bunk. My tent mates were all gone, so I couldn't ask them. I knew one of the cooks, a guy called Ed. He dished me out a big bowl of vegetable soup and sat and talked with me.

I remember he said, "If you ever come to Tulsa, just ask for Ed the cook."

I didn't think he was truly that well known in Tulsa or any other place. Out on the fence line, one morning three men wearing Stetsons and boots rode up on horseback.

"What the hell are you doing?" One of the rangers explained that the Department of the Interior had decided that this would no longer be free range. (Besides fencing this rocky area, we were also fencing off a canyon leading to a grass-covered valley.) This was like the Old West with range wars between the cattlemen and the clod busters. Each rider had a rifle on his saddle. I hoped they wouldn't start shooting. I was ready to hit the ground if one of them reached for his gun.

"We'll see about that," the rancher said and they rode off down the fence line. The rest of the day I kept a vigilant look out for their return. I was even nervous about them coming to our camp that night. I had seen a movie where the ranchers had shot up a railroad gang's camp. My fears abated the next day under the yolk of post hauling, hole digging, and sweat.

We finished the fence, packed up the tents, and were trucked back home.

Working, Playing, Becoming

I stepped right back into the social swing of things at Colt's Corner, once in a while getting a date, but most of the time hanging out with the guys. One Saturday afternoon one of the guys said that there had been a pajama party of one of the girl's houses. "They're probably still over there. Let's go see."

We crashed the party. The girls were receptive. There was music on the phonograph and the parents were not at home. We paired off a guy with a girl, some dancing, some just sitting. I was on the sofa with my arm around Genene Myers. I leaned my face toward her, and we kissed.

"That's not a real kiss." She pulled me in close to her and pressed her lips to mine while hugging me with all her might, her mouth opened, and my tongue sled in. I was never so excited. A few more of those plus some breast feeling topped off the afternoon. I never dated Genene after that because she went steady with and wore the letter jacket of one of the football players.

Three of my best friends at that time were Chuck Franklin, Bob Lacey, and Billy Mudd. Chuck and I used to go down to the Alamo Hotel on Sunday afternoons and go in a side door on Cucharras street and listen to jam sessions. It was a free event where a bunch of musicians, black and white, from as many walks of life got together and really wailed. Any musician could set in. This was real jumpin' jive you couldn't hear on the radio. I didn't feel I was good enough for this group. The audience was always a small faithful group of jazz enthusiasts. I learned later that the strange smell in that place was marijuana. The common recreational drugs of our generation were nicotine and alcohol.

"You know, if you take a Benzedrine inhaler apart and soak the cardboard stick in black coffee, it'll keep you awake twenty-four hours a day for a long time," one of the pundits at Colt's told me while we were exchanging pearls of knowledge.

I tried a stick in some coffee. It kept me awake all one night even though I was feeling painfully tired and sleepy. Never again. The real dopeheads were those who shot up Blue Velvet; Paragoric, an over-the-counter opium derivative for rubbing on baby's gums when teething, was mixed with an antihistamine and injected in the arm. I only heard of this. I didn't know of any users. We had heard that Spanish Fly was a drug used to make female cattle hot for sex. We wondered if it would work on girls. We didn't have any. We didn't know where to get any and even if we had, we would have been afraid to use it.

Chuck wasn't a musician, but he sure liked jazz. He was a red headed guy, rather slight of build, very smart but lived on the outer fringe of the in-groups. He fit, but not quite. Chuck's father was a traveling optometrist who was on the road all week fitting and selling eyeglasses in the small rural towns who had no such service. He evidently made a pretty good living at it. They lived in a big house on the north side.

Bob and I some nights would get dressed up in our top coats and white silk scarves. We'd go down to Todd's Shoe shop for a shine on our Cordovan colored shoes with black double soles. We were the epitome of hip sophistication. We would make a showing at Colt's first, next we'd drive Bob's parent's car down to the drive-in on south Nevada Avenue. We would usually wind up in the all night restaurant drinking coffee and sharing our common wisdom with each other. I always enjoyed telling the story of Grandpa running for land in the great Oklahoma land rush on the Cherokee strip and telling of my father doing time for grand larceny. Actually I don't know what he did time for but grand larceny had the sound of excitement. The story set me apart from the hum drum family life of my peers. One night one of the guys with us came up with: "Did you know that the word *fuck* was an abbreviation of "found under carnal knowledge" in the old common law of England? Sexual intercourse was against the law for unmarried couples." Actually, adultery was against the law in Colorado at that time. Another "did you know" was that in Colorado Springs, you couldn't build a house that would block your neighbor's view of the mountains. I don't know if that was true or not.

One Christmas Eve Bob and I went out cattin' around before going to midnight mass with his parents. We had a few beers and we both fell asleep during the mass to the ire of his mother. While driving me home, Mrs. Lacey lectured us all the way to my house and was still berating Bob as the car pulled away. About the only other time I wore a top coat was when Uncle Walt would ask me if I would like to go with him up to Denver in the evening to pick up Eileen and the boys at her Mother's house. I enjoyed these trips riding along the highway talking with my uncle. He was witty and funny. I think I respected him more than any other man I had met. To me he was a surrogate father I guess. In later years he would become like an older and wiser brother to me.

Billy could always beat me shooting pool. Once in a while he would hustle some stranger into playing for money. He looked much younger than his seventeen years and many a grown man was sucked into a money game with him, only to lose. He was natural in all that he did. He had transferred to the high school from Saint Mary's and even though he was short, he was an excellent varsity basketball player. He generally used his left hand, but he was totally ambidextrous, a gift which served him well in pool shooting and in basketball. He also had that talent to make people laugh. He did funny impressions of people we all knew: teachers, coaches, other students, and many celebrities and movie cartoon characters. He stayed overnight with me once.

In the morning Mom said, "I heard you boys laughing in there very late. Did you ever get any sleep?"

We must have laughed ourselves to sleep. Billy and I hitchhiked down to Pueblo one night because our common knowledge led us to believe that the steel mill town was loose, easy and loaded with action. When we got to downtown Pueblo, it was locked up tight as a drum. The stores were all dark and locked up. There wasn't a bar in sight and the easy streetwalkers were totally absent. Another myth exposed as false. It was in the wee hours of the morning when we got back home. We used to talk about hopping a freight train just for the fun of it, riding somewhere and hopping one back. We never did. Billy said the nuns at Saint Mary's were strict.

"They always threatened to whack us with the ruler or send us to the principal's office who they said would use a paddle on us. But I never knew of anyone who got whacked or paddled."

I asked Billy, "Why are Catholics supposed to eat fish on Friday?"

"I don't know, maybe because Saint Peter was a fisherman and he wanted to sell fish."

I don't know where we got the idea, but one night Ozz, Billy, and I went up into the belfry of the Baptist Church on East Kiowa Street and threw pigeon eggs down at cars. The drivers never knew where the splattered eggs came from. Another stupid thing we did at night was go over east on Platte Avenue where there was a small apple orchard and pick out some real mushy rotten apples and toss them at passing cars.

On one occasion a driver stopped and took off running toward us. We scattered and went three different directions. Once I felt he was not chasing me, I slowed down and went on home.

Next day at Colt's we three met up. The guy had picked Billy to chase, but never caught him. Billy said he ditched him by hiding in the bushes at the Deaf and Blind School.

A Car, a Restaurateur, a Better Car

"Harveys, All the pancakes you can eat 50 cents," read the sign in front.

I was hired as a fry cook to make pancakes, fluffy eggs, and other breakfast delicacies. After breakfast, and for the rest of the day, we served a vast number of sandwiches with various cute names, only one of which I can remember: "Humdinger," which was a huge triple-decker concoction of assorted meats, cheeses, and other things I can now only guess at. I drove to work in my newly acquired car, a 1931 Dodge coupe, which Grandpa was getting rid of before he went to California. The price was one hundred dollars, and I was to pay him twenty-five dollars a month. At work I parked the car to the side of the restaurant in a driveway next to the riding stable. The stable wranglers ate stack after stack of pancakes each morning. There were two of us manning the two large grills. We dropped the pancake batter with steel dispensers. When not grilling cakes, we made the popular fluffy scrambled eggs made with milk and constant whisking in a sauce pan. The hours were long and the pay was short.

I got to thinking I could run a short-order place like this. The lunch counter attached to the old bowling alley was owned by Randy, a guy I knew when he had a candy store on El Paso Street. He wanted to sell the lunch counter. I saw myself as a restaurateur, in business for myself, driving a new car, maybe a Cadillac. The picture danced in my head of all the guys and girls saying in awe: "Doak has his own business." What would I call the place?

Speedy Allen, my landlord, loaned money for bail bond, so I went to him and asked if he would loan me the money to buy out Randy.

"Pull up a chair, Jack."

I pulled up a wooden ladder-back chair to the side of Speedy's big rolltop desk.

"Do you know how much money the place takes in?" Before I could say no, he went on, "Do you know what his expenses are? Do you know what a pound of hamburger costs him? Do you know how many hamburgers you can get from a pound? If it's making money, why is he selling it?" Speedy went on and on for about fifteen minutes, and I sunk lower and lower. "When you can answer all these and it adds up to a profitable conclusion, then you might be ready to consider a purchase."

I realized I didn't know anything about buying any business of any kind. I thanked him and walked out filled with humility caused by my ignorance. At the time I didn't really realize the valuable lesson I had been given.

I traded the old 1931 Dodge in for a 1934 Dodge four-door sedan. It was upholstered in brown sheepskin. It wouldn't match the hot rods owned by some of the guys I knew. I didn't drag race with it, and it wouldn't burn rubber. The car was equipped with a Southwind gasoline heater, which some previous owner had installed. This was pure luxury since my old car had no heat at all. I did though play with the car on the streetcar tracks on Colorado Avenue. The tracks to Manitou were still in place and when there was little or no traffic present, we used to see if we could get our cars to ride in the imbedded tracks so we could let loose of the steering wheel.

The wheel base of the cars was a little too wide, so the car would ride the rail on one side for only a short time before it jumped out. The gear shift on the floor of the cars enabled an awkward boy to let his hand slip off the gear shift knob and fall on the knee of the girl sitting next to him. If she didn't move her knee away, a boy could be emboldened to go further. If she sat real close to you the gear shift would be between her legs. I was told that this provided the possibility of a very exciting evening.

That old Dodge was far from being a hot rod, but I did often take it out on the Eighth Street cutoff, an old country road that ran from Cimarron Street on the west side, past the County Poor Farm over to Cheyenne Boulevard. There was hardly ever any traffic on this road, so I would roll down the windows and push the gas pedal clear to the floor and watch the speedometer. By the time I went by the poor farm I was tearing ass at the exhilarating speed of seventy miles per hour.

One night I was driving home a car full of drunk guys when a cop pulled me over. We scurried around in panic trying to hide beer cans. I rolled down the window and waited. "Did you know one of your tail lights is out?' I said:

"No, sir," very tight lipped trying to conceal my beer breath.

From the back seat came, "Tell him to shove it up his ass, Doak." *Oh Jesus*, I thought for sure that cop was going to lock us all up. "You better get your friend home."

"Yes, sir."

"And get that taillight fixed."

"Yes, sir."

He walked back to the squad car. I had been tensely holding my breath. I let go with a big, audible exhale and sucked air back in.

"Ronnie, you dumb shit, you almost got us all jailed."

The other guys got on him too. Ronnie's response was to throw up on the floor of my car. The smell was sickening. We rolled down all the windows, and I drove all the guys home. Ronnie needed help getting to his front porch. I put him down on a porch chair and rang the doorbell.

"Ronnie is sick," I told his mom.

She went to Ronnie. I hurried to the car and got out of there. It took the garden hose to clean out my new car and left it overnight with all the windows open to get rid of the stench. I could kick Ronnie's butt.

This Is a High-Class Place

In order to make my car payments to the General Finance Company, I would need an additional job. I interviewed with Bill Hartford owner of the House of Oscar, a supper club up north on Nevada Avenue. They had a job available for an all-around busboy, bar boy, and kitchen helper.

"This is a high-class place, so we need someone who knows what they're doing."

I ran down my experience at Pebble Beach.

His response was, "When can you start?" I started the following night.

The kitchen was run by Bill's brother, Oscar; the hostess was Bill's sister Irene. There were about four or five waiters. When I wasn't bussing dishes, pouring water, or stocking the bar, I worked in the kitchen washing dishes and making antipasto plates freezing my butt off inside a walk-in refrigerator.

Oscar, it turned out was an alumnus of the Stratton Home. He was a happy guy and fun to work with. He not only was the chef, he washed pots and pans and did other chores in the kitchen as did I.

Once in a while he would send me to the bar to get him a whiskey. "And get whatever you like, Jack." I usually just got a bottle of Coke. For about a month I worked both at Harvey's during the day and at Oscar's at night. I paid off the car and quit Harvey's.

I liked working behind the bar. When it wasn't too busy, Tony, the bartender, would teach me how to mix drinks. A popular drink of the time was the Moscow Mule, a concoction of vodka, ginger beer, and lime juice served in a copper mug. There were other exotic offerings like the Pink Lady, Irish Coffee, and the Cuba Libra, to name a few. I thought that being a bartender was the greatest ever. I knew that when I became twenty-one I was going to go to bar-tender school.

The House of Oscar had a five-piece band and a dance floor. The band leader was Rocky Ford. One of their numbers was "Little Baby Trumpet," which Rocky would sing. I remember the phrases:

> I've got a little baby trumpet,
> And it's only seven inches long
> It plays high, and it plays low
> It plays fast, and it plays slow

Then he would reach inside his jacket and pull out this smallest of trumpets. It was about seven inches long. It had the full sound of a normal-size trumpet. He also did a little comedy shtick in between musical numbers, mostly old vaudeville stand up stuff like, "We just flew in from LA-boy are my arms tired." This was followed by a base drum beat. Another one was: "This is our first time in Colorado Springs. I like the way it's laid out-I don't know how long it's been laid out, but I like it anyway." Snare drum roll followed by base beat. There was a freelance cigarette girl who came in each night going from table to table offering cigarettes for sale. She wore a short skirt and a pill box hat. The cigarettes were displayed on a tray held up by a neck strap. Also a photographer would make the rounds offering to take patron's pictures.

One night Irene told me that Ruth Etting had reserved a booth in the lounge and that I should give especially good care in serving her. I asked Oscar: "Who is Ruth Etting?"

"She was a very big singing star of the '20s and '30s. She ran around with some Chicago gangster called the Gimp. They split up and he was pissed that she was running with this other guy, who he shot. The guy, Myrl Alderman, wasn't killed, so he and Ruth ran away and settled here. They own the Carriage House Restaurant and come here once in a while." Miss Etting showed up with a man who I assumed was Myrl Alderman. The lights were low in the lounge, so

I didn't get a real good look at her, but I do remember that I thought she was pretty and I remember she smiled and thanked me when I poured water for them and each time I refilled their coffee cups. When I went home that night I asked Mom if she had ever heard of Ruth Etting. "Are you kidding? She was the biggest singing star ever. Why do you ask?"

I told Mom I had served her that evening.

Mom pumped me, "What does she look like? What is she like? What does she drink? Was she with somebody?" and on and on. A few years later the Ruth Etting story would be made into a movie titled *Love Me or Leave Me*, starring Doris Day with James Cagney playing the Gimp.

One busy Saturday night in late September Oscar had me making antipastos in the refrigerator when Bill came to the kitchen and told me to stop what I was doing and go help out at the bar. He and Oscar had words, but Bill won out. While I was stocking the bar, Irene came and told me to go clear a couple of tables. I told her Bill told me to stock the bar.

"I don't care what he told you. I'm telling you to go clear those tables."

All this frustrated and angered me to the point that I told Irene, "You can go clear those tables yourself because I quit."

I walked out through the kitchen and out the back door. That Sunday I hung out at the pool hall "drinkin' Cokes and tellin' jokes." Colorado Springs was dry on Sunday. Businesses who offered hot meals were exempted. Some taverns stayed open on the strength of serving steamed hot dogs from a small steamer on the back bar. Only in America.

Monday morning I applied for work at the Timken Roller Bearing factory and was hired to start work that evening on the swing shift, three to eleven.

News Break
December 1949
Miller Wins Pulitzer and Tony
Playwright Arthur Miller's *Death of a Salesman* is the recipient of the Pulitzer Prize for Drama and Tony Award for best play.

News Break
December 8, 1949
Nationalist China Moves to Formosa
The Nationalist government of China, facing defeat by the Communists on the mainland, has shifted its capital to Taipei on the island of Formosa.

About the Author

J ack Walker calls Colorado Springs, Colorado his home town, having spent most of his first 30 years there. His formative years were spent in a home for needy children. He dropped out of high school in his sophomore year and took jobs from the oil fields of Wyoming to a fishing boat in California. Even though a high school drop-out, he achieved a Bachelor of Arts degree in Political Science from Colorado College on the GI bill. He served on the flight deck of an aircraft carrier during the Korean war. Following the war and graduation, he with pregnant wife and three children moved to Chicago Where he became the only white officer in a predominately black labor union during the civil rights turbulence of the 60s. He did graduate research at Roosevelt University for the book: "Roles of the Labor leader."[49] And later taught in the University's labor Education Division while attending night classes at Chicago Kent College of Law. The 70s were spent as a civil rights investigator for the Office for Civil Rights, U. S. Department of Health, Education and Welfare. He has been homeless in the bitter Wyoming winter and he has lived on Chicago's north lake shore in a luxury apartment while driving a Jaguar. "I've been rich and I've been poor-Rich is better." Jack is also a ranked member of the International Yang Family T'ai Chi Association. Jack having retired from the Porter County Indiana Library System, now lives with his wife Pat in Valparaiso, Indiana.

---

[49] Beeler, Duane, Roles of the Labor Leader, Chicago, Roosevelt University Press, 1969

CPSIA information can be obtained
at www.ICGtesting.com
Printed in the USA
BVHW03s1949190618
519451BV00001B/8/P